Apple Training Series

Desktop and Portable Systems

Third Edition

Marc Asturias / Moira Gagen

Apple
Certified

Apple Training Series: Desktop and Portable Systems, Third Edition
Copyright © 2007 by Apple Inc.

Published by Peachpit Press. For information on Peachpit Press books, contact:

Peachpit Press
1249 Eighth Street
Berkeley, CA 94710
(510) 524-2178
Fax: (510) 524-2221
www.peachpit.com
To report errors, please send a note to errata@peachpit.com.
Peachpit Press is a division of Pearson Education.

Authors: Marc Asturias and Moira Gagen
Editors: AppleCare Worldwide Service Training Group
Apple Series Editor: Nancy Peterson
Apple Worldwide Training Series Editor: Rebecca Freed
Project Editor: Whitney Walker
Developmental Editor: Justine Withers
Technical Editors: Jim Bontempo, Beth Collison, Julianne Douglas, E. Lisette Gerald-Yamasaki, Michael Huckabone, Carol Ketteridge, Lew Laurent, Suzanne Perry, Jeremy Scheffee, Steffani Woo
Copy Editors: Darren Meiss and Emily K. Wolman
Production Coordinator: Laurie Stewart, Happenstance Type-O-Rama
Compositor: Kate Kaminski, Happenstance Type-O-Rama
Indexer: Karin Arrigoni
Cover Art Direction: Charlene Charles-Will
Cover Illustration: Mimi Heft
Photographs: Stan Young
Cover Production: Maureen Forys, Happenstance Type-O-Rama
Media Reviewer: Eric Geoffroy

ISBN-13:   978-0-321-45501-7
ISBN-10:   0-321-45501-0
9 8 7 6 5 4 3 2
Printed and bound in the United States of America

Contents

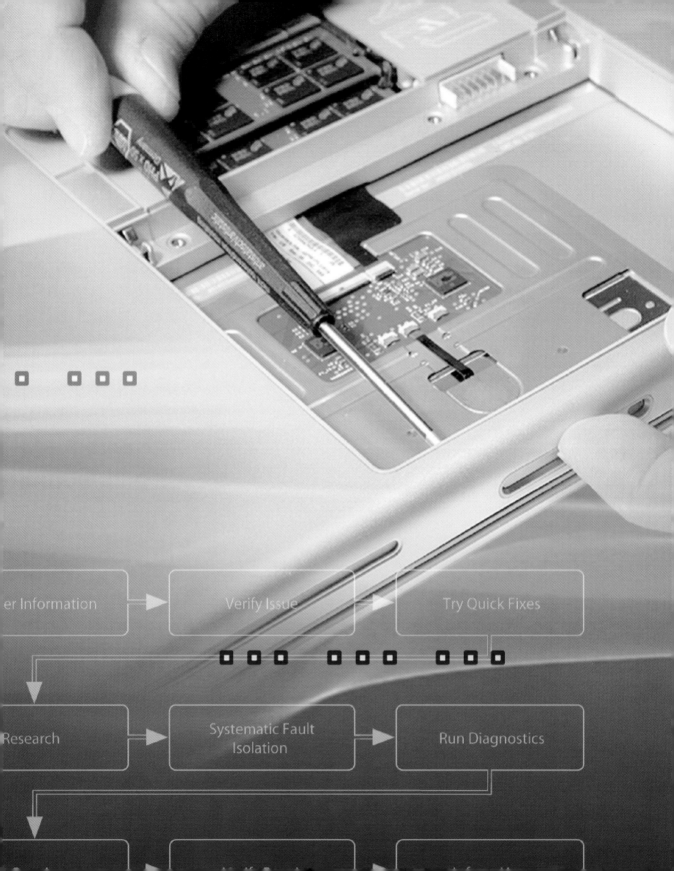

er Information → Verify Issue → Try Quick Fixes

Research → Systematic Fault Isolation → Run Diagnostics

Getting Started

This book introduces the procedures for supporting and servicing Apple computers. The materials in this book are equally helpful in classroom and self-paced situations, and point to further resources that are available only to those enrolled in Apple-authorized service training programs.

The primary goal of the Apple-authorized service training curriculum is to prepare a technician to knowledgeably address customer service-related concerns and questions. This includes the ability to return a Macintosh computer to normal operation using the proper and authorized tools, resources, and troubleshooting methodology.

Whether you are an experienced technician or someone who just wants to dig deep into your Macintosh, you'll find in-depth technical service information as well as a comprehensive overview of the service tools and procedures used by Apple-certified service technicians to diagnose, upgrade, and maintain Macintosh computers.

Warning: Voiding Your Warranty

Please note that, in most cases, any support or repair work performed on any Macintosh computer by an uncertified individual will void the manufacturer's warranty on that equipment. Throughout this book, we describe detailed upgrade, repair, and disassembly procedures. These are intended as learning tools only. Apple and Peachpit Press are not responsible for any damage to any equipment that occurs as a direct or indirect result of following the procedures described in this book. Please be aware that all repairs should be performed by an Apple-certified technician.

Course Structure

This book covers much of the required course material for Apple Desktop Service and Apple Portable Service certification exams. The lessons are designed to let you learn at your own pace. You can progress through the book from beginning to end, or dive right into the lessons that interest you most. It's up to you.

If you are enrolled in a leader-led Apple-authorized service training program, this book will serve as a reference and guide during your training experience.

The book is divided into four sections:

▶   Lessons 1–5: Tools and practices

▶   Lessons 6–8: Common hardware and technologies

▶   Lessons 9–20: Desktops

▶   Lessons 21–28: Portables

In the Desktops and Portables sections, we start with an overview of the recent models, organized in product families. Then we focus on a specific model and go into detail on a typical upgrade procedure, disassembly procedure (called Take Apart), and troubleshooting. The five models we cover are:

▶   iMac (24-inch)

▶   Mac mini (Early 2006)

▶ Mac Pro

▶ MacBook (13-inch)

▶ MacBook Pro

At the end of each lesson, you can take a test to help review the material you've learned. Refer to the various Apple troubleshooting resources, such as the Knowledge Base and included service material, as well as the lessons themselves, to help you answer these questions. In the case of the Taking Apart lessons, rather than a test we have provided a list of review points, since the only successful way to test your skills with these procedures is by actually doing the job.

This book assumes a basic level of familiarity with the Macintosh operating environment. All references to Mac OS X refer to Mac OS X 10.4.

Reference Files

The lessons in this book are designed to help you learn by doing, completing exercises and tasks as you go. Register at this book's companion website (www.peachpit.com/ats.deskport3) for access to a variety of reference files, including procedures, flowcharts, and diagnostic utilities. Most important, it includes the service manuals for the Macintosh models that are used as examples throughout this book.

Reference files are listed at the beginning of each lesson and occasionally within the text of those lessons, and are located in the lesson folders on the website. Filenames shown in blue within the lesson refer to a file that is included online.

The companion website also provides several completely revised fundamental technology and product overview lessons. We recommend that you read them in chronological order along with the lessons in this book. The online lessons are:

▶ Lesson 5a, "Basic Computer Theory and Terms"

▶ Lesson 5b, "Underlying Technologies"

▶ Lesson 6a, "Liquid Crystal Displays"

- ▶ Lesson 9a, "About eMac Models"
- ▶ Lesson 17a, "About Power Mac Models"
- ▶ Lesson 17b, "About Xserve Models"
- ▶ Lesson 21a, "About iBook Models"
- ▶ Lesson 25a, "About PowerBook G4 Models"

We refer to many Knowledge Base documents within this book. Most of these files are readily available online. We encourage you to read them there, as the online documents are updated whenever new information becomes available.

Some Knowledge Base material is marked as available to the "Apple extended audience." This audience includes members of Apple Authorized Service Provider (AASP) organizations, those who have a self-servicing account, and owners of the Apple Technician Training (ATT) program.

Further Learning

If, after reading this book, you have a thirst for more knowledge of Macintosh computers, you have a couple of options: Apple Technician Training (ATT) and Apple Authorized Training Centers.

The ATT program is a self-paced program, which includes a year of access to continually upgraded online materials. This online training includes a baseline study of Xserve. For more information, please visit www.apple.com/support/products/techtrain.html.

For those who prefer to learn in an instructor-led setting, Apple offers training courses at Apple Authorized Training Centers worldwide. These courses, which typically use the Apple Training Series books as their textbooks, are taught by Apple-certified trainers, and balance concepts and lectures with hands-on labs and exercises. To find an Apple Authorized Training Center near you, refer to Apple Knowledge Base documents 305055, "Americas: Service Training and Testing Centers," and 304101, "Europe: Service Certification Training and Testing Centers."

Certification

Apple offers two hardware service certifications:

▶   Apple Certified Desktop Technician (ACDT)

▶   Apple Certified Portable Technician (ACPT)

These certifications qualify technicians to perform warranty repairs on Apple products while working at Apple-authorized service facilities.

This book covers the majority of the course material for, and is mapped to the learning objectives of, the Apple Desktop Service and Apple Portable Service certification exams. The remaining learning objectives can be found in the Xserve section of ATT. It is designed to help you prepare for those exams. Successfully passing these exams is part of the requirement to be certified as an ACDT or ACPT.

For more information, visit http://train.apple.com/certification/hardware.html.

Apple offers a number of other certification paths, including:

▶   Mac OS X and Mac OS X Server Certifications

▶   Certifications for Pro Application Users and Technicians

You may also refer to Knowledge Base document 113612, "Apple Certifications: Getting Certified — CA/LA/US."

The use of ATT materials and the successful completion of Apple service certification exams do not imply any authorization by Apple to perform repairs or to conduct business directly with Apple or on its behalf.

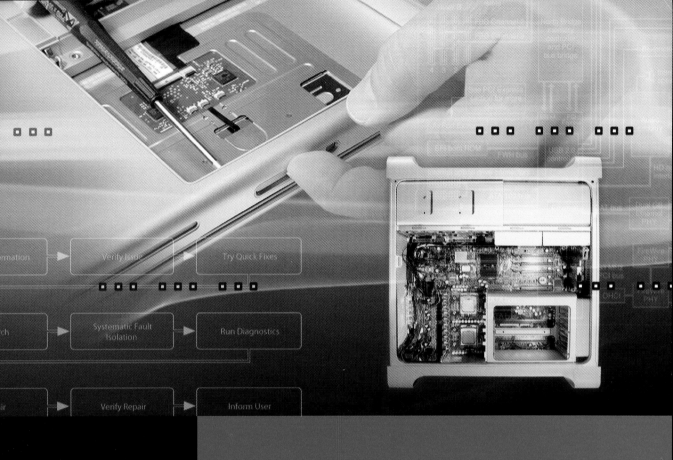

Verify Issue → Try Quick Fixes

Systematic Fault Isolation → Run Diagnostics

Verify Repair → Inform User

Tools and Practices

1

Reference Files	Mac Pro (macpro.pdf)
	Apple General Troubleshooting Flowchart (AGTFwithNotes.pdf)
	iMac (24-inch) (imac_24in.pdf)
Time	This lesson takes approximately 2 hours to complete.
Goals	Locate all the charts, part numbers, images, and safety/troubleshooting information for a specified Apple product
	Familiarize yourself with the service and user's manuals
	Identify which Apple reference will produce the most informative results

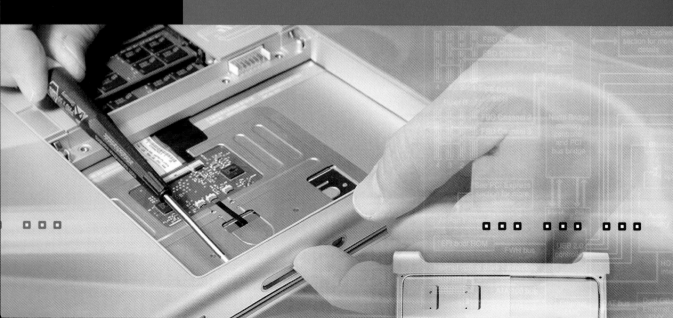

Reference Materials

Motivated people—ready and eager to get into the details of hardware repair and maintenance—might be tempted to skip a lesson called "Reference Materials." Do not succumb to that temptation! Even the most self-reliant, self-starting individual needs the right tools for the job. Just as you wouldn't send your adventure video game character into a cave without a magic health potion, you shouldn't pick up your screwdriver or don your electrostatic discharge (ESD) wrist strap without the information that will save you time and frustration as you service and support Apple products.

This lesson describes some Apple technical and troubleshooting materials, including the Knowledge Base, diagnostic software, service manuals, discussion forums, hot issues, product specifications, and compatibility notes.

Some of these materials are available only to certified Apple technicians, students in the Apple Technician Training (ATT) program, and technicians associated with an Apple Authorized Service Provider (AASP). If you are not in one of those groups, you will not have full access to the sites or be able to complete some of the exercises in this lesson. However, you will still get a good overview of the available materials. To help you gain familiarity with many of the processes, the companion website for this book (www.peachpit.com/ats.deskport3) contains Apple proprietary diagnostic software, service manuals, and other technical materials for several Macintosh models that are used as examples throughout the book.

> **MORE INFO** ▶ For information about Apple authorized training and service provider programs, try the following sites:
>
> http://train.apple.com
>
> www.apple.com/contact/reseller.html
>
> www.apple.com/support/products/techtrain.html

One-Stop Shopping

Apple Service Source is the starting point for many useful reference materials for Apple Authorized Service Providers and for students in Apple Technician Training.

> **NOTE** ▶ The screen shots in this lesson come from the AASP version of Service Source, and we discuss the features of that version.

The Service Source home page links to information on all the service-oriented Apple products and programs. As of this book's publication date, the main categories include Macs, Mac Pro, Power Mac & Xserve, MacBook Pro & PowerBook, MacBook & iBook, Displays, Other Products (AirPort, iPod, and iSight), Service Programs, and Service Training. Below each of the different products is a pop-up menu with choices including Tech News, Service Manuals, and Support Pages.

Text links on the right side of the Service Source page lead to a wide variety of necessary information for Apple technicians. This area of Service Source varies as new items are added or changed but generally includes links to news about the service program and Apple products, a customized support page, the Knowledge Base, discussions, and software updates.

> **NOTE ▶** Service Source is a resource reserved for AASPs and students who have purchased the ATT kit. Although this book does not provide you with access to Service Source, it does examine the components of this reference and reviews how you can use these components.

Finding Support Information

Apple offers a number of resources to help you answer questions and otherwise support your customers, including the following:

- ▶ Configuration information
- ▶ Warranty status
- ▶ Compatibility information
- ▶ User's manuals
- ▶ Product specifications

Configuration Information

Configuration information is a detailed description of the specific model a customer bought. It's more specific than product specifications, because specifications covers all configurations of a product, not any one specific configuration. Most of Apple's newer products are available in a single configuration that can be configured to order to incorporate customer-specific choices.

Warranty Status

Global Service Exchange (GSX) provides Apple Authorized Service Providers (AASPs) with multiple references and tools for troubleshooting and servicing Apple products. Authorized Service Providers use GSX to access Service Source, Knowledge Base, and Apple Service Training. The easiest way to check the status of an Apple product is to type the serial number in the serial number field in GSX and click Coverage Check.

You can also help your customers find the warranty status of their products by directing them to the Apple Support site (www.apple.com/support). After typing the serial number in the field in the lower right, your customer will see warranty information similar to this:

Compatibility Information

When a customer asks about upgrade possibilities, and you need to find compatibility information for a product, start at the Apple Support page.

1   Open https://service.info.apple.com in your browser window.

2 Choose the support page for the product in question from one of the Product Service pop-up menus.

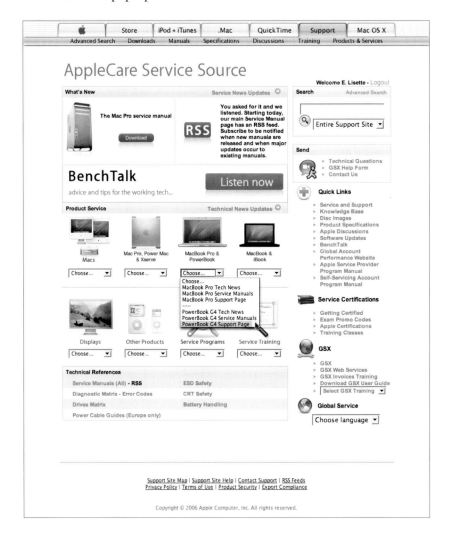

3 Type *compatibility* in the search field. Make sure the Restrict to [product] checkbox is selected.

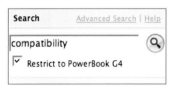

A list of Knowledge Base documents pertaining to your product appears.

User's Manuals

Product manuals are the user's manuals that ship with a product when it is purchased. Unlike service manuals, product manuals provide information, such as product setup and configuration, that is intended to help a customer set up and use the product.

Product manuals are, of course, available to all users, not just AASPs. You need to be familiar with product manuals so you are aware of the instructions that customers use to set up their computers.

To access product manuals (in this case, for the iMac), do the following:

1 Go to the Apple Support page (www.apple.com/support).

2 Click the Computer + Server product icon.

3   Click Intel-based iMac.

4   Under Support Resources, click Download an iMac manual.

5   Skim the manual.

Product Specifications

The Specifications resource offers a quick means of locating the technical specifications of Apple's many different products. Everyone can access the Apple Specifications site at: http://support.apple.com/specs/. In addition, you can access product specifications from Service Source: the link is located in the bar section of the Service Source home page.

After you select it, you will see a screen similar to this one:

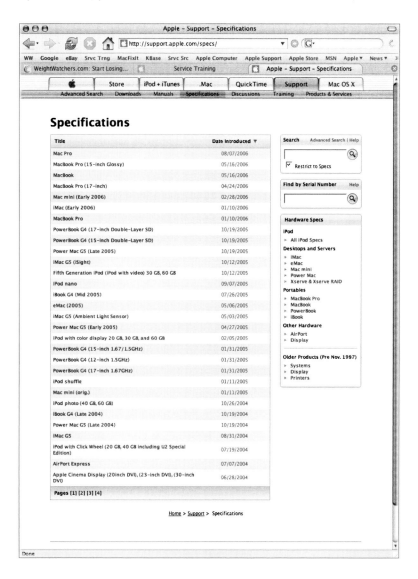

From this page, you can access the specifications for most Apple products. Here is a portion of the Mac Pro specification:

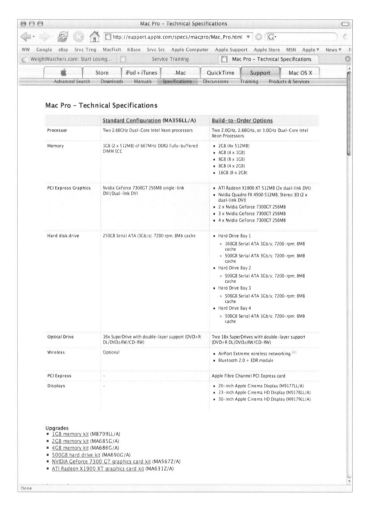

The fastest way to find the general "speeds and feeds" of a product is to look up that product's technical specification.

1   Access Specifications from the Apple Support page.

2 Locate and compare the memory specifications for the following systems:

iMac (Mid 2006 17-inch)

MacBook

MacBook Pro (17-inch)

Power Mac G5 (Late 2005)

Mac mini (Early 2006)

Specifications Quiz

▶ An iMac G5 (17-inch 1GHz) customer is concerned that her non–air-conditioned worksite may be too warm for her iMac to operate properly. She needs to know the temperature range in which the iMac can operate. What can you tell her? Where could she have found the information herself?

Answer Key

Environmental requirements for an iMac G5 (17-inch 1GHz) are as follows:

▶ Operating temperature: 50° to 95° F (10° to 35° C)

▶ Storage temperature: –40° to 185° F (–40° to 85° C)

▶ Relative humidity: 5% to 95% noncondensing

The necessary information is available to the public by following the path iMac G5 Support > Find specifications for your iMac > iMac (17-inch 1Ghz). The information is contained in document iMac (17-inch 1Ghz) - Technical Specifications.

Upgrade Information

When it comes time to upgrade your customer's computer—that is, to install an optional configure-to-order component—you'll find it helpful to review the product specifications (discussed above) and Take Apart procedures in the service manuals.

Apple service manuals are organized around a basic outline and usually provide these features:

▶ Take Apart—This section describes complete procedures for removing and installing system components.

▶ Troubleshooting—This section includes symptom charts that provide specific diagnostic procedures to follow for common symptoms.

▶ Upgrades—Here you have the procedures for installing optional components, such as additional memory and AirPort cards.

▶ Exploded View—This section provides exploded views (sometimes with part numbers), input/output (I/O) ports, and screw matrices with pictures of the screws used in the system.

Apple service manuals are delivered in the industry-standard Portable Document Format (PDF). You can view these files in the Preview application in Mac OS X, in Safari, as well as in Adobe Acrobat or Adobe Reader.

Using Bookmarks

Apple produces the service manuals with bookmarks so you can easily navigate to the topic you're interested in.

1 Open Service Source in a browser window.

2 From the "Mac Pro, Power Mac, & Xserve" pop-up menu, choose Intel & G5 Service Manuals.

This opens Knowledge Base document 86424, "Mac Pro and Power Mac G5 Service Manuals."

NOTE ▶ Sometimes banners at the top of Knowledge Base documents indicate that material is restricted; ATT users have access to some material that is not available to the public.

3 Locate the service manual for Mac Pro.

If you do not have access to Service Source, you can open the service manual on the book's companion website, www.peachpit.com/ats.deskport3.

4 Download the service manual by clicking its PDF icon.

5 Use Preview to open the service manual you just downloaded.

6 Choose Drawer from the View menu (if it is not already open).

Your screen will look similar to the following figure:

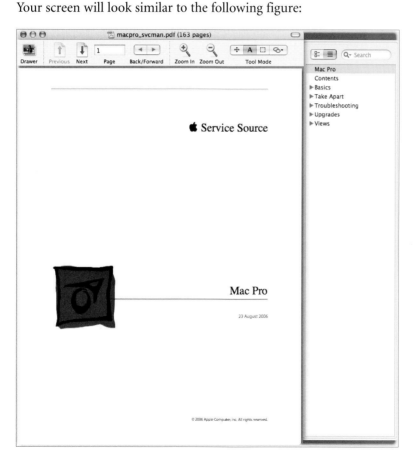

Adding a Bluetooth Card to a Mac Pro

This exercise assumes that you have Service Source open in a browser window. If you are not affiliated with an AASP, have not purchased ATT, or otherwise do not have access to Service Source, skip to step 2.

Let's assume you have to upgrade a Mac Pro with a Bluetooth Card. Do the following steps:

1   Find and download the Mac Pro service manual, if you have not done so already.

2   Open Upgrades in the Mac Pro service manual.

3   Select Bluetooth Card from under the Upgrades heading in the Bookmark pane.

Upgrade Quiz

1.   Where do you find Take Apart instructions?

2.   What tools do you need to add a Bluetooth Card to a Mac Pro?

3.   What component do you need to remove before beginning the addition?

4.   What were the stock hard drive options for the Power Mac G5 (Original)?

Answer Key

1. Service manuals; 2. Magnetized jewelers Phillips #1 screwdriver; 3. You don't have to remove any components; simply lay it on its side with the access side facing up; 4. 80 and 160 GB

Resources for Locating Trouble

Apple defines troubleshooting as isolating and resolving an issue. Many of the tools you use to isolate are also the tools you use to resolve. You will learn more about Apple's recommended troubleshooting process in Lesson 3,

"General Troubleshooting Theory." In the meantime, these resources will help you when you are trying to pin down the source of trouble:

▶ Service News

▶ Apple General Troubleshooting Flowchart

▶ The Knowledge Base

▶ Symptom charts

▶ Disc images

▶ Diagnostic software

Service News

AppleCare Service News are bulletins about new or revised service programs and policies. Diagnostics tools updates are communicated through Service News.

You can access Service News through Service Source.

Service technicians can search the Knowledge Base for Service Tech News articles by using the keyword *ksshot*.

Apple General Troubleshooting Flowchart

The Apple General Troubleshooting Flowchart documents Apple's recommended troubleshooting process. You will learn more about this process in Lesson 3. ATT owners and AASP technicians can find the current Apple General Flowchart with notes through the Service Training website at http://service.info.apple.com/service_training/training.html. The flowchart is also on this book's companion website, www.peachpit.com/ats.deskport3.

The Knowledge Base

The Knowledge Base is the primary reference resource that Apple supplies. It is available online and is free to anyone who needs to research issues that involve Apple hardware or software, although access to some Knowledge Base documents is restricted to AASPs, internal Apple personnel, and Apple developers. In this lesson, you'll be logging in to the Apple website as part of learning how to search the Knowledge Base effectively.

The varied natures of these audiences and the differences in their needs have influenced the structure of the Knowledge Base. Here, of course, we concentrate on the best way for AASPs and technicians to use this resource.

Access to the Knowledge Base requires the following:

▶ A JavaScript-capable web browser (such as Safari), with JavaScript enabled

▶ Cookies enabled in the web browser

▶ An Apple ID

Apple ID is an account-management system that Apple requires for all users of the Knowledge Base, Apple Discussions, and the Apple Store. Once you register with Apple and establish an Apple ID, you can sign on to any of those Apple resources.

To perform a basic search of the Knowledge Base, go to www.apple.com/support, enter a term in the Search field, and then click the magnifying glass icon. If you click the Advanced Search link near the top of the page (http://search.info.apple.com), you will see a screen similar to the one shown on the following page.

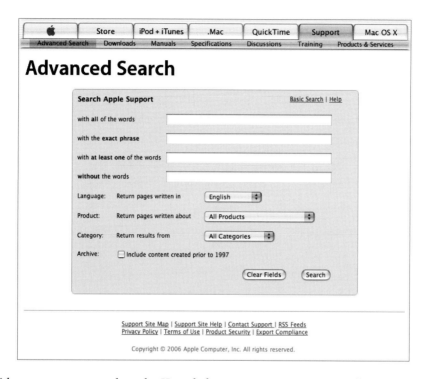

Take a moment to explore the Knowledge Base so you can use it effectively when you need to research an issue.

1   Open Knowledge Base.

2   Review the Help document for Advanced Search by clicking the Help link in the upper-right corner of the Search box.

3   Enter *keywords* in the search text field and press Return.

4   Open Knowledge Base document 75178, "How to Use Knowledge Base keywords."

TIP ▶ You may want to bookmark this document if you have to perform frequent product-specific searches.

5   Review the document and find the keyword for iMac G5.

6   Do a new search using that keyword (*kimacg5*) along with the word *ksshot*.

7   Skim Knowledge Base document 304091, "iMac G5: Fans are running at a constant high speed."

Knowledge Base Quiz

1.   What controls the fans in an iMac G5 system?

2.   You need to review the Do-It-Yourself (DIY) procedures for a Power Mac G5 (Late 2004) system. Which is the *best* resource to check?

Answer Key

1. The System Management Unit (SMU) manages the fans in response to thermal conditions in the iMac G5. You can find necessary information by searching the Knowledge Base for *imac g5 fans*, then following the links to documents 304091 and 301733; 2. Knowledge Base

Symptom Charts

For the following exercises, you will use the Mac Pro and other service manuals you just opened in Preview, as well as other manuals specified in the exercises.

NOTE ▶ Page numbers in the manual that comes on the companion website may be somewhat different from what you see here.

Let's assume that you have a Mac Pro that is completely nonfunctional. A number of issues could lead to this symptom. To systematically troubleshoot it, do the following:

1   Refer to the Apple General Troubleshooting Flowchart. (We discuss the flowchart in more detail in Lesson 3.)

For purposes of this exercise, you have already gathered information and verified the issue. One quick fix is to check the Symptom Charts section of the service manual.

2   In the Navigation pane of your Mac Pro service manual, open the Troubleshooting heading, then open Symptom Charts.

3   Open Startup Failures.

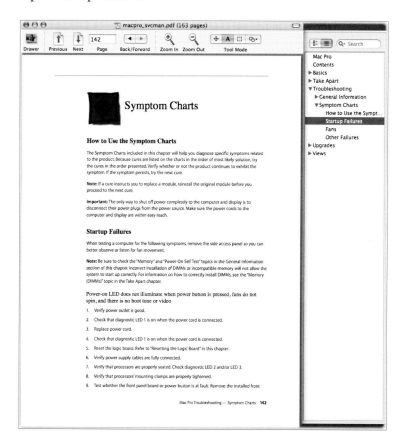

4   Review the contents of this page and the rest of the Startup Failures section.

Notice that the procedures go from the simple and easy to the complex and difficult.

Diagnostic Software

Apple supplies a suite of diagnostic software tools for troubleshooting its products. AASPs can use Service Source to update their collection of such tools. Click the Diagnostic Matrix link at the bottom of the Service Source page to open the Service Diagnostics Matrix window.

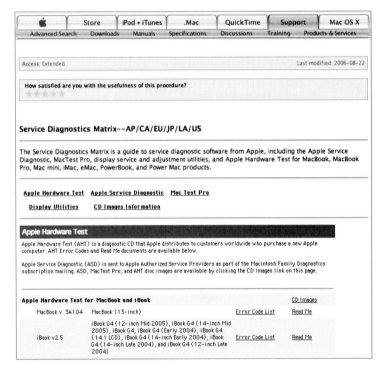

From this page, AASPs can access updates for Apple Service Diagnostic and Apple Hardware Test, as well as display adjustment utilities for a variety of Apple products. You'll learn about using Apple software tools in Lesson 2, "Software Tools."

NOTE ▶ The diagnostics area of Service Source is available only to AASPs. However, the companion website for this book includes diagnostic software for several Apple products.

Diagnostics Quiz

▶ What version of Apple Service Diagnostics should you use with a Power Mac G5 (Late 2004)?

Answer Key

▶ 2.5.8

Disc Images

A number of references and software tools are best used in a bootable CD format. Apple supplies a wide variety of disc images that its AASPs can use in making CDs for reference or testing.

The Disc Images page includes file-download links and detailed information on how to burn bootable versions of diagnostic CDs.

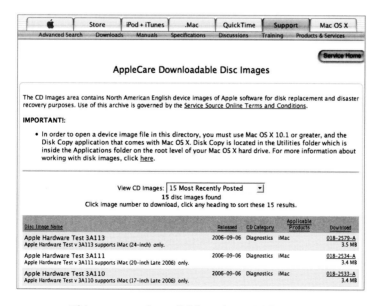

NOTE ▶ This resource is available only to AASPs.

Resources for Resolving an Issue

When you have located the trouble, and you're ready to fix it, be aware of these resources:

▶   Safety and MSDS information

▶   Screw matrix

▶   Take Apart procedures

Safety Information

As a service technician, you will work with materials and equipment that require special handling. Items such as CRT displays, power adapter boards, and batteries require certain precautions to ensure your safety. In addition, you must take measures to ensure that ESD does not damage the equipment you work on.

You can find necessary information on the CRT and ESD Safety Information page, accessible from the Technical References links at the bottom of the Service Source page. This book provides detailed coverage of most safety topics, including ESD, in Lesson 4, "Safe Working Procedures and General Maintenance."

> **MORE INFO** ▶ Some components, such as batteries, have Material Safety Data Sheets (MSDS) with detailed safety and environmental information. Search the Knowledge Base for *MSDS*.

Screw Matrix

A screw matrix, sometimes also called a screw reference sheet, lists all the screws in an Apple product, along with their dimensions, part numbers, and the location where each is used. You can find the screw matrix in the product's service manual, although not all products have a screw matrix.

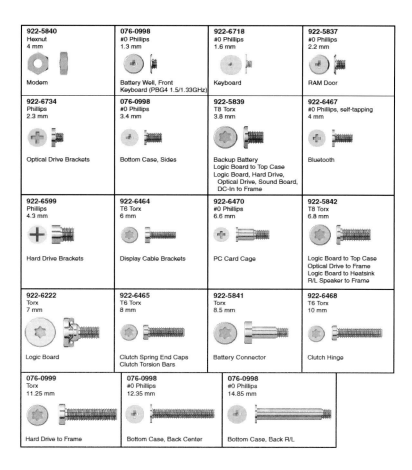

Take Apart Procedures

You worked with a Take Apart procedure earlier in this lesson. Before a product is introduced, a lot of time and effort go into developing service and trouble-shooting procedures for it. The results of this effort are published in the service manual that Apple provides to its AASPs. These service manuals can be one of your best tools.

Now let's assume that you need to replace the hard drive in a Mac Pro. You'll need to review the procedures necessary to open the unit and access the hard drive.

1   In the service manual, open Take Apart in the Bookmark pane.

2   Select Hard Drives.

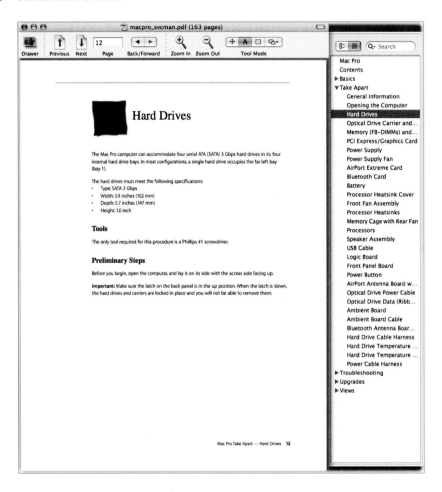

Resolving Quiz

1. What is the part number for the 1.25 GHz logic board for the Power Mac G5 (Late 2004)?

    TIP You will need access to GSX or a copy of the service manual, because part numbers are listed in the Exploded Views section.

2. What tools do you need to remove the hard drive from a Mac Pro?

3. When you handle the drive in a Mac Pro, which side of the drive should you avoid touching?

4. You need to replace an internal DVD drive in an iMac (24-inch). What parts do you need to remove before you can remove the drive?

Answer Key

1. 661-3335; 2. Phillips #1 screwdriver; 3. Avoid touching the printed circuit board on the bottom of the drive; 4. To replace an internal DVD drive in an iMac (24-inch), first you must remove the access door, front bezel, and LCD panel. The necessary information is available in the Take Apart section of the iMac (24-inch) service manual, which is on this book's companion website, www.peachpit.com/ats.deskport3.

Lesson Review

1. You need to review the DIY procedures for an eMac (USB 2.0). Which of the following resources would be the best one to check?

   a. Specifications

   b. Knowledge Base

   c. Featured Software

   d. Apple Support site

2. Where do you find Symptom Charts? (Choose the best answer.)

   a. GSX home page

   b. Service Source

   c. Discussions

   d. Service manuals

3. How do you determine the tools you need to take apart an iMac (Late 2006)? (Choose the best answer.)

   a. Do a search on *tools* in Parts and Configs.

   b. Call Apple.

   c. Review the service manual.

   d. Search Knowledge Base.

4. While taking apart a MacBook, you mix up the screws you removed. What is the best resource for determining where the screws are used?

   a. Knowledge Base

   b. Discussions

   c. Specifications

   d. Service manual

5. While assisting a customer, you give her the number of a Knowledge Base
    article you looked up after signing on to GSX. Later the customer calls and
    states that the article is not available when she looks for it. What has hap-
    pened? (Choose the most likely answer.)

    a. The customer does not know how to access Knowledge Base.

    b. The article was removed after you first found it.

    c. The article is intended for AASPs and not for the public.

    d. There was a system failure at Apple.

Answer Key

1. d; 2. d; 3. c; 4. d; 5. c

2

Reference Files	Isolating Startup Items.pdf
	Isolating Kernel Extensions.pdf
	Mac OS X Logs.pdf
	From Hardware to Software: The Evolution of Features (Distinguishing_Hardware_from_Software_Issues.pdf)
	Apple Hardware Test
	Service Diagnostics Matrix
	Apple LCD Tester
Time	This lesson takes approximately 2 1/2 hours to complete.
Goals	Describe how and when to use Apple troubleshooting tools and techniques
	Use the Service Diagnostics Matrix to determine the appropriate diagnostic software to use for a specific system
	Interpret trouble reports

Software Tools

No single diagnostic tool is the best solution for every troubleshooting situation. The successful troubleshooter is proficient with multiple tools to address the widest range of issues. This lesson concentrates on software tools (some supplied by Apple, some by third-party developers) that are readily available and often used by technicians restoring Macintosh computers to normal operation.

Software Tools

Software Tool or Technique	Used To
System Profiler	Gather information
Safe Relaunch	Try quick fixes
Safe Mode	Try quick fixes, try systematic fault isolation
Startup Manager	Try quick fixes
Target disk mode	Try quick fixes, repair
Repair Disk Permissions	Try quick fixes, repair
Software Update	Try quick fixes, repair
Force quit	Try quick fixes, repair
Single-user mode	Try quick fixes, try systematic fault isolation
Verbose mode	Try quick fixes, try systematic fault isolation
Disk Utility	Run diagnostics, repair
Network Diagnostics	Run diagnostics, repair
Apple Service Diagnostic (ASD)	Run diagnostics, verify repair
Apple Hardware Test (AHT)	Run diagnostics
Apple LCD Tester	Run diagnostics
Server Monitor	Run diagnostics, inform user
Console	Research, repair
Install/restore CDs and DVDs	Try quick fixes, repair

NOTE ▸ This lesson concentrates on the basic tools that you as a technician should understand. It does not cover all available diagnostic software.

System Profiler

As you will learn in Lesson 3, "General Troubleshooting Theory," the first step in the troubleshooting flowchart is to gather information. One of the best tools to use for this is System Profiler.

System Profiler gathers detailed information about system software versions; types and number of hard drives and other peripherals; internal hardware components; and installed memory, extensions, and applications. These details are very useful when you try to track down the source of a particular issue, and it's usually a good idea to save this information for later reference (to do so, choose File > Save As).

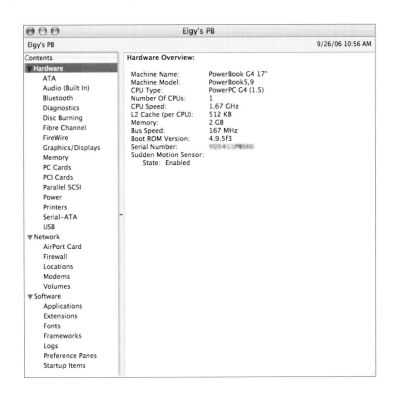

The View menu has a Refresh option. When you select Refresh, System Profiler gathers information again, so you don't have to quit and reopen System Profiler if you connect or disconnect a device, or add or remove software.

There are four ways to access System Profiler:

▶ From the Apple menu, choose About This Mac and then click More Info.

▶ Launch System Profiler from Applications/Utilities.

▶ Use the command line (enter */usr/sbin/system_profiler*). This is helpful for remote computer administration.

▶ While started from the Install disc, choose System Profiler from the Utilities menu.

  MORE INFO ▶ To learn more about how to use System Profiler, choose System Profiler Help from the System Profiler Help menu.

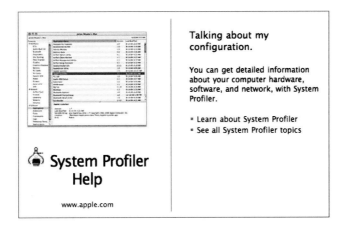

Practice using System Profiler and interpreting the Profiler reports.

1   Open System Profiler on a test computer with no peripherals attached.

2   Review the Hardware section, which for FireWire will resemble the
following screen:

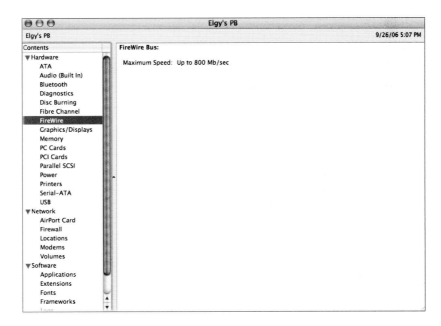

3 Attach a USB or FireWire peripheral, such as an iSight camera, a USB printer, or a USB or FireWire storage device.

4 Review the Hardware section again to see the changes.

System Profiler Quiz

1. If you attach a device to the computer after you've opened System Profiler, does the newly attached device appear? If not, what must you do to have it appear?

2. The computer described in the following screen shot has two built-in USB ports. Identify which devices are connected to each.

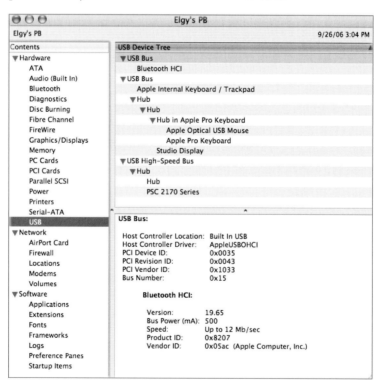

Write your answers to the System Profiler Quiz in the space provided below.

USB Port	Connected Device

Answer Key

1. No, you must choose View > Refresh; 2. One built-in port is used by a hub, which in turn is connected to a display and a keyboard, and the keyboard is connected to a mouse. The other built-in port is used by a hub, which is used by a printer and perhaps additional devices.

Quick Fix Tools

In Lesson 3, you'll learn what makes something a quick fix. In the meantime, here's a list of the common quick fixes we'll cover:

▶ Safe Relaunch

▶ Safe Mode

▶ Startup Manager

▶ Target disk mode

▶ Repair disk permissions

▶ Software Update

▶ Force quit

▶ Single-user mode

▶ Verbose mode

Safe Relaunch

When an application unexpectedly quits, the Safe Relaunch feature is a way of restarting with a fresh, default preferences file. This should help resolve situations in which a corrupt preferences file caused an application to quit unexpectedly. However, not every issue can be traced to a bad preferences file, so you should use probing questions to isolate the issue. For example, does the application quit only when working with a particular file? If so, the file itself may be corrupted instead of the application's preferences file.

1   If your application unexpectedly quits, a dialog will appear allowing you to relaunch it. Click Reopen.

2   If the application quits unexpectedly the next time you open it, another dialog appears. Click Try Again to "Safe Relaunch" the application with default preferences.

The Safe Relaunch dialog appears only when an application quits unexpectedly a second time. If you force-quit an application, this dialog does not appear.

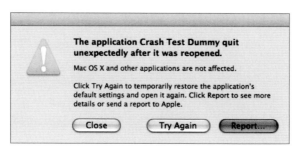

The Safe Relaunch option sets aside the application's preferences and creates a new preferences file.

If the new preference allows the application to work, when you quit the application you'll be asked whether you want to keep the new preferences file.

3 If you click Yes to keep the new preferences file, the old file is renamed, with .saved added to the filename.

For example, in the application shown in the preceding screens, the old preferences file would be renamed com.apple.crashtestdummy.plist.saved. If you need to restore the old preferences file, rename it by removing .saved from the end of the filename.

NOTE ▶ Remember that while some preferences files can be safely moved aside, applications such as Mail store a lot of information in them. Setting the preferences aside may cause other issues. Probe to find out if an application has quit recently and the application settings have changed.

Safe Mode

A Safe Boot is a good way to start troubleshooting when you suspect that software or a damaged directory on the startup volume is causing an issue. Safe Boot works in Mac OS X 10.2 or later. Safe Mode is the state Mac OS X is in after a Safe Boot.

Starting up into Safe Mode in Mac OS X 10.4, Tiger does several things to simplify the computer's startup and operation:

▶ Forces a directory check of the startup volume

▶ Loads only required kernel extensions (some of the items in System/Library/Extensions)

▶ Disables all fonts other than those in System/Library/Fonts

▶ Moves to the Trash all font caches normally stored in Library/Caches/ com.apple.ATS/(uid), where uid is a user ID number such as 501

▶ Temporarily turns off automatic login (if turned on)

▶ Disables all startup items and any login items

To start up in Safe Mode:

1 Ensure that the computer is completely shut down.

2 Press the power button.

3 Immediately after you hear the startup chime, press and hold the Shift key until you see the spinning gear progress indicator.

The login window indicates when you have started up in Safe Mode; "Safe Boot" will appear in red. Since starting up in Safe Mode also disables automatic login, you should always see the login window.

TIP ▶ When not performing a Safe Boot, hold down the Shift key during the "Welcome to Mac OS X" startup screen to prevent automatic login.

Many features of Mac OS X still work while in Safe Mode. For example, you can still connect to a TCP/IP network using the computer's built-in Ethernet connection.

However, some features of Mac OS X do not work while in Safe Mode, including:

- ▶ AirPort
- ▶ DVD Player
- ▶ Video capture
- ▶ Internal and external modems
- ▶ Audio input and output
- ▶ Video card acceleration (including Quartz Extreme)
- ▶ IP over FireWire

MORE INFO ▶ For more information about Safe Boot, Safe Mode, and devices or features that don't work in Safe Mode, see Knowledge Base document 107392, "What is Safe Boot, Safe Mode?"

If an issue isn't reproducible in Safe Mode, there are four possible reasons:

- ▶ Directory corruption on the startup volume
- ▶ Unusable font cache
- ▶ A startup item issue
- ▶ A kernel extension issue

If you restart after a Safe Boot and the issue is no longer reproducible, then there was a problem with the volume's directory or there was an unusable font cache. If the issue persists, startup items or kernel extensions are the most probable causes.

MORE INFO ▶ To practice isolating startup items or kernel extensions, see **Isolating Startup Items.pdf** and **Isolating Kernel Extensions.pdf** on this book's companion website, www.peachpit.com/ats.deskport3.

Startup Manager

Startup Manager enables you to choose the startup volume on the fly. (A startup volume is a disk or partition of a disk that contains a usable copy of the Mac OS.) You may want to use Startup Manager when you're troubleshooting a startup issue or an issue with the normal boot drive.

To launch Startup Manager:

1   Turn on or restart the computer, and immediately press and hold the Option key.

     After a few seconds, the Startup Manager screen appears (similar to the one below), and the Startup Manager scans for available volumes.

2   Do either of the following:

     ▶   Click the circular arrow to rescan for other volumes, including NetBoot Server volumes.

     ▶   To eject any disc in the drive or open an empty tray-loading drive, hold down the Eject key (F12 or key with eject symbol). On models that do not have an Eject key, hold down the Command (Apple) and period (.) keys. Ejecting the disc will also close the tray. After inserting a disc that is capable of starting up the computer, you can rescan for volumes.

3   Click the startup volume you want to use.

In the previous example, three startup volumes are available: a hard disk, a USB disk, and a DVD-ROM disc.

4   Click the right-arrow button to start up the computer from the volume you selected.

Target Disk Mode

Target disk mode allows the internal disk of a Macintosh computer with a FireWire port (the target computer) to be used as an external hard disk connected to another computer (the host). The computer will not go into target disk mode if Open Firmware Password has been enabled.

Target disk mode has these primary uses:

▶   High-speed data transfer between computers

▶   Diagnosis and repair of a corrupted internal hard drive

▶   Access to optical drive–based diagnostics for systems that do not have a functioning optical drive

> **NOTE** ▶ Target disk mode works with internal optical drives that are connected as master to the internal ATA (AT attachment) bus. Target disk mode connects only to the master ATA drive on the Ultra ATA bus. It will not connect to slave ATA, ATAPI (AT Attachment Packet Interface), or SCSI (Small Computer System Interface) drives. This means you can use a Macintosh's built-in optical drive as an external FireWire optical drive to start up a host Macintosh into optical drive–based diagnostics or a Mac OS X Install disc, using target disk mode and Startup Manager combined.

To use target disk mode:

1   Unplug all other FireWire devices from both computers.

2   Make sure that the target computer is turned off.

If you are using a PowerBook or iBook as the target computer, plug in its AC power adapter.

3   Use a FireWire cable to connect the target computer to a host computer.

The host computer does not need to be turned off.

4   Turn on the target computer, and immediately press and hold the T key until the FireWire icon appears.

The target computer's internal hard disk should become available to the host computer and will likely appear on the desktop.

TIP ▶ If the target computer is running Mac OS X 10.4 Tiger, you can also open System Preferences, choose Startup Disk, and click Target Disk Mode. Then restart the computer and it will start up in target disk mode.

5   When you are finished copying files or otherwise troubleshooting, drag the target computer's hard disk icon to the Trash, or choose File > Eject.

6   Press the target computer's power button to turn it off.

7   Unplug the FireWire cable.

Do not plug in any FireWire devices until after you have disconnected the two computers from each other, or have stopped using target disk mode.

TIP ▶ To mount an Intel-based Macintosh in target disk mode, the host computer must be running Mac OS X 10.4 or later. If you attempt to mount an Intel-based Macintosh in target disk mode on a Macintosh running Mac OS X 10.3.9 or earlier, you'll see an alert message.

MORE INFO ▶ For more information, see Knowledge Base document 303118, "Intel-based Macs: 'You have inserted a disk containing no volumes that Mac OS X can read' alert message." To further familiarize yourself with target disk mode, you can also review Knowledge Base document 58583, "How to use FireWire Target Disk Mode," and Knowledge Base document 75414, "What to do if your Mac doesn't enter FireWire Target Disk Mode."

Repair Disk Permissions

When you install software using Apple's Installer application, the Installer places a receipt on the hard disk in Library/Receipts. This receipt contains a bill of materials, which lists all the files the Installer put on the hard disk, where it put them, and their original permissions. If these permissions are ever changed (perhaps due to software malfunction, user modification, and so on), the application that was installed may operate slowly, malfunction, or quit unexpectedly.

Applications sometimes install many files, so it would be inefficient and time consuming to check and reset permissions on each of these files manually. The easiest and most effective way to do this is to use the Repair Disk Permissions function, which is part of Disk Utility.

When you use Verify or Repair Disk Permissions, Disk Utility looks at certain receipts in Library/Receipts on the drive from which the computer started and compares the permissions to what is located on the drive. Disk Utility uses only an internal list of relevant receipts, not all of the receipts in that folder.

Here are some things to keep in mind:

▶   If a file isn't created or modified by the Installer application, Repair Disk Permissions does nothing to it. Repair Disk Permissions will not change the contents of the Home folder, so it is unlikely to resolve any issue isolated to a particular user.

▶   If you remove some or all of the files in Library/Receipts, Repair Disk Permissions may not function.

   MORE INFO ▶ For more information about using Repair Disk Permissions, see Knowledge Base document 25751, "About Disk Utility's Repair Disk Permissions feature."

In general, you should not use Repair Disk Permissions unless you are troubleshooting a known permissions-related issue documented in the Knowledge Base or you see an error in the console.log related to permissions.

To run Repair Disk Permissions:

1 Open Disk Utility.

2 Select a disk or volume.

3 Click Repair Disk Permissions.

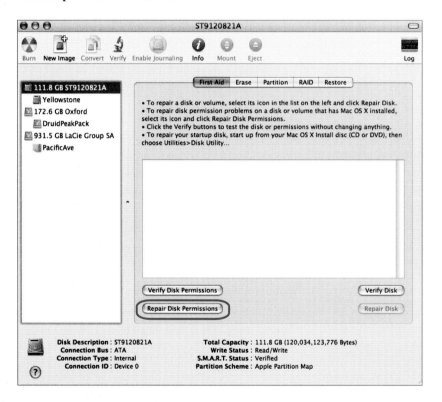

Software Update
Software Update checks Apple's software download site for the latest software updates for Mac OS X. It also looks for any installed Apple applications, such as those in iLife or iWork, and lists all of the available updates.

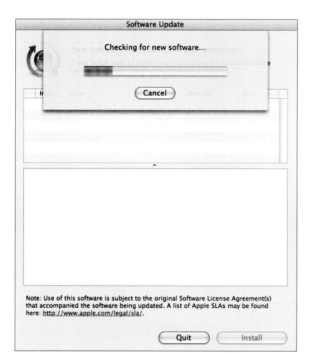

Whenever you're troubleshooting a software or operating system (OS) issue, run Software Update to verify that the computer has the latest software installed.

Software Update is configured by default to automatically check for updates periodically. The user can control when these checks occur. So if you're working on a Macintosh that other people use, you cannot assume that all software updates have been installed on it. You may need to run Software Update multiple times to be sure that all updates have been installed, because some updates are required to be installed and operational before other updates can be detected.

Software Update provides some options for handling an update. If you don't want to install a particular update, select it and choose Update > Make Inactive; Software Update will ignore that application when it checks for available updates.

To verify whether a software update was installed successfully, look for its receipt in the folder Library/Receipts. The Installed Updates pane of Software Update also lists the updates that have been installed. Click Open as a Log File to see installed updates and any errors encountered.

Force Quit

If an application isn't responding, you can force it to quit, but you will lose any unsaved changes to documents that are open in the application.

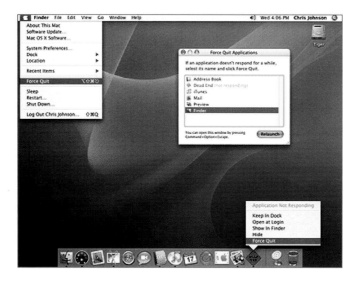

There are several ways to force an application to quit:

▶ From the Apple menu, choose Force Quit, select the application in the list, and click Force Quit.

▶ Hold down the Command and Option keys and press Esc, select the application in the list, and click Force Quit.

▶ Hold down the Option key and click the application icon in the Dock, then choose Force Quit from the menu that appears.

After you force-quit an application, try using it again. If the application still doesn't work, try restarting the computer. If you continue to have problems, you may need to install the application again or contact the application's maker for more help.

TIP ▶ If you select the Finder in the Force Quit Applications window, the Force Quit button changes to Relaunch. You cannot quit the Finder, but you can force-quit it as needed, and it will relaunch automatically.

Single-User Mode

Single-user mode is a way to start the computer so that you can troubleshoot the startup sequence of the computer using UNIX commands.

To troubleshoot in single-user mode:

1 Turn on the computer, and immediately press and hold Command-S.

   You have successfully entered single-user mode when you see white text appear on the screen.

2 Examine the system log by typing the following:

   more /var/log/system.log

   The system log shows where the startup sequence is failing.

   TIP ▶ Corrupted system, login window, or directory services preferences can cause long delays and possibly stop the computer from completely starting up. You can troubleshoot these preferences by starting up the computer in single-user mode, moving them to a temporary location, and restarting. These are the preferences files you should watch:

   ▶ Library/Preferences/SystemConfiguration/preferences.plist

   ▶ Library/Preferences/com.apple.loginwindow.plist

   ▶ Library/Preferences/DirectoryService

   ▶ ~/Library/Preferences

   MORE INFO ▶ To learn more about single-user mode, read Knowledge Base document 106388, "Mac OS X: How to Start up in Single-User or Verbose Mode."

Verbose Mode

Verbose mode enables you to see all the internal computer messages that get created during startup—if you can read really quickly. Unlike single-user mode, verbose mode continues to a normal login window without stopping to accept UNIX commands.

Verbose mode is mainly useful when you are troubleshooting a Macintosh that consistently does not respond (hangs) and does not finish starting up. If there is an issue with one or more of the many software processes that start during Mac OS X startup, you may see these internal computer messages stop, leaving the last of these messages on the screen. This may provide a clue for the cause of the unresponsiveness.

To start up the computer in verbose mode, press and hold Command-V during startup.

> **MORE INFO** ▶ To learn more about verbose mode, read Knowledge Base document 106388, "Mac OS X: How to Start up in Single-User or Verbose Mode."

Diagnostic Software

Diagnostic software is another term for applications that help you test the computer's hardware components. You use these tools after you've exhausted the appropriate quick fixes, assuming the issue you're investigating involves a computer that at least turns on.

You should also use diagnostic software to verify complete hardware functionality after completing a repair. Run a complete set of diagnostic tests instead of just those tests that pertain to the components that were replaced.

Apple offers a few diagnostic applications. We've arranged the utilities in this section in rough order of least to most invasive and most commonly to least commonly used.

Disk Utility

Using Disk Utility, you can:

▶ Obtain information about a hard disk, including its format, capacity, and number of files

▶ Verify and repair any Mac OS Standard (HFS), Mac OS Extended (HFS Plus), or UFS formatted disk

▶ Erase the contents of a hard disk, CD-RW disc, or DVD-RW disc

▶ Partition a hard disk

▶ Set up a Redundant Array of Independent Disks (RAID)

▶ Create disc image files, such as from hard disks or optical discs

▶ Burn (write) disc image files to optical discs

WARNING ▶ You must use Disk Utility from a Mac OS X 10.4–compatible Install disc to verify and repair a volume that has Mac OS X 10.4 Tiger installed. Older Install discs are likely to erroneously report errors on a Tiger volume. This issue extends to third-party disk utilities as well. Before using a third-party disk utility on a Tiger volume, verify that it is certified for use with Mac OS X 10.4. Failure to do so may lead to data loss and irreparable damage to the drive's directory.

Disk Utility is installed with Mac OS X in the Applications/Utilities folder. To launch Disk Utility, double-click its icon. By default, Disk Utility displays the startup disk at the top of the list on the left, with additional mounted hard disks, optical discs, and disk images below.

You will probably use Disk Utility's First Aid tab more than any other tab in troubleshooting. The First Aid tab has two main functions: hard disk and disk permissions inspection and repair. When you click Repair, Disk Utility verifies the disk and repairs any damage it finds.

Try these troubleshooting techniques:

▶   Start up from the Install disc to verify or repair the disk.

▶   Use Safe Boot. Safe Boot checks the startup disk, repairing any errors it finds. If you have a startup issue but are able to start up after using Safe Boot, the issue was likely resolved when the disk was repaired.

Self-Monitoring Analysis and Reporting Technology (SMART) status reporting provides feedback when a drive is failing. If a volume's name is displayed in red in Disk Utility's main window, the drive is reporting a hardware error. When SMART detects that a drive is failing, it will not let you erase, repair, or perform any other functions on that disk. Immediately back up all important data from that drive to another, because drive failure is usually imminent.

> **MORE INFO** ▶ For more information about using Disk Utility, see Knowledge Base document 106214, "Resolve startup issues and perform disk maintenance with Disk Utility and fsck."

Here's a technique that combines using Startup Manager and Disk Utility:

1   Insert the Mac OS X Install disc into a sample Macintosh.

2   Turn on the computer while holding down the Option key.

Startup Manager appears.

3   Select the Install disc and click the right-arrow button to open the Installer.

4   In the window that appears, choose a language.

5   Choose Utilities > Disk Utility.

6   In the Disk Utility window that appears, select the internal hard disk and click Repair Disk.

7   When the repair is complete, quit Disk Utility.

8   Quit Installer.

9   Click Startup Disk.

10 Select the internal hard disk and click Restart twice.

Network Diagnostics

In Mac OS X 10.4 Tiger, when an application has trouble accessing your network or the Internet, it may display an alert message and offer to diagnose the issue using Network Diagnostics. Although the exact alert message may vary, take a look at this iChat example of a network error alert. It provides you with the option to diagnose the issue:

To open Network Diagnostics, click the Diagnose button in the alert message.

> **TIP** If you have accidentally dismissed the error message by clicking the OK button, you can open Network Diagnostics from the Network system preferences by clicking the Assist Me button at the bottom of the preferences pane, or by navigating to System/Library/CoreServices.

Network Diagnostics is a powerful tool for diagnosing network connection issues. It should be your first tool of choice, although it does not diagnose all connectivity issues; it troubleshoots only Ethernet, internal modem, and

AirPort connections. If your network connection uses a Bluetooth modem, IrDA (Infrared Data Association), or built-in FireWire, you can't diagnose that connection with Network Diagnostics.

> **TIP** ▶ If Network Diagnostics can't fix your network connection, try creating and configuring a new location in the Network system preferences pane.

Network Diagnostics can troubleshoot a connection to your AirPort Base Station or other router. However, this tool cannot diagnose the router or base station. If possible, isolate the network by removing other devices.

Apple Service Diagnostic

One of the major issues you'll face when troubleshooting is determining whether the symptom is due to software or hardware. The evolution of modern processors has made this determination increasingly difficult. As computer processors and memory become more powerful they can accommodate software that can perform more hardware-like functions. Misdiagnosing an issue wastes time and may lead to unnecessary replacement of service parts. Worst of all, it may not resolve the root cause of the problem.

> **MORE INFO** ▶ For a longer discussion on the transition from specialized circuits to software, read From Hardware to Software: The Evolution of Features (**Distinguishing_Hardware_from_Software_Issues.pdf**) on the companion website for this book, www.peachpit.com/ats.deskport3.

Apple Service Diagnostic (ASD) detects hardware problems with all newer Macintosh models, including Xserve. Like Apple Hardware Test (discussed in the following section), ASD works within Open Firmware (PowerPC) or EFI (Intel) to perform low-level hardware tests. It was first introduced in June 2002 for use with Xserve systems and is not available to the general public.

NOTE ▶ Starting with the introduction of Intel-based Macintosh desktops and portables, ASD (and AHT) version numbering changed. All ASD discs are numbered sequentially, starting with the prefix "3S," as in 3S107. AHT discs are numbered sequentially, tarting with the prefix "3A," as in 3A115. This approach provides each diagnostic release a unique version number and eliminates confusion between the same version across different product lines. ASD and AHT discs for PowerPC Macs will continue to have version numbers, such as 2.5.8.

If you suspect the computer has a hardware issue, ASD provides information that can help identify the problem. If ASD detects an issue, an error is displayed. Make a note of the error before proceeding. If ASD does not detect a hardware failure, the issue may be software related.

ASD discs are typically configured as dual-boot discs, with one partition set up to execute Open Firmware or EFI diagnostic tests and the other partition set up to execute additional diagnostic tests that require a minimal Mac OS X system. Therefore, to run a full set of tests in ASD, you must use Startup Manager with ASD discs to access and start up from both partitions and execute all diagnostic tests in each.

Apple Authorized Service Providers (AASPs) can download the appropriate version of ASD, along with a Read Me file and either a test results guide or a user's guide.

MORE INFO ▶ The public and ATT users do not have access to the Service Source area where CD images are stored. For details on Apple Service Diagnostic, if you are a service provider or user of AppleCare Technician Training, refer to Knowledge Base document 112125, "Service Diagnostics Matrix."

Apple Hardware Test

Apple Hardware Test (AHT) works with code in Open Firmware (PowerPC) or EFI (Intel). AHT enables you to identify hardware issues and to test only the hardware. It is useful in any situation in which you need to confirm that compatible Macintosh computer hardware is operable—particularly when a system turns on but does not boot to the Finder. It's also extremely helpful to confirm that you've properly performed a hardware upgrade or repair.

As of early 2000, Apple includes an AHT disc with the software supplied to consumers with each new Macintosh. Recently AHT has been included as a separate partition on the Mac OS X Install disc rather than as a separate disc.

AHT is model-specific, so be sure you are using the version designed for the particular Macintosh being tested. For a list of the available versions, if you are a service provider or user of AppleCare Technician Training, check Knowledge Base document 112125, "Service Diagnostics Matrix." If your customers can't locate the copy of the AHT CD that corresponds to their computer, keep in mind that AASPs can download all versions from the CD images section of Service Source.

To use AHT on a PowerPC-based Mac, you must boot from the AHT CD using the same procedure used for starting up from any CD:

1   Insert the AHT CD into the optical drive on the system that you need to check.

2   From the Apple menu, choose Restart.

3   Press the C key until the Mac displays a small "loading" icon.

To use AHT on an Intel-based Macintosh:

1   Insert the AHT CD into the optical drive on the system that you need to check.

2   From the Apple menu, choose Restart.

3   Press the D key until the Mac displays a small "loading" icon.

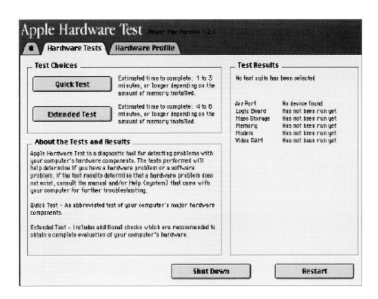

If you have the AHT CD and a supported computer system:

1   Read Apple Hardware Test: Technical FAQ (Knowledge Base document
    58624; you will be able to access this document if you're affiliated with
    an AASP or have ATT).

2   Start up the computer from the Apple Hardware Test CD.

3   Run a Quick Test on the computer.

4   Run an Extended Test on the computer.

5   Enable test looping and run at least three loops of a Quick Test.

6   Access the Hardware Profile tab and read the information.

The tests that AHT performs are all pass/fail. If a component checks out fine, it
passes, and AHT moves on to the next component. If it fails, further tests are
halted, and AHT produces an error code to let you know what has failed and
the appropriate action to take. The error code appears in the Test Results portion of the AHT window.

The error code consists of three parts:

▶ The abbreviated name of the hardware test (for example, "cpu_")

▶ The function ID (for example, "26")

▶ The error number (for example, "12345")

> **MORE INFO** ▶ For a complete explanation of error codes, if you are affiliated with an AASP or have ATT, refer to Knowledge Base documents 31195, "Apple Hardware Test: Tests and Error Codes," and 112125, "Service Diagnostics Matrix."

> **TIP** ▶ If you have access to both AHT and ASD for a given computer, use ASD. If you don't have access to ASD (for example, if you are not affiliated with an AASP), use AHT.

Apple LCD Tester

Apple LCD Tester displays black, white, red, green, and blue screens to facilitate viewing and locating screen pixel anomalies. You can download Apple LCD Tester from the Service Diagnostics Matrix.

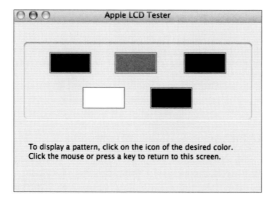

Server Monitor

Server repairs present challenges that most other repairs do not. Servers are normally used for mission-critical functions, and they handle data that is expensive and sensitive. When a hardware repair is completed, the owner or administrator of a server may demand confirmation that the system hardware is completely functional, so you need a method of quickly addressing the customer's concerns. That's where Server Monitor comes in.

Server Monitor provides detailed status of Xserve hardware functionality and can generate reports for the customer's records. Although Server Monitor will run on most Macintosh models, it can monitor only Xserves. Server Monitor can be run either directly on the Xserve being monitored or, more typically, through a local network from another Macintosh. Server Monitor reads the status of power supply voltages, temperatures, fan speeds, and many other hardware and software components on an Xserve.

Apple supplies Server Monitor via Internet download. It is part of the Mac OS X Server Admin Tools available at www.apple.com/support/downloads/serveradmintools1047.html.

If you have access to an Xserve:

1   Install the Server Admin Tools, if you haven't already.

2   Open Server Monitor.

3 Gather the following information:

▶ Server name or IP address

▶ Name of an authorized user

▶ Password for that user

4 On the upper-left side of the Server Monitor window, click Add Server.

5 Select the server to see its status.

This screen is a starting point for detailed information on the hardware status of the Xserve.

6 In the Server Monitor window, click Show Log.

7 In the Log window, click Save.

This will create an RTF file that you can email or transfer to the customer.

Diagnostic Tools Quiz

1. Can ASD check an external FireWire drive?

2. What two looping options does ASD offer?

3. What two steps does Apple recommend you take before starting up from the ASD disc?

4. Read ASD (Dual Boot) v3S109 Read Me, if you haven't already. What key command do you use to start testing using ASD (Dual Boot) v3S109?

5. What families of products are compatible with Apple Hardware Test?

6. Which of the following items should not be connected to a system while using AHT? (Choose all that apply.)

   a. SmartMedia reader

   b. USB floppy disk drive

   c. Apple keyboard

   d. External FireWire drive

7. How do you open Apple Hardware Test on a MacBook?

8. What is the difference between the Quick Test and the Extended Test?

9. Which of the following hardware components does AHT check? (Choose all that apply.)

   a. AirPort Card

   b. Keyboard

   c. Inverter board

   d. Display module

   e. Memory

   f. Video

10. If you haven't already, read Apple Hardware Test: Tests and Error Codes (Knowledge Base document 31195). What does an error code of "mem_/X/ X" signify?

11. What keyboard command toggles looping mode on and off?

12. You are using AHT to check an iMac (17-inch 1GHz) and get a test error code of "2GMC/a/b/xxxx." What is the first step Apple recommends you take?

13. You are helping a customer troubleshoot her computer over the phone. You've followed all the troubleshooting flowchart steps up to Run Diagnostics without resolving the issue. The issue does appear to be hardware-related. Do you run ASD or AHT? Why?

Answer Key

1. No; 2. Number of looping tests and elapsed time of looping tests; 3. Turn the computer off and on, and check cables, peripherals, and user controls; 4. d; 5. iBook, iMac/eMac, PowerBook, MacBook, MacBook Pro, Power Mac G4/G5, Mac Pro, Xserve, and Mac mini. Refer to Knowledge Base documents 25165, "Apple Hardware Test: Support FAQ," 58624, "Apple Hardware Test: Technical FAQ," and 31195, "Apple Hardware Test: Tests and Error Codes," as well as the Service Diagnostics Matrix and accompanying Read Me files on the companion website; 6. a, b, d; 7. Restart the computer with the AHT disc in the drive and hold down the D key until the "loading" icon appears. When the AHT main screen appears, follow the onscreen instructions and recommendations; 8. Quick Test is an abbreviated test of the computer's major components and takes only a few minutes to complete. You should use it when you don't have time to run the Extended Test, which is more thorough and is recommended for obtaining a complete evaluation of the computer's hardware. The test usually takes about four to eight minutes to complete, but could be longer. The length of the test mainly depends on the amount of RAM installed in the computer; 9. a, e, f; 10. It signifies that memory should be replaced; 11. Control-L; 12. Make sure that there is no Ethernet cable connected; 13. You should have the customer run AHT. Unless she happens to have ATT or is a service technician affiliated with an AASP, she won't have access to ASD.

Other Apple Troubleshooting Tools

After you try the appropriate quick fixes and run the appropriate diagnostics, you may need to use the following tools to research and/or repair the issue.

Console

Console, an application for viewing log files, is installed with Mac OS X in the Application/Utilities folder. Double-click its icon to launch Console, which immediately opens a window displaying the Macintosh computer's log files.

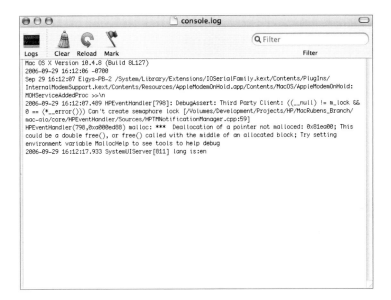

These log files record error messages from applications and background processes. These files can help you troubleshoot problems because they might contain:

▶ More detailed information than what you see in error messages

▶ Informative messages that are not displayed anywhere else

▶ Progress messages

▶ Messages that might be useful to a developer or technician assisting you with an issue

TIP ▶ To minimize the amount of information to sort through in a log, it's often best to open the Console, click Clear in the toolbar, and then reproduce the issue.

Log files and their contents sometimes appear a bit mysterious. Here is an example error message that the graphical user interface (GUI) would provide:

Here is what that error message looks like in the system.log file of the Console:

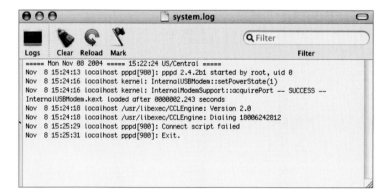

The Console system.log provides a lot more information than a two-sentence error message. But you have to understand how a log file message is structured before you can get meaning out of it. Generally speaking, you will get the most important information from checking which process provides what message, and in what order.

Let's look at the next to last line in the preceding example:

Nov 8 15:25:29 | localhost | pppd[980]: | Connect script failed

▶ The log entry starts out with the date and time of the log message: Nov 8 15:25:29.

▶ The next section is the hostname where the error occurred: localhost (local means "this" and "host" means "computer").

▶ The next part is the name of the process and the process ID number in brackets: pppd[980].

▶ After the process ID number is a colon and the message reported by the process: Connect script failed.

Looking at the messages reported from the processes listed in the system.log file, here is some of the information we can reasonably gather:

▶ acquirePort — SUCCESS — InternalUSBModem.kext loaded: The kernel extension that drives the modem loaded successfully.

▶ Dialing 18006242812: The modem has attempted to dial.

▶ Connect script failed: The connection script, which includes the information from the PPP and TCP/IP tabs in Network, didn't get the modem connected.

Since the modem actually attempted to dial, you can eliminate a hardware issue with the modem itself, and the system software that makes the modem work properly. You can take further isolation steps to ensure that your customers have the proper connection information to connect to their Internet service providers (ISPs). Perhaps they have to dial 9 to get an external line, or they have the wrong phone number to dial into their ISP's modem bank.

TIP ▶ Permission errors are often logged in the Console or system logs.

To experiment with Console:

1   Launch Console.

2   Click Logs in the upper-left corner, then double-click system.log. Note the date and time of the last entry (if one exists).

3   From the Apple menu, choose System Preferences.

4   If necessary, move the System Preferences window so that you can see the Console window.

5   In the System Preferences window, click Network.

6   From the Show pop-up menu, choose Built-in Ethernet, and from the Configure IPv4 pop-up menu, choose Using BootP.

7   Click Apply Now.

You should see some new messages in the Console window.

MORE INFO ▶ To learn more about the logs Mac OS X creates, read **Mac OS X Logs.doc** on the companion website for this book.

Install and Restore Discs

Currently Apple supplies Software Restore and Software Install CDs and DVDs with many of its computers. These discs are important troubleshooting and service resources. They are bootable, which enables you to start up a Macintosh that has a damaged OS on its drive. The discs that come with a system are normally the best known-good startup source, since they were designed specifically to work with that system.

TIP ▶ One noteworthy use of Software Install discs is resetting passwords in Mac OS X. If you forget the password to a user account, boot from the Mac OS X Install disc and choose Installer > Reset Password. This will work only if Open Firmware password protection is not enabled.

When using Software Install or Software Restore CDs, back up any customer data before proceeding. Do not take the risk of losing customer information.

Software Restore procedures erase all the information on a drive and replace it with the factory default software. This means that any data or customer-installed software will be lost.

Software Install procedures are designed to allow discrete installation of specific software. While they do not totally erase a drive, it is still a good idea to back up any important customer data before doing the installation. If you are not sure of the importance of customer data on a system, check with the customer before proceeding.

> **WARNING** ▶ The following steps require a Macintosh with a hard disk that can be erased, and the Software Install and Software Restore discs that came with that computer.

To practice conducting Software Install and Software Restore procedures:

1 Boot the system from the Software Install disc.

2 Reinstall the default OS.

3 Restart the system and verify that the installation was successful.

4 Boot the system from the Software Restore disc.

5 Following the directions, restore the system to its factory default configuration.

6 Restart the system and confirm that the restoration was successful.

Lesson Review

1. You need to restore the Mac OS X system on a Power Mac G5 (June 2004). The customer has very important files on the system. Can you use the Software Restore disc that came with the system?

   a. No, if you restore you will erase the drive.

   b. No, the restore disc doesn't have an OS on it.

   c. Yes, this will fully restore the OS on the system.

   d. Yes, but make sure you use only disc 1.

2. To boot into Safe Mode, when should you hold down the Shift key on boot?

   a. While logging in

   b. Right after the startup chime

   c. When you see the Mac OS X startup screen

   d. When you see the gray apple and progress indicator

3. Apple Hardware Test (AHT) does not need the Mac OS because:

   a. The Mac OS is included on the AHT CD.

   b. AHT relies on code that resides in Open Firmware (PowerPC) or EFI (Intel).

   c. The Mac OS ROM file is on the AHT CD.

4. A customer calls you and states that he has run AHT on his Power Mac G4 (FW 800). He asks what error code "cpu_/26/-49909" means and how he can fix the system himself. What should you tell him?

   a. The system needs its PRAM reset.

   b. He needs to bring in the computer for a possible power supply replacement.

   c. He needs to bring in the computer for a possible processor module replacement.

5. You are attempting to determine if a PowerBook G4 (Double-Layer SD) is working correctly after performing a logic board replacement. Which of the following diagnostics is the best one to use for looping tests?

    a. Network Diagnostics

    b. System Profiler

    c. Apple Service Diagnostic

    d. Apple Hardware Test

6. You are servicing a Power Mac G5 (Late 2005) and need to reformat the hard drive. Which Apple utility do you use?

    a. Software Update

    b. Disk Utility

    c. System Profiler

    d. Apple Hardware Test

7. True or false: You can use the Software Restore CD to reinstall Mac OS X on an iMac G5 without erasing important data files on the hard drive.

8. What is the function of Console?

    a. It enables you to read log files.

    b. It is used for command-line input.

    c. It shows you currently active processes.

    d. You use it to delete corrupt preferences files.

Answer Key

1. b; 2. b; 3. b; 4. c; 5. c; 6. b; 7. False; 8. a

3

General Troubleshooting Theory

If you are experienced in troubleshooting and supporting computers, you probably have your own approaches and procedures, and don't feel that the Apple troubleshooting process has anything new to offer. Experienced technicians are adept at recognizing symptoms that match what they have seen before and checking to confirm that the issue is the same. They use their experience and intuition to determine the steps necessary to address a particular situation and resolve it very quickly.

But when a situation is outside of their experience, even the best technician can get stuck. That's when the need for a systematic approach becomes evident. So read on: The troubleshooting steps in this lesson give you a proven method to use when more random approaches fail. When you finish this lesson, you will have a proven process to back up your ever-increasing experience.

Goals and Processes

Let's get into the practice of being systematic by making sure we all agree on the basic goals of the process and by reminding you of some important ideas and tasks to keep in mind as you work.

Success and Speed: Two Troubleshooting Goals

We believe that how you go about a process is as important as its outcome—in this case, that an efficient and logical approach to troubleshooting will help you find and resolve an issue. To that end, bear in mind these two equally important goals:

► Fix a product properly.

► Fix a product quickly.

Fixing a product properly results from many elements working together. These elements include:

► Following systematic troubleshooting procedures

► Following proper procedures for taking apart and reassembling a product

► Using up-to-date references and tools

► Not creating new issues

This process helps you reach the goal of giving your customer a product that works completely and correctly.

The second major goal of the efficient troubleshooter is to fix the product quickly. This does not mean taking shortcuts or doing sloppy work. It means making sure that you are not wasting time. Customers want their products back as soon as possible, so the faster you can troubleshoot a situation, the more satisfied your customers will be.

Winging It

Suppose that you are attempting to determine why an iMac is not displaying any video. The last time you saw this situation, the computer had a bad main logic board, so your experience suggests that this iMac has a similar issue. If you have had experience with a number of iMac computers that had no video, you may also be aware that resetting the power management unit (PMU) chip can address this issue. And you may know that resetting parameter random-access memory (PRAM) is a recommended step.

If you try resetting PRAM and that does not work, you might then open up the system and reset the PMU. If that has no effect either, perhaps you'll swap out the main logic board and find that the system is working now. You have resolved the issue…or have you? Later, you could find that the main logic board was perfectly okay and that you conducted an expensive repair that may have been unnecessary.

What happened here? You got the system working, but the main logic board you replaced is a good part. Your approach fixed the computer, but now you have a new mystery. The explanation: The video issue was due to the logic board not being seated correctly. Replacing the logic board automatically resulted in seating it properly, but it did not need to be replaced.

So the lesson here is that experience and intuition aren't always a substitute for a systematic method. It is not easy or practical to automatically know all the possible resolutions to a specific troubleshooting issue, and that's when it's time to address the issue in a careful, systematic way.

Troubleshooting To-Do List

Be sure to use the following suggestions throughout the troubleshooting process. One or more of these might provide inspiration for an otherwise difficult issue:

▶ **Keep notes:** What starts out as a simple troubleshooting session can sometimes develop into a major task. Start taking notes from the very beginning of the troubleshooting process, even if it seems like a simple issue to fix. Write down each piece of information you gather, the results of each test you perform, and your proposed solution.

▶ **Consult resources:** In addition to experience and techniques, a good troubleshooter possesses product knowledge. Consulting available resources is a vital part of obtaining knowledge about the product and about the specific issue you are troubleshooting. Browsing through references such as Apple Service Source or the Apple Knowledge Base can be particularly helpful when you find yourself stuck without an idea of what to try next in your troubleshooting research. It can stimulate new thoughts and ideas about the source of the issue.

▶ **Consider the human factor:** When you have been working long and hard on a situation that has you stumped, take a break (coffee is optional). Frustration can impair your ability to think logically and rationally. But after a short rest, you may be surprised at the solutions that come to mind.

Troubleshooting Process

Now that you are well equipped with troubleshooting goals and processes, you are ready to embark on the systematic journey. There are two major stages in Apple's recommended troubleshooting process:

▶ Identify the issue.

▶ Perform the actual repair (or take other steps that identifying the issue has made clear).

To identify the issue, you must:

1 Gather information.

2 Verify the issue.

3 Try quick fixes.

4 Use appropriate diagnostics.

5 Follow systematic fault isolation.

6 Use additional resources to research the issue.

7 Escalate the issue (if necessary).

After you have identified the issue, you must:

1 Repair or replace the faulty item.

2 Verify the repair by testing the product thoroughly.

3 Inform the user of what you have done and complete administrative tasks (yes, really).

We review these processes in detail in the following sections of this lesson. Keeping the steps of the troubleshooting process straight is sometimes difficult for new technicians. Apple has produced a General Troubleshooting Flowchart as a reference.

> **NOTE** ▶ This flowchart (**AGTFwithNotes.pdf**) is also available on this book's companion website (www.peachpit.com/ats/deskport3).

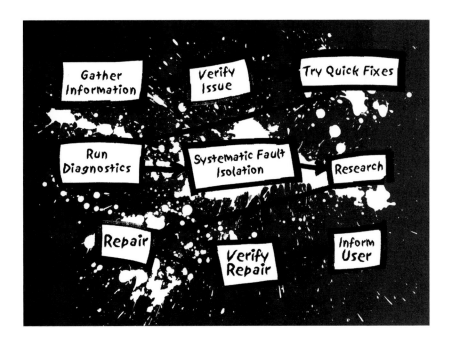

Gather Information

It is important to know as much as you can about the situation before you jump headlong into trying to fix it. Gathering information is the first step in successful troubleshooting.

If the computer is functional, run System Profiler (discussed in Lesson 2, "Software Tools") to compile useful technical information on the Macintosh and its components. In some cases, the customer is available to explain the nature of the situation. In those cases, the following tips will assist you in getting accurate and useful information from your customer.

When you question customers who are having trouble with their computers, you have to understand that they are probably not happy with their situation. Your courtesy and professionalism will make the circumstances better and enable you to gather information to repair the product. Be patient. Be polite. Be conscious that you are there to help the customer. Furthermore, be aware that customers may not share your level of technical expertise or understand the terminology, so try to talk to customers at their level.

Follow these tips when gathering information from customers:

▶ Start with open-ended questions such as "What is the issue?" Open-ended questions generally start with words like *how, why, when, who, what*, and *where*. They cannot be answered with "yes" or "no."

▶ Let customers explain in their own words what they have experienced. Do not interrupt the customer—interrupting generally prompts someone to start over.

▶ As you begin to understand the basics of the issue, start using close-ended questions that require more limited, specific answers and can often be answered with "yes" or "no," such as "What operating system are you using?" The customer will either tell you what the Mac OS version is or tell you that he does not know.

▶ Verify your understanding of what the customer has told you. Restate what you have been told and get the customer's agreement that you understand the issue, such as "So what's happening is that when you try X, Y happens. Is that correct?"

▶ If the customer agrees that you understand, continue to gather information. If the customer does not agree that you understand, clarify what you misstated and again verify your understanding. Do not continue until the customer agrees that you understand the issue.

When troubleshooting an issue, you need to know how the computer is supposed to start up so you can compare that against what's being described, and ask the appropriate questions. Here's a visual description of the startup process.

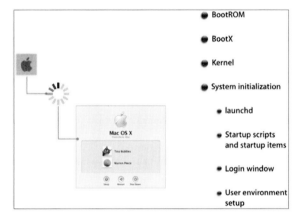

The following table lists the startup sequence for Intel-based Macintosh systems.

Startup Sequence Stage	Cue
Power On, Boot-ROM/RAM check is initialized	You may hear a click, fans or hard disks spinning, or CRT crackling
BootROM—POST: POST runs diagnostic on memory and processor POST or BootROM failure ▶ One beep: No RAM installed. ▶ Two beeps: Incompatible RAM types.	Black screen, power LED on

Startup Sequence Stage	Cue
▶ Three beeps: No good memory banks. ▶ Four beeps: No good boot images in the boot ROM. ▶ Five beeps: Processor is not usable. ▶ Power LED flashes once per second = ▶ Bad RAM, no RAM ▶ Power LED continuously repeats a series of three flashes and a pause = Marginal RAM	
BootROM—EFI ▶ Metallic Apple: Found boot.efi. ▶ Circle with slash: Could not load boot.efi, or some other issue.	Boot chime
BootROM—EFI ▶ Flashing globe: Looking for booter/kernel on NetBoot server. ▶ Metallic Apple with spinning earth: Found booter/kernel on NetBoot server. ▶ Folder with blinking question mark: No bootable device has been found.	Boot chime
Kernel	Gray screen with Metallic Apple and spinning gear
launchd	Blue screen
loginwindow	Login window appears.
User Environment Setup	The text "Logging In" appears in login window along with a progress bar upon successful login. Desktop and Dock appear.

There are two abnormal behaviors around startup that you should be aware of so you can probe effectively:

▶   No power

▶   No video

Follow these steps to learn about troubleshooting these two behaviors in an iMac (24-inch):

1   Open the service manual for the iMac (24-inch).

2   Click the Troubleshooting disclosure triangle.

3   Click the Symptom Charts disclosure triangle.

4   Click Power Issues.

5   Skim the descriptions of symptoms and solutions.

6   Click No Video.

7   Skim the descriptions of symptoms and solutions.

Common Symptoms Quiz

1.   You are troubleshooting an iMac (24-inch) with a customer over the phone. The customer says the computer won't turn on. What power-related probing questions should you ask?

2.   You're working on an iMac (24-inch) a customer brought in because the display isn't working. What video-related questions should you ask to gather information and verify the issue?

Answer Key

1. "Can you see any light, even from the back, in the display? Can you hear any fans or hard drives spinning?"; 2. "Does the computer turn on? Can you hear the boot chime? Does a white LED appear on the front bezel? Can you hear sounds from the fan or drive activity? Does the display show any picture or color?"

▶ Isolating to Software or Hardware

Typically, your first task when trying to get a computer working again is to figure out whether the issue is caused by hardware or software. If you want to be efficient, your best bet is to start with software. In fact, to locate the problem, consider these four categories in order:

1. User issues
2. Software issues
3. OS issues
4. Hardware issues

For each category, follow these steps:

1. Quick fixes: These troubleshooting steps are inexpensive, fast (shorter than 20 minutes), and non-destructive (to user data).
2. Diagnostic software/tools: These are Apple or third-party software or tools that can diagnose and/or correct faults. Usually they take longer than quick fixes.
3. Systematic fault isolation: This is a potentially painstaking search procedure that successively eliminates half the system as a possible trouble source. It is used in only less than 1 percent of cases.

User Errors

You check for user errors in the course of gathering information, duplicating the problem, and trying quick fixes. Yet keep in mind the possibility of incorrectly set preferences, incompatible equipment, and incorrect assumptions on the user's part. Take nothing for granted.

Continues on next page

► **Isolating to Software or Hardware** *(continued)*

Software-Related Issues

Incompatible or damaged software, viruses, and other software problems can all cause symptoms that look like hardware problems. But replacing hardware won't solve them—and it costs time and money. Always check for software problems before replacing any hardware. Remember that you need to be checking both application packages and the Mac OS.

Mac OS X stores six things in PRAM:

► Display and video settings such as refresh rate, screen resolution, and number of colors

► Time zone

► Startup disk

► Speaker volume

► DVD region setting

► Kernel panic information (only on first reboot after a panic)

If the symptom you're troubleshooting is related to these, try resetting PRAM.

Open Firmware contains the startup disk information, artificial limits on RAM or CPUs, and persistent settings for safe, verbose, or single-user modes. Open Firmware also keeps a *device tree*, which is a record of hardware chips and devices. The device tree is how the operating system knows which hardware is available through which controller chips. If you're experiencing a device-related issue, you can try resetting Open Firmware.

A computer's PMU or SMU is relevant to sleep/wake issues, battery issues (such as not charging at all), power-on issues, power issues with a built-in display (no video at all), or port issues (USB/FireWire ports appear dead). If you're troubleshooting symptoms relating to these items, try resetting the PMU or SMU.

Continues on next page

▶ **Isolating to Software or Hardware** *(continued)*

Run Repair Disk Permissions if you're troubleshooting a confirmed permissions-related issue. How do you know when you have a permissions issue? Use Console to see if it reports a permissions-related error. If you are trying to copy, move, or otherwise modify a file to which you should have access and you receive a message that you don't have permission, this would be a permissions-related issue. Even if you are having a permissions-related issue, if the affected file is in your Home folder, repairing permissions will have no effect.

When Disk Utility can't repair the directory on a volume, an Archive and Install will not resolve those issues. In fact, it can make the situation worse. The disk directory is not something that is installed, but rather it is a way of cataloging what is stored on the disk. If you have an issue that Disk Utility can't repair, a more robust disk utility may be able to repair the issue. However, if these fail, the only way to obtain a new directory is to erase the drive.

If it appears that the hard drive is failing, particularly if Disk Utility is reporting a Self-Monitoring Analysis and Reporting Technology (SMART) failure, AHT fails on the mass storage test, or when the drive is making loud audible noises, zeroing all data won't resolve the issue. While zeroing all data on a disk may reveal bad sectors, it doesn't fix them. Generally, if a standard format of the drive doesn't resolve the issue, there may be a hardware failure.

Hardware Issues

Remove external devices and internal cards (except the video card, if needed for display) and test the main unit alone. If the issue remains, you have isolated it to the computer itself. If the issue disappears, reinstall the cards and peripherals one by one, until the symptoms reappear. When they do, you have found the culprit—or at least a clue.

Verify the Issue

Verifying the issue is extremely important in successful troubleshooting. It gives you a chance to objectively confirm the extent and the nature of the situation. In the long run, it saves you from wasting time working on the wrong issue.

Using the information you have gathered, set up the system and try to re-create the issue. Here is an example: "When I am using my spreadsheet program and try to print in landscape mode to my inkjet printer, the Mac OS 9 system stops responding halfway through the first page. It doesn't matter what else the system is doing or what spreadsheet I try to print—the same thing happens every time. It first occurred yesterday. I used to be able to print this way without any trouble."

Start up the system, open the spreadsheet program, and try to print. Does the system truly stop responding or could it be something else? For example, maybe you'll discover:

- ▶ A long delay that the user perceives as the system not responding
- ▶ The system waiting for a response to a dialog on the screen (such as clicking an OK button)

For every issue, there can be other explanations for the system's behavior. Make sure you aren't trying to troubleshoot a nonexistent issue or an issue that has not been well defined.

If you are helping someone troubleshoot, the act of verifying the issue is crucial. Sometimes the issue can be solved merely by watching a person go through the process of re-creating it and observing that she is operating the system incorrectly.

In other cases, watching a person re-create the issue yields additional information about the circumstances under which the issue occurs (that is, the person forgot to tell you some things about when and how the issue occurs). Or, your observation of the issue may be quite different from the description you are given.

The customer's actions give you insight into the customer's technical expertise and may answer some of the other questions.

▶ **Step Back and Ask More Questions**

Before you continue to troubleshoot, ask your customer (or yourself, if the customer is not available) the following questions:

1. What is the product model and serial number?

    With this information, you can immediately match the product against any possible known issues for that product.

2. Can you reproduce the situation now?

    Intermittent issues can be very hard to isolate. Probe for circumstances or environmental factors that may be significant.

3. What version of the operating system are you using?

    There may be specific issues with the version of the Mac OS that the customer is using.

4. When did the issue start? Has the product ever worked? What was the last thing changed or added to the system?

    With these questions, you can determine whether the introduction of new hardware or software may have contributed to, or caused, the issue.

5. How is this feature intended to work?

    Here you can determine whether the customer is confused or misinformed about a feature's proper function.

6. Does the issue occur only with one specific application?

    In this case, you are trying to determine whether the issue is systemic or affects only one program.

7. Does the issue disappear if you restart the system (Mac OS 9) with extensions disabled (by holding down the Shift key at startup) or with Apple-only extension sets?

    You want to determine whether there are third-party software conflicts or corrupt software components.

Continues on next page

▶ **Step Back and Ask More Questions** *(continued)*

8. Does the issue disappear if you restart the system with all external devices removed?

    You want to determine whether a hardware device may be the cause of the issue.

9. Does the issue disappear if you restart the system with all third-party internal devices (RAM, PCI card, SCSI/USB/FireWire devices) removed?

    By doing this, you can determine whether a third-party hardware device may be the cause of the issue.

10. Does the issue disappear when the system is restarted from the system CD or a Disk Tools disk?

    By working with known-good system software, you can determine whether the installed system software is the cause of the issue.

11. What devices are used with this system?

    Understanding the system's operating environment can provide you with helpful indications of where the issue may be based.

12. What have you done to try to resolve the issue?

    The customer's actions gives you insight into the customer's technical expertise and may answer some of the other questions.

Try Quick Fixes

A quick fix is not necessarily the most likely solution to the issue, but because it is easy to perform and involves little time or expense, it is worth trying. There is nothing more frustrating than spending hours isolating an issue only to find out later that a quick fix solves it.

A quick fix is defined here as a repair action that can be performed quickly, involves little or no risk of harm to the system, and has little or no cost. An experienced, efficient troubleshooter will try one or more quick fixes before taking on the more time-consuming tasks involved with isolating the issue.

> **NOTE** ▶ "Quick fix" does not imply a temporary, substandard, or sloppy repair.

Let's take another look at the printing issue we just considered. Possible quick fixes in this situation include:

▶ Turn the printer off and back on again, then try to print.

▶ Restart the system and try again.

▶ Disconnect and securely reconnect the printer cable (being careful to follow safety precautions).

▶ Take the paper out of the paper cassette and reinsert it to be sure that it is inserted properly.

Here are some more examples of quick fixes:

▶ Disconnect and reconnect power cables, printer cables, monitor cables, and so forth. (Make sure that the Macintosh and its devices are turned off when you do this, except when dealing with USB and FireWire devices, which are hot-pluggable.)

▶ Rebuild the desktop by holding down Command-Option as the Finder loads in pre–Mac OS X.

▶ Completely shut down the computer (in as proper a manner as possible), wait at least 10 seconds, and then turn it back on. Better yet, turn off the computer and all of its connected peripherals, wait a bit, then turn everything back on.

▶ Adjust physical user controls (such as brightness and contrast knobs on a display) as well as software controls (such as the output volume setting in Sound preferences).

This is only a partial list of quick fixes. The situation and your experience will determine which quick fixes make sense for troubleshooting the issue you are working on.

A good source of quick fixes is the troubleshooting symptom charts in the Troubleshooting lesson of the product's service manual. You should consider any steps that fit the criteria for quick fixes. Then, as you gain experience, you will develop your own collection of quick fixes.

Quick Fixes for Mac OS X

Mac OS X has a lot of settings and toggles that you can work with to help quickly determine and isolate issues. There are so many, in fact, that you might not have discovered them all. This section lists other quick fixes that might be appropriate for systems running Mac OS X. Some of them can affect data on the customer's system, so you must consult with the customer to determine whether he has a current backup and weigh the advantages of the quick fix against the possible inconvenience or time required.

To help you keep your tests as low-impact as possible, we've broken the Mac OS X quick-fix tests into three categories, which you should try in order.

Innocuous/No-impact Tests

▶ Restart or shut down.

▶ Run System Profiler.

> **TIP** ▶ If you have access to Service Source, you can check to see whether any of the Top Support Questions look similar to the situation you're seeing. (You'll find these from the Service Source main page, by opening the product menu and then choosing the product's support page.)

▶ Start up in Safe Mode (Mac OS X 10.2 and later), which loads only the minimum necessary files and performs an elaborate directory check of the hard disk (which is why it can take a long time to start up). After you hear the startup sound, press Shift and hold it until the progress indicator displays "Safe Boot." To end the Safe Boot and get back to typical operation, just restart as normal.

▶ Suppress Auto-Login (in Login or Accounts preferences) if you suspect that the issue lies within the default user's system configuration, and then restart and log in as a different user.

▶ Suppress Login items by holding down the Shift key as soon as the Finder appears in Mac OS X.

▶ Start up from a known-good disc such as Install Mac OS or Restoration CD.

▶ Click Repair Disk Permissions in the First Aid tab of Disk Utility.

▶ Start up in single-user mode by pressing Command-S during startup. After displaying a bunch of technical text, the Macintosh should show a UNIX command-line prompt (#). Enter any UNIX commands you want, or type *exit* and press Return.

▶ Start up in verbose mode by pressing Command-V during startup. This forces the Macintosh to display text that explains what UNIX is doing before the customary graphical user interface (GUI) appears. You'll need to understand at least basic UNIX for this to be of any use.

▶ Start up in another Mac OS by selecting a different volume in Startup Disk preferences.

▶ Relaunch Finder by Option-clicking the Finder icon in the Dock and choosing Relaunch from the menu that appears.

▶ Disconnect all external devices.

▶ Turn off Screen Saver and Energy Saver (if troubleshooting an installation issue) in System Preferences.

▶ Verify with other users (if troubleshooting a network issue).

▶ Connect to another device or volume (if troubleshooting a network issue).

▶ Connect to PPP test server (if troubleshooting a modem issue).

Moderate Impact Tests

▶ Adjust user settings.

▶ If troubleshooting a network issue, check the settings in the Firewall tab in Sharing preferences.

► In Network preferences, choose Show > Network Port Configurations. Make sure necessary ports (such as Ethernet or AirPort) are activated.

► In System Preferences, check the Startup Disk selection (if troubleshooting a startup issue).

► Force-quit a troublesome application by choosing Force Quit from the Apple menu.

► In Accounts preferences, log in as a (new) test user. Since most user settings are tied to the user account, you can create a new account with which you can test a more standardized user environment, presumably with no conflicting or corrupted system resources.

► Launch the Disk Utility, select the startup disk, click the First Aid tab, then click Repair Disk Permissions. If any repairs were necessary, repeat the process.

► Move, rename, or delete potentially problematic preferences files. The applications that use the preference files will automatically re-create clean copies as necessary.

► Update the printer driver (if troubleshooting a printing issue).

► Update the firmware for peripherals (such as AirPort Base Station or an internal optical drive) if possible.

► Move a troublesome device from one port to another to determine whether the port or the peripheral is at fault.

► Use known-good peripherals (for example, monitor, disk drive, printer).

Invasive/High-impact Procedures

► Reinstall the suspect application.

► Reset the PRAM.

► Reset the PMU or system management unit (SMU) chip (see the service manual). Always reset the main logic board before resetting the PMU or SMU a second time.

► Replace current RAM with known-good RAM.

Run Diagnostics

If trying quick fixes doesn't resolve the problem, your next step is to run appropriate diagnostics. (This step is on the flowchart.)

As you learned in Lesson 2, diagnostic tools are software packages that allow you to check the performance of a system. In that lesson you reviewed and used Apple's primary diagnostic software.

These, and other diagnostic packages, enable you to determine if the system components are functioning correctly.

Systematic Fault Isolation

Systematic fault isolation is a technique for systematically isolating the source of an issue. You start by eliminating roughly half of the items you are checking, then trying to re-create the issue. Continue halving your search group until you find the source of the issue. To do this, you must apply your knowledge of the product, its common issues, and the symptoms as you check one possible cause after another, in a logical order.

This part of the troubleshooting process can be the most difficult and the most time-consuming, so don't take the time to try systematic fault isolation unless all the following conditions apply:

▶   You've tried all the appropriate quick fixes and diagnostic tools and still don't know what's causing the issue.

▶   You've checked the service manual, Knowledge Base, and other references, and still don't know what's causing the issue.

▶   There is data on the boot hard drive that you can't get off and can't erase.

Here are some ways to "halve" the problem:

▶   Find the functional area—sometimes called a "problem space"—that the issue affects. For instance, the general functional areas for a typical Macintosh could be considered software, logic and control, memory, video, input/output (I/O), and power.

If you can narrow down the issue to, for example, the video area, you can narrow your search to the parts that relate to video: the monitor, cables and connectors, video random-access memory (VRAM), video card (if present), and logic board.

▶ Work from largest to smallest components of the system. For example, if you suspect there is an issue with a component of the OS, you would want to first check the complete Mac OS by starting the system from a known-good CD with the same version of the Mac OS. Only when you know that the rest of the computer system is working correctly would you want to start investigating the components of the Mac OS.

▶ It is ultimately more efficient to methodically test one thing at a time than it is to try two or three things at once. This means reinstalling the original part if a replacement part does not correct the issue.

Component Isolation

Component isolation is a systematic fault isolation technique with which you can accurately and decisively determine the source of hardware issues. That is, after you've eliminated user error, software, and the OS as potential sources of the issue, and you've applied the appropriate hardware quick fixes and diagnostics, you can turn to component isolation.

Here's how it works: Using a minimal system, you start up a computer and observe its behavior. Armed with an understanding of the normal power flow sequence (discussed later in this lesson), the symptoms you observe may direct you to add or replace components in a specific sequence until you can determine the hardware component that is causing the issue.

Don't confuse this procedure with randomly swapping modules until a system finally works; component isolation works in a much more systematic manner. You should use component isolation when you are attempting to isolate intermittent, hard-to-find hardware issues or when other approaches have not worked, and you need to make sure that the system hardware is working correctly.

NOTE ▶ Component isolation requires an electrostatic discharge–compliant work area, appropriate tools for taking apart the product you are testing, and job aids identifying components of the system and the steps of the procedure for that system.

Understanding the Power Flow Process

When a computer starts up successfully, a large number of different activities occur. Let's look at a desktop Macintosh as it starts to boot. The following steps are a very simplified description of a complex process, but they will help you understand:

1. When you press the power button on your desktop computer, power flows through the power cord to the power supply. When you press the power button on a PowerBook G4 (15-inch FW800) while plugged into a power adapter, power flows through the power cord to the power adapter and then to the sound/DC-in board. If the power cord or power button is defective, the system will not boot.

2. On a desktop, the power supply feeds power to the logic board. If the power supply or the connection from the power supply to the logic board is defective, the system will not boot.

   On a portable, the sound/DC-in board feeds power to the logic board and the removable battery. If the sound/DC-in board or the connection from the sound/DC-in board to the logic board is defective, the system will not boot.

3. In both Macintosh models, the logic boards feed power to a processor. If the logic board or the processor is defective, the computer will not boot.

4. The logic board feeds power to the RAM as well. If the RAM is defective, the computer will not boot. Instead, you will hear an error chime for defective RAM.

5. The logic board sends a boot chime or signal to the speaker assembly in the Front Panel board if the POST is successful. If this boot chime occurs, you know that the components in this power chain are working correctly.

Starting with a Minimal System

In the power flow description earlier in this lesson, we made no mention of hard disk drives. This was intentional, because when setting up a minimal system for the component-isolation technique, you start with only the components necessary to hear a startup sound or see a flashing question mark on the monitor.

You do not need a hard disk drive when testing power flow in a minimal system. The POST does not rely on any components of the Mac OS residing on the hard disk. Likewise, if you have a working power button on the Macintosh itself, you do not even need a keyboard.

Removable components include the hard drive, optical drive, modem, Bluetooth module, AirPort Extreme card, display, inverter board, additional RAM, power adapter (if running from battery), and battery (if running from AC adapter).

> **NOTE** ▶ For some Macintosh models, RAM is not a required component because a minimal amount of RAM may already be part of the main logic board on those models.

Here are some common portable components:

▶ The logic board in most portables contains what in desktop systems would be entirely separate cards. This can include the processor, video chipset, and, in some cases, RAM. All currently shipping portable systems have processors soldered onto the logic board. Some older systems had processor cards that could be separated from the logic board. Since so many components are built onto the logic board, it has many potential ways to fail. When isolating a video issue to the on-board video chipset, make sure to test using external displays. If the issue persists on both built-in and external displays, then most likely the video chipset on the main logic board is faulty. If external video is good then the issue is likely isolated to the built-in display.

▶ The hard drive is a permanent data storage mechanism. It's one of the major power draws in a portable computer and one of the few moving parts in most portable systems. Common issues with the hard drive can include loss of data, crashing, freezing, excessive noise, and slow performance.

▶ The optical drive is used to read optical media. It's one of the few moving parts in most portable systems. When in use, it can be fairly loud and can use a large amount of power. Common issues include not reading media, not ejecting media, failure to burn media, or damaging media when read.

▶ RAM is temporary data storage. It's faster than a hard drive and is used to cache information, so as soon as power is gone the data is gone. Portables generally use small outline dual inline memory modules (SO-DIMMS). Common issues include kernel panics, crashing, and freezing.

▶ The DC-in board is where the alternating current (AC) adapter plugs into the computer. This is required to start the computer even if there is a battery present. Common issues are not charging the battery, not lighting up the ring on the power adapter, and not supplying any power to the system. If used improperly, AC adapters or other items end up stuck in the DC socket.

▶ The inverter board converts and supplies power to the fluorescent lamps that provide backlighting inside the display module. Common issues include noise when adjusting brightness, or no backlight on displays.

▶ The display is the main output device on portable systems, so this is where you will see what is going on. Common display failures are pixels stuck on or off, tinting, lines on the display, or physical damage.

▶ The low voltage differential signaling (LVDS) or time division multiplexed signaling (TDMS) cable transfers video information from the on-board video chipset to the display. Sometimes you can identify cable failures easily by moving the display back and forth. If the issue changes, the LVDS or TDMS cable is most likely the issue. Common failures include lines in the display, tinting, and loss of video.

▶ The battery allows a portable to be portable. Some portables allow you to hot-swap batteries. Common issues include not allowing the computer to power on, short battery life, and incorrectly reporting battery life.

▶ The AC adapter converts the AC voltage coming from the wall to DC voltage that the components can use. It acts as the power supply would in a desktop system. Common issues include no power, the charge ring not lighting, the tip getting broken off in the DC port, and getting tripped over and causing physical damage to the computer.

How Do I Isolate Components?

In general, component isolation consists of the following steps:

1   Set up a minimal system by removing *all* system components that are not needed for the system to boot and produce a boot chime and/or a flashing question mark.

2   Boot the system and observe/listen for what occurs.

3   If you get a boot chime and/or a flashing question mark, the system is operating correctly.

This tells you that one (or more) of the components you just removed may be the root cause of the original issue.

4   If you do not get a boot chime and/or a flashing question mark, check the components of the minimal system by replacing them with known-good parts in a specified order.

The advantage here is that now you have only a small number of components left to replace, instead of having to guess which component to replace from among perhaps over a dozen components in a fully configured unit.

5   Whenever you replace a part, reset the PMU before rebooting.

Doing this ensures that the PMU will not have any issues that may mimic and therefore mask your original problem.

Component Isolation Quiz

1. What are the five components of a minimal system for a PowerBook G4 (15-inch FW800)?

2. When you first start up a minimal system, you do not get any sound. What component should you check first?

3. If a minimal system is starting up correctly, what component do you add first?

4. You get no startup sound from a system after swapping the main logic board. What components are likely at fault?

5. Why is it important to check cables?

Answer Key

1. AC power adapter or main battery, DC-input board, logic board, speaker assembly, and CPU with heat sink; 2. Power adapter; 3. The display; 4. DC-input board; 5. A bad connection due to a defective cable acts just like a bad component.

Research in Additional Resources

At the start of this lesson you learned that, along with good troubleshooting technique, product knowledge and experience are the basis for efficient, professional troubleshooting. If you have completed the steps described so far and still can't determine the source of the issue, it is time to research additional resources.

In situations in which you may not have in-depth experience or product knowledge, you can use such references as Service Source and the Knowledge Base. These resources are collections of the best information assembled by Apple. There is a good chance that solutions to your issues are documented in one or both of these references.

Escalate the Issue

If you still cannot troubleshoot an issue despite your best efforts, you may need to escalate your problem to Apple. How you do this depends on where you are located, and the practices and policies of your business or agency.

Repair or Replace the Faulty Item

After determining the source of a service issue, it is time to repair or replace the faulty item. There are several steps that you must take before starting to replace software or hardware:

▶ Make a full backup of the customer's hard disk before updating, reinstalling, or otherwise modifying the software on a system. This ensures that you can restore the system to its original state if you need to do so.

▶ Use known-good software when modifying a system. Avoid introducing new issues while trying to solve the original one.

▶ Look for the latest versions of software when updating or reinstalling software. This is particularly important for System folder components such as extensions, control panels, and peripheral drivers. At the same time, you should be careful not to add new software components that can adversely affect applications and other software that the customer has placed on the system.

▶ Follow all safety guidelines for working on computer systems. This includes powering down systems before connecting or disconnecting peripherals.

▶ Observe all appropriate ESD precautions before working on hardware. (You will learn about ESD in Lesson 4, "Safe Working Procedures and General Maintenance.")

Verify the Repair

To ensure a positive customer experience, thoroughly test every product you repair and ensure that the computer is functioning correctly before returning it to the customer. Sometimes you may resolve one issue only to find another, or you may have repaired the right module but left a cable unplugged when reassembling the product. You need to make sure that the entire issue has been resolved, no new issues have been introduced during troubleshooting and repair, and the computer will continue to function after the repair.

> **TIP** When verifying repairs for central processing units (CPUs), use Apple Service Diagnostic (ASD) or Apple Hardware Test (AHT) to test the entire system, even if you repaired only one part of the system. If possible, run looping tests for several hours, to catch any intermittent issues.
>
> When verifying repairs for peripherals, if there is a diagnostic available for the product, use it! For example, many printers have built-in self tests; read the product's manual to determine how to initiate this useful feature.

Repair Verification Quiz

1. You replaced the main logic board of a computer that was having intermittent issues. The situation seems to be resolved. How should you verify that the intermittent issues no longer occur?

2. A customer's iMac was not printing to a third-party color inkjet printer. You have reinstalled the printer driver and generated a black-and-white test page on this printer. Do you need to verify further? If so, what should you do?

Answer Key

1. Conduct looping tests of the system over an extended period using ASD or a similar diagnostic; 2. Print a color test page. You have checked only part of the system's performance so far.

Inform the User and Complete Administrative Tasks

Once you have returned the computer to normal operation or escalated the issue, inform the user of the work that you completed. Also, give customers information to improve their computing experience. Taking time to teach customers how to avoid future issues adds value and improves their experience.

Keep in mind the following suggestions for giving your customer the best possible information:

▶ Print out diagnostics that you have completed and show them to the customer.

▶ Explain any steps the customer can take to avoid having situations recur. For example:

  ▶ If the customer has shut off the system incorrectly, explain the hazards of not shutting down properly.

  ▶ If the customer's system was made unusable by a virus, teach the customer how to avoid viruses in the future.

  ▶ If the customer has lost data, describe some backup methods.

Your final step is to complete any administrative tasks. Each Apple Authorized Service Provider (AASP) has different administrative procedures for documenting service and handling parts. How you complete the administrative tasks for servicing an Apple product depends on where you are located and the internal policies of your business or agency.

Lesson Review

1. A customer tells you that her iMac has stopped working. The first thing to do is:

    a. Run ASD.

    b. Try quick fixes.

    c. Reduce the computer to a minimum system.

    d. Gather more information.

2. A MacBook is not recognizing the additional RAM that a customer just installed. You cannot resolve the issue over the phone, so the customer brings the system to you for repair. What items would be useful for resolving the issue? (Choose all that apply.)

    a. Replacement keyboard and mouse

    b. ASD

    c. System software CDs

    d. Replacement RAM SO-DIMM

    e. Tools

3. Which of the following is not an example of systematic fault isolation?

    a. Check for software issues before replacing any hardware.

    b. Remove external devices and internal cards, and test the computer by itself.

    c. If a module is easy to replace, swap it right away.

    d. Inspect components visually.

4. A customer's Power Mac G4 running Mac OS X 10.2.6 does not turn on. What is the first step to take after gathering information from the customer?

    a. Run ASD.

    b. Refer to Service Source.

    c. Check the power source and cable connections.

    d. Reset the PRAM.

5. What is the first step to consider when a computer with a cathode-ray tube (CRT) display starts up to a black screen?

   a. Run AHT.

   b. Adjust the brightness and contrast controls.

   c. Rebuild the desktop.

   d. Reset the PRAM.

6. You cannot solve an issue after trying quick fixes, running diagnostics, and consulting the troubleshooting charts in Service Source. What is the next step to take?

   a. Call Apple.

   b. Look up the issue in the Knowledge Base.

   c. Check the cable connections.

7. Which of the following steps should you take before escalating an issue? (Choose all that apply.)

   a. Verify the issue.

   b Systematic fault isolation.

   c. Verify the repair.

   d. Try quick fixes.

8. A customer brought you an iMac that is not working. Which of the following questions would be the most helpful to start with?

   a. What is the serial number?

   b. What seems to be the issue?

   c. Have you had this issue before?

   d. Where do you use this computer?

9. What are the three characteristics of a quick fix?

   a. Can be performed quickly

   b. Involves little or no risk of harm to the system

   c. Has little or no cost

   d. Uses Apple-approved third-party diagnostics

10. You cannot start up an iMac. What two things do you need to check first?

    a. Power supply and power board

    b. Internal cabling and board seating

    c. Power outlet and power cord

    d. Keyboard and mouse

11. Which of the following items qualifies as a quick fix?

    a. Format the hard drive.

    b. Power cycle a cable modem.

    c. Carry the computer into a service provider.

    d. Upgrade the OS from 10.1 to 10.4.

12. You have just replaced the logic board in a PowerMac G4 (Mirrored Drive Doors 2003) due to it not recognizing the hard drive. The replacement drive has been tested as working. What is your next step?

    a. Inform the user the repair is complete.

    b. Return the bad part and close the repair.

    c. Check that no new issues have been introduced.

    d. Mail the computer into the repair center to confirm the issue is resolved.

13. Which item is not an element of resolving an issue properly?

    a. Isolating an issue to hardware or software

    b. Following proper procedures for take apart and assembly

    c. Using up-to-date references and tools

    d. Using the minimum number of tools

14. A previous technician was researching an issue with an iMac G5. He was unable to find the answer, and you are unable to find one as well. Using the Apple General Troubleshooting Flowchart, what is the next step in your troubleshooting?

    a. Repair or Replace

    b. Escalate

    c. Gather Information

    d. Run Diagnostics

15. Can you remove the video card from a system to test a minimal configuration?

16. Where does power flow on a PowerBook G4 (15-inch FW800) after it reaches the processor?

    a. Logic board

    b. RAM

    c. Hard drive

    d. Display

17. Is component isolation a type of systematic fault isolation?

18. What qualifies as passing a minimal configuration test? (Choose all that apply.)

    a. A RAM tone

    b. Booting to an OS

    c. Powering on

    d. A flashing question mark

    e. A normal startup chime

19. Why is a video card not required for a minimal configuration?

    a. Video cards in some systems draw power and can confuse the test.

    b. A startup chime can also indicate a good boot in a minimal system.

    c. All you need is fans kicking on to tell you the minimal system has passed.

    d. Video cards complicate the issue by giving you a display to look at.

Answer Key

1. d; 2. b, c, d, e; 3. c; 4. c; 5. b; 6. b; 7. a, b, d; 8. b; 9. a, b, c; 10. c; 11. b; 12. c; 13. d; 14. b; 15. Yes; 16. b; 17. Yes; 18. c, d, e; 19. b

4

Time This lesson takes approximately 1 hour to complete.

Goals Practice ESD damage prevention

List the basic equipment needed to reduce the risk of damage from ESD and explain how this equipment works

Set up a conductive workbench mat

Identify the risks of working with CRTs

Locate CRT safety, discharge, and disposal procedures

State the eight CRT safety rules

Discharge a CRT using Apple-recommended procedures

Explain safety and first-aid procedures related to the leaking of liquid coolant

Describe the hazards of working with an iMac power supply

Describe the risks of booting into EFI

Care for the translucent plastics on Apple products

Clean and maintain a monitor screen

Back up files

Check for viruses

Dispose of batteries safely

Optimize a hard disk

Safe Working Procedures and General Maintenance

Whether the computers you're taking care of belong to you, a customer, or a large group, this lesson provides the information you need to approach any situation safely and with the proper tools.

In this lesson, you will learn about the risks to you and the computer when you service computers, as well as general maintenance tasks you might perform during the "verify repair" step in the Apple General Troubleshooting Flowchart. While these may seem like unrelated topics, safe workstations and conscientious work practices are all part of keeping computers, customers, and yourself happy.

ESD Prevention

Whenever you open a Macintosh or other electrical device, you are exposing its internal components to potential damage from the static electricity that builds up in your body through normal activity. Electrostatic discharge (ESD) occurs when static electricity is discharged from one conductor (such as your finger) to another conductor (such as a memory chip) of a different potential. Exposing an integrated circuit (IC) to as little as 10 volts of static electricity can damage the IC irreparably—and you wouldn't even know it happened, because humans can't perceive static electricity less than 1500 volts. When you do feel an electrical shock, you are feeling a minimum of 3000 volts.

Since imperceptible ESD can damage ICs found in computer and communications equipment, you must be particularly careful when working on Macintosh hardware. Plastics, utensils, polystyrene products, polyester clothing, and even the ungrounded touch of your hand carry sufficient electrostatic charges to damage electronic components, even if you don't feel a spark. This section provides guidelines for preventing ESD damage and describes how to set up an ESD-compliant workstation.

ESD Safety Guidelines

Follow these guidelines to reduce the risk of ESD damage:

▶   Before working on any device containing a printed circuit, ground yourself and the equipment you are working on to an earth or building ground. Use a grounded conductive workbench mat and a grounding wrist strap or heel strap, and ground the equipment to the mat.

   WARNING ▶ Make sure you are *not* grounded when you:

   ▶   Work on plugged-in equipment
   ▶   Discharge a cathode-ray tube (CRT)
   ▶   Work on an unplugged CRT that has not been discharged
   ▶   Perform live adjustments on a CRT

   See "CRT Safety Procedures," later in this lesson, for more information.

▶ Handle all ICs by the body, not by the pins. Do not touch the edge connectors, exposed circuitry, or printed circuits on boards or cards. Handle ICs, boards, and cards by the edges, or extract them using an ESD-compliant pair of pliers or other appropriate tool.

▶ Never place components on any metal surface. Metal surfaces can hold a static charge that will damage sensitive electronic parts. Use antistatic, conductive, or foam rubber mats.

▶ Do not touch anyone who is working on ICs. If you touch someone who is properly grounded, your "zap," or body charge, might cause damage. Always keep your own body charge away from other technicians.

▶ Use static-shielding storage bags for boards and ICs. Before you leave your bench to take a board to a storage place, put the board in a static-shielding bag. Leave all Apple replacement modules in their ESD-compliant packaging until you need them.

▶ Don't wear polyester clothing or bring plastic, vinyl, or Styrofoam into the work environment. The electrostatic field that surrounds these nonconductors cannot be totally removed without the use of an ionized air generator.

▶ If possible, keep the humidity in the service area between 70 and 90 percent, and use an ionized air generator if available. Charge levels are reduced (but not eliminated) in high-humidity environments. Using an ionized air generator helps neutralize the charge surrounding nonconductors. However, this type of device can't provide total protection: the static charges often cause ESD damage before the neutralizing process eliminates the charge.

Workstation Setup

Before you start to work on any task involving circuit boards, you must verify that your workstation is ESD-compliant—that is, that it has equipment and materials designed to prevent ESD damage.

You need the following equipment to set up an ESD-compliant workstation:

Wire lead with alligator clips

Ground/polarity tester   Wrist strap   Mat

▶ A conductive workbench mat and wire lead—When properly grounded, the workbench mat provides a safe place on which to set sensitive components and equipment.

> **MORE INFO** ▶ Refer to Knowledge Base document 50077, "ESD Prevention Rules" for more information on setting up a conductive workbench mat.

▶ A wrist strap with a built-in 1-megohm resistor and wire lead—The wrist strap grounds you so that you can touch sensitive components without zapping them.

▶ An equipment wire lead with alligator clips—This wire lead grounds the equipment so that an electrostatic charge cannot build up. It is especially important when you are working on CRTs, which can build up an electrostatic charge even when they are not plugged in.

▶ A ground/polarity tester—This tester verifies proper grounding of power outlets.

A Note on Working Off-Site

When you work at a customer site, you must take the same precautions to avoid ESD damage. Take time to make the work area ESD-compliant. Take a workbench mat and a wrist strap with you. (For travel convenience, you may want to use a mat that folds up.) Be sure everything is properly grounded and never set parts on the floor.

> **WARNING** ▶ Do not wear a wrist strap when discharging a CRT. See "CRT Safety Procedures," later in this lesson, for more information.

ESD-Compliant Workstation Quiz

Read Knowledge Base document 50077, "ESD Prevention Rules", and answer the following questions:

1. When there is a risk of contacting high voltage, such as when you discharge a CRT or work with a powered-on CRT, do you wear a grounding wrist strap?

2. When there is a risk of contacting high voltage, do you work on a grounded pad?

3. What items do you need to set up an ESD-compliant workstation?

4. For what do you use a ground/polarity tester?

Answer Key

1. No; 2. No; 3. A conductive workbench mat, a wrist strap with 1-megohm resistor and ground cord, a wire lead with alligator clips, and a ground/ polarity tester; 4. To verify proper grounding of the power outlet.

CRT Safety Procedures

Over the last few years, cathode-ray tube (CRT) displays have been used in fewer and fewer computers. In the Macintosh systems, only one model, the eMac, has been available. From June 2002 until mid-2006, the eMac was sold to schools and some private parties. While CRT-based Macintosh systems are no longer sold, they will be a part of the supported product line for years to come. At some point, you may have to service a CRT system.

Between the changing and improving technology and the lowering of prices, attempting to fix a CRT unit should rarely be your first option. If you are not an Apple Authorized Service Provider (AASP) or in a certified training course, you should not attempt to do so at all.

Risks

The CRT is one of the most dangerous pieces of equipment you'll repair. Happily, there are very few occasions when you should have to open a display and expose a CRT. Yet because of the risks inherent in working with CRTs, it is extremely important that you know what to do and what not to do when troubleshooting and servicing Macintosh computers that contain them.

CRTs are glass vessels that have the air pumped out of them. They have very thick glass in the screen area and thinner glass in the narrow neck area. This makes a CRT fairly fragile when it is not encased in a computer or bezel. The neck area is particularly easy to break or crack.

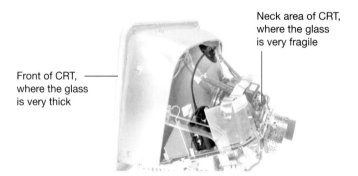

Neck area of CRT, where the glass is very fragile

Front of CRT, where the glass is very thick

The vacuum tube in a CRT can implode if it is broken or punctured. The surrounding air will rush violently into the unsealed vacuum in the CRT, spraying broken glass in every direction.

Color CRTs may contain mercury or other potentially toxic materials. If the CRT is broken or cracked, these materials may be released and pose a risk of toxic exposure.

A charged CRT carries high voltage—about 27,000 volts in a color unit. You could electrocute yourself unless you handle the display using the appropriate safety procedures.

Safety

If you handle a CRT properly, neither you nor the display will come to any harm. There are several CRT safety procedures that can keep you safe.

Handling CRTs correctly consists of not placing stress on the neck portion of the CRT assembly. Since the neck has thinner glass, you should never lift a CRT by the neck. It is also important to handle CRT modules carefully when lifting them or putting them down.

If you must transport a CRT module, always make sure that it is in a shipping package or installed in the computer.

> WARNING ▶ A CRT can carry a charge even when the display or system is turned off, and can build up a secondary charge after the power is removed.

These areas of a CRT can present a shock hazard:

- ▶ Anode cap and connector
- ▶ High-voltage cable
- ▶ Yoke assembly
- ▶ Flyback transformer
- ▶ Any exposed soldered connections

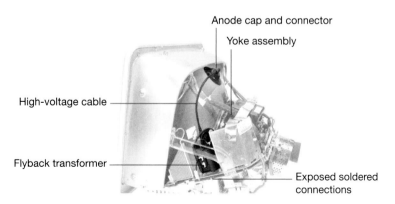

Dangerously high voltages flow through these parts until the display is disconnected from its power source and properly discharged. Do not touch any of these parts inside the product housing until after the display is disconnected from its power source and properly discharged.

In typical repair situations, you should always follow ESD precautions while working inside a Macintosh. This means setting up an ESD-compliant workstation and consistently following all ESD rules.

However, working around a CRT inside a Macintosh, or working around the inside of any Macintosh while it is powered on, can bring parts of your body dangerously close to hazardous voltages. Thus doing so requires an exception to the ESD rules.

Being grounded in these situations is extremely dangerous because your grounded ESD wrist or heel strap and grounded ESD workbench mat create a path through your body to ground. If you accidentally contact high voltage, the current has a clear path through your body and can electrocute you.

To work safely on a CRT inside a Macintosh, follow these safety rules every time:

1. Never work alone. Having someone nearby in case of an accident could save your life.
2. Turn off the power and disconnect the AC power cord before you remove the CRT cover.
3. Remove any metal jewelry.
4. Remove the grounding wrist or heel strap until the CRT has been discharged.
5. Disconnect the snap fastener on the grounded workbench mat until the CRT has been discharged.

6.   Wear safety goggles.

7.   Discharge the CRT immediately after removing the case and before touching anything inside the system or display. (The CRT-discharge procedure is discussed next.)

8.   After discharging the CRT and turning off the CRT power, reconnect and wear a grounding wrist or heel strap.

Discharge

By now you shouldn't have to be reminded that CRTs carry a high voltage and can be dangerous. But you still have to work on them sometimes. So how do you do that without electrocuting yourself?

Newer Apple CRT displays are equipped with a bleeder resistor (contained in the flyback transformer) that automatically drains the charge from the CRT when the power is shut off. However, if the resistor fails, the anode may retain a charge. For that reason, Apple requires all service technicians to discharge all CRTs before performing repairs.

The Apple discharge procedure is a precautionary measure to confirm that the CRT has been discharged prior to working on it.

After completing this section, you will be able to safely discharge the high voltage from a CRT.

WARNING ▶ The CRT discharge component of this lesson is intended for service technicians working under the direct supervision of an AASP. Do not attempt the CRT discharge part of this lesson if you are studying AppleCare Technician Training.

When discharging a CRT, you need the following equipment:

▶   Safety glasses

▶   Ungrounded foam pad

▶   Needlenose pliers

▶   Wire lead with alligator clips at both ends

▶   CRT discharge tool

To ensure your safety, follow Apple-recommended CRT discharge procedures. Search the Knowledge Base and Service Source for the display or Macintosh you are servicing.

Before you do anything, including discharging a CRT, turn off and unplug the display or Macintosh. Then follow these steps:

1. Follow the first six CRT safety rules, listed in the preceding section, to prepare to discharge the CRT.

2. Remove the housing.

If you have access to them, refer to the Take Apart instructions in the appropriate service manual for your Macintosh or display.

3. Put one hand behind your back.

> **NOTE** ▶ Putting one hand in your pocket or behind your back helps to prevent current from passing through your heart if you touch a high-voltage area.

4. Using the Apple CRT discharge tool shown below, connect the alligator clip from the lead to the ground lug on all-in-one systems.

> **NOTE** ▶ If you do not have a discharge tool, you can use an insulated screwdriver attached to a wire lead with alligator clips on both ends.

5. Slide the discharge tool probe under the anode cap and into the anode aperture. As soon as you can feel the metal of the probe touching the metal of the aperture, the CRT is discharged.

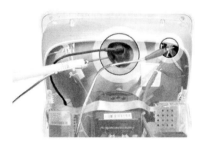

If a discharged CRT must remain exposed for any length of time, establish an ongoing lead between the anode and ground.

> **MORE INFO ▶** Refer to Knowledge Base document 50078, "About CRT Safety," for instructions on establishing an ongoing lead.

When discharging a CRT, use only the ground lug to make your ground connection on a Macintosh to prevent damage to the logic board. Any high voltage that may be present is safely discharged to ground circuits (on the power/sweep assembly), which are designed to handle such voltage.

Disposal

Use the following instructions for returning color CRTs, whether in-warranty or out-of-warranty.

Some dead CRT assemblies, specifically color CRT assemblies, cannot be thrown away with regular trash because they have the potential of becoming hazardous waste.

As with dead lithium, lead-acid, nickel-hydride, and nickel-cadmium batteries, AASPs should return dead Apple color CRT assemblies directly to Apple if the original packaging is available.

When returning dead color CRT assemblies:

▶   Do not release the vacuum.

▶   Enclose them in the packaging in which they were originally shipped.

If you no longer have the original packaging, do *not* return color CRTs to Apple. Instead, dispose of CRT assemblies according to your local hazardous waste ordinances.

Similarly, broken CRTs (for example, monitors with cracked glass) must not be returned to Apple. Dispose of any broken color monitor CRT assemblies according to your local hazardous waste ordinances.

Remember that CRT displays present these basic dangers:

▶   CRT displays may implode if mishandled.

▶   CRT displays may contain hazardous materials.

CRT Safety Quiz

1.   Name the major risks of working on CRTs.

2.   Is carrying CRTs by the neck recommended?

3.   Name one toxic material that can be found inside CRTs.

4.   You are troubleshooting an eMac for a no-video issue. You want to open the system to check internal cabling. What is the *first* recommended step you take?

5.   What are the eight CRT safety rules?

6.   You have an Apple CRT that is cracked and you do not have the original packing for the part. How do you dispose of it?

Answer Key

1. Implosion (flying glass), hazardous materials if CRT is cracked or broken, lethal shock hazard; 2. No; 3. Mercury; 4. Make sure someone is in the room with you; 5. a) Never work alone; b) Turn off the power and disconnect the AC power cord before you remove the CRT cover; c) Remove any metal jewelry; d) Remove the grounding wrist or heel strap until the CRT has been discharged; e) Disconnect the snap fastener on the grounded workbench mat until the CRT has been discharged; f) Wear safety goggles; g) Discharge the CRT immediately after the case has been removed and before touching anything inside the system or display; h) After you have discharged the CRT and turned off the CRT power, reconnect and wear a grounding wrist or heel strap; 6. According to your local hazardous waste ordinances

Liquid Coolants

Traditionally Macintosh computers have been air-cooled by attaching large aluminum or copper heatsinks over the processor. These heatsinks have fins that are fan-cooled.

The Power Mac G5 (June 2004) Dual 2.5 GHz model was the first Power Mac to include a liquid cooling system, which is considered a "closed-loop system." This means the cooling fluid is completely sealed within the tubing and you don't have access to the fluid to refill or change it.

The liquid cooling system fluid is predominantly water (80 percent or greater) with a mixture of corrosion inhibitors, antifreeze, and bacterial growth preventatives.

Although having a closed-loop liquid cooling system provides a higher degree of safety when using liquid cooling, there still can be some circumstances in which the liquid cooling system is defective and causes a leak.

You might visually identify a coolant leak if you happen to be near the computer when it is on. Since the liquid is under pressure, you may see or hear squirting. Once the processor reaches a certain temperature (due to a lack of cooling), the computer will power itself off to prevent further damage.

If you ever suspect that a liquid cooling system fault is present or involved, you should pull the power cord from the computer or wall socket immediately. Don't just turn off a power strip. Once the computer is powered off, you can open the case to determine if there is an overt leak.

Evidence of leaks includes corrosions around fittings in the liquid coolant system, the presence of a light green or red liquid, or a slick or slimy feel when handling the part. If you perceive any indication of a leak, service the computer immediately (if you're an AASP technician).

Wear nitrile or rubber gloves when handling a liquid cooling module that is leaking or suspected to be leaking.

Place the failed liquid cooling module (leaking or not) in the bag the replacement came in, seal it, and return it to Apple.

For coolant leaks or spills, absorb the material using rags, paper towels, or other suitable materials. Contain and dispose of all cleaning materials according to local antifreeze-disposal laws and regulations. Do not combine used coolant with any other chemical.

For complete instructions on working with liquid coolants, refer to the Material Safety Data Sheet (MSDS) for the liquid:

1   Open www.apple.com/environment/resources/msds.html.

2   Click the MSDS link for the Power Mac G5 Dual 2.7GHz, red liquid.

3   Skim the document.

Liquid Coolant Safety Quiz

Read the MSDS for liquid coolants and answer the following questions.

1. What should you do if you get some liquid coolant from a Power Mac G5 in your eyes?

2. What happens if you get some liquid coolant on your hands?

Answer Key

1. Rinse the eyes with water, get immediate medical attention; 2. The skin on your hands could get slightly irritated

iMac Power Supply

A number of iMac computer models contain a power supply board that requires extra caution. These models include:

▶ iMac (iSight)

▶ iMac (Early 2006)

▶ iMac (Mid 2006 17-inch)

▶ iMac (Late 2006)

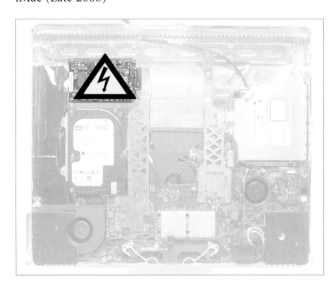

The AC/DC power supply board is a high-voltage source when the unit is under power, and remains powered up whenever the system is plugged in, whether or not the system is turned on. The voltages pose a potential hazard to your personal safety.

Observe these precautions:

▶ Make sure the unit is unplugged when working on it with the front bezel removed. *Never* work on or near the power supply with the unit powered on.

▶ Never work alone. In the event of an electrical shock, it is important to have someone present who can provide assistance.

▶ Keep one hand in your pocket or behind your back when working on any computer that is plugged in. This will help ensure that your body does not provide a path to ground in the event that you accidentally make contact with the line voltage.

▶ Don't wear jewelry, watches, necklaces, or other metallic articles that could present a risk if they accidentally make contact with the power supply circuitry.

Booting to EFI

While you might think booting to EFI on an Intel-based Macintosh is the same as booting to Open Firmware on a Power PC–based Macintosh, there are some critical differences.

On a Power PC–based Macintosh, booting into Open Firmware yielded a shell command prompt where a savvy troubleshooter could do many useful things, such as reset the nonvolatile memory (NVRAM), eject a CD, set up Open Firmware password protection, and even disable one of the processors in a multiple-processor Macintosh for testing purposes.

The firmware in an Intel-based computer uses EFI technology. When Apple introduced the earliest Intel Macintosh models, they did not have a shell. All the diagnostics and key commands at startup functioned as they did for Open Firmware, but without a shell. Enterprising, if uninformed, users could irreparably damage the logic board.

Since those earliest Intel-based Macintosh models were introduced, Apple has made available a few key tools:

▶ Boot Camp, so you can boot Macintosh computers into Windows

▶ A firmware restoration utility, available through the Downloads section of the Apple Support page (www.apple.com/support/downloads)

Depending on what you're trying to achieve, use one of these two tools, or the diagnostic and key commands; do not boot into EFI.

> **NOTE ▶** Attempts to use firmware in a manner that Apple does not explicitly endorse may damage your computer's logic board. Any repairs that are necessary because of this damage will not be covered under the terms of the Apple One-Year Limited Warranty, AppleCare Protection Plan, or other AppleCare agreement.

General Maintenance

A lot of general maintenance falls to end users. It's always a good idea to remind them to give their computers the "spa treatment" to help ensure reliability and good performance. This section presents guidelines and hints to help maintain computer equipment in good working order.

Caring for Translucent Plastics

Many Apple products are made with translucent or transparent polycarbonate plastic. This plastic is designed to be both aesthetically pleasing and tough; it should wear quite well.

Yet while translucent plastics are as durable as those used in other computer equipment, scratches and other kinds of minor cosmetic damage may be more visible than in opaque plastics.

When servicing products that use translucent plastics, follow these general guidelines:

▶ Do not scratch the plastic with sharp items or rub it with abrasive materials.

▶ Do not drop anything heavy on the product or drop the product on the floor.

Cleaning Computer Equipment

There are specific instructions for cleaning the plastics of Apple computers and displays. Search the Knowledge Base for *cleaning plastics*. You'll find articles like the following:

▶ Knowledge Base document 30889, "How to clean the plastics on your Mac"

▶ Knowledge Base document 58036, "iMac: Servicing and Take Apart Issues"

▶ Knowledge Base document 86399, "Apple Cinema HD Display: How to Remove Adhesive Residue"

▶ Knowledge Base document 304058, "About white MacBooks' palmrest area"

▶ Knowledge Base document 93270, "iSight: About the Mount Adhesive"

▶ Knowledge Base document 60446, "How To Clean an LCD Panel"

> **WARNING** ▶ Do not clean any part of the display with a cleaner that contains alcohol or acetone. Never spray cleaner directly onto the screen. Liquid could drip inside the display and cause electrical shock.

Maintaining the Display

Since glass is a main component of Apple displays, and since they are designed to minimize weight, it is easy to crack or break an LCD display panel.

Some sources maintain that defective LCD pixels can be restored by rubbing the screen around the defective pixel. This procedure does not work and is very likely to create further problems. In fact, given the great complexity of LCD displays, such a procedure will likely make more pixels defective. For example, rubbing too hard can crush some of the tiny spacers that keep several of the LCD layers apart, causing even more pixel anomalies to appear. Simply put, don't rub LCD screens. If you have to clean an LCD screen surface, be sure to do so carefully and only with gentle pressure.

To maintain a display, follow these basic procedures:

▶ Turn off the display or turn down the brightness whenever the display is turned on but not being used; otherwise, the image on the screen could "burn in" and damage the screen.

▶ Use the Energy Saver pane of System Preferences to set the display to go to sleep after a specified period of inactivity. Screen Effects (in System Preferences) or a third-party screen saver program is another option. However screen savers aren't as effective at maintaining the LCD. (Refer to Knowledge Base document 10639, "Screen Savers: Using With Liquid Crystal Displays." Also, search the Knowledge Base for *screen saver* for more information.)

▶ Make sure the vents on the computer and display are clear and unobstructed.

▶ Don't let liquid get on or into the display.

If you are trying to eliminate a persistent image from an LCD screen, refer to Knowledge Base document 88343, "Avoiding image persistence on Apple LCD displays."

Backing Up Files

Of course no one ever expects to lose data, whether for technical or other reasons. This is precisely why you should make backing up a standard part of any workflow. Backing up files helps you prevent the loss of important documents, applications, and other software.

You can back up your files using a dedicated application, such as Retrospect (www.dantz.com), that automatically archives the contents of your hard disk (or any portion you specify). Alternatively you can back up important documents every day by copying the files to another disk, a volume on a network, an external hard disk, or a writeable optical disc.

> **MORE INFO** ▶ For detailed information on backup methods, refer to Knowledge Base document 106941, "Mac OS X: How to back up and restore your files," and Knowledge Base document 301239, "How to back up and restore your important Mac OS X 10.4 files."

There are some special things you should consider when backing up an iPod, or more accurately, an iTunes library.

With iTunes 7 you can easily back up the entire iTunes library, including ratings and play count. You can also restore the entire library using the disc(s) you created.

To perform a library backup, follow these steps:

1   Open iTunes.

2   Choose File > Back up to disc.

You are presented with a window with three options:

Select "Back up entire iTunes library and playlists" or "Back up only iTunes Store purchases." With either option, you can choose to back up only those items added or changed since the last backup.

iTunes begins processing the library and determines which items to back up. The size of the iTunes library determines the length of time this step takes. The larger the library, the longer it will take.

The processing step completes, and iTunes begins burning the backup to disc. If your backup is too large for a single disc, a dialog appears letting you know the backup will or will not fit on one disc:

3   Insert a blank CD or DVD into your computer's optical drive.

   NOTE ▸ When a disc is finished burning, iTunes closes the disc and verifies the information. This step may take up to an hour. When a disc is full, iTunes prompts you to insert another disc.

   A dialog notifies you when your library backup is complete.

   TIP ▸ When working with iTunes and iPod customers, it's important to remind them of the benefits of using this backup feature to help preserve their entire iTunes library. This is especially helpful in the event that there is a need to reinstall the computer's operating system or move a library to a new computer.

Proper Battery Disposal

Whenever you replace a battery—whether from inside a Macintosh computer or a common flashlight—it is important that you dispose of the old batteries appropriately, according to local hazardous waste ordinances. For current instructions, search for *battery disposal* in the Knowledge Base. Also refer to Knowledge Base document 50079, "Battery Handling."

Checking for Viruses

A computer virus is a program, usually hidden within another (seemingly innocuous) program, that produces copies of itself to insert into other programs and often performs malicious actions such as destroying data.

Use an antivirus program regularly to check for and delete viruses on the hard disk, especially if you download files from the Internet or share files with others. Choose an antivirus program that alerts you when an email attachment, shared file, or Internet download is infected.

Check periodically for updates to your antivirus program to ensure that the program scans for the latest known viruses. Also search the Knowledge Base for *antivirus*. You'll find documents such as these:

▶ Knowledge Base document 4454, "Mac OS: Antivirus Utilities"

▶ Knowledge Base document 11907, "Macintosh: Lists of viruses"

Optimizing the Hard Disk

As you may know, smaller hard disks have a habit of becoming full, and the operating system deals with this by writing bits and pieces of files wherever it can find free space. Although they are fully written, the files are logically fragmented over the surface of the disk. Because the drive's magnetic head has to move all over the place to read or write fragmented files, performance suffers.

Disk optimization is a process in which the physical locations of files on a volume are streamlined. Files and metadata are rearranged to improve data access times and minimize time moving a hard drive's head.

Fortunately all of this has changed in recent years. Multigigabyte drives are common and inexpensive, so the lack of storage space that led to fragmentation rarely occurs. Furthermore, Mac OS X contains intelligent routines that, in essence, optimize the hard disk during normal use.

> **MORE INFO ▶** To find out more about disk optimization, refer to Knowledge Base document 25668, "About disk optimization with Mac OS X."

General Best Practices

Even if you have plenty of experience taking apart computers, it can't hurt to take a moment to review some common-sense suggestions to keep in mind while working on Macintosh hardware:

▶ Consider making a full backup before attempting any significant hardware change.

▶ Always properly shut down the Macintosh computer before opening its case.

▶ As you remove screws, take care not to lose them. Place them in a small ESD-safe container or stick them on a strip of duct tape in the order they're removed as an aid for reassembly. Some Macintosh computers have "captive" screws that can't be removed; take care not to strip these.

▶ If you don't have a printed reference to guide you, take your own pictures with a digital camera to remind you of the proper placement and orientation of components.

▶ Wearing eye protection and a nose and mouth filter, use a can of compressed air to clean dust from the interior of the Macintosh computer. Every Macintosh with a fan inside draws air through it to keep the components cool, but this can also suck in a lot of dust. That dust coats the components like a thin blanket and clogs air vents, causing the interior to operate at higher-than-ideal temperatures.

TIP ▶ Blowing out accumulated dust can extend the useful lifespan of your Macintosh, but be sure not to blow dust into sensitive components like magnetic or optical drives.

▶ Be gentle. If a part to be removed is stuck, wiggle it back and forth. If you're trying to install a part and it appears not to fit, don't force it. Double-check the orientation, look for alignment tabs, and make sure you have the right part.

Lesson Review

1. What does ESD stand for?
   a. Electronic surveillance device
   b. Electric shock damage
   c. Electrostatic discharge

2. ESD can damage a computer by:
   a. Decalibrating the CRT
   b. Damaging sensitive chips
   c. Starting a fire in the enclosure

3. Which three of the following should you keep away from an ESD-compliant workbench? (Choose all that apply.)
   a. Plastics
   b. Magnets
   c. Polyester clothing
   d. Styrofoam

4. Which of the following tasks requires that you *not* wear a grounded wrist strap or heel strap?

    a. Discharging a CRT

    b. Handling a logic board

    c. Opening a computer case

5. How should you handle integrated circuits to reduce the risk of ESD damage?

    a. By the pins

    b. By the edge connectors

    c. By the body

6. How should you reduce the risk of ESD damage?

    a. Ground yourself.

    b. Make sure the equipment is on.

    c. Keep the equipment on a metal surface.

7. Which one of the following is not one of the four basic pieces of equipment needed to reduce the risk of damage from ESD?

    a. Grounded mat

    b. Wrist strap

    c. Plastic storage bags

8. Which general step(s) do you take to clean a monitor screen safely? (Choose all that apply.)

    a. Disconnect the power cord.

    b. Turn off the monitor.

    c. Use a mild, nonabrasive cleaner.

9. Which of the following is most likely a symptom of a fragmented hard disk?

   a. Download errors

   b. Insufficient memory errors

   c. Slow disk access

10. True or false: Always wear a grounding wrist or heel strap when discharging a CRT or performing live adjustments.

11. True or false: Whenever you work around a live CRT, keep one hand behind your back or in your pocket.

12. True or false: The CRT carries a charge even when the display or system is turned off, so you must discharge a CRT before you can work safely.

Answer Key

1. c; 2. b; 3. a, c, d; 4. a; 5. c; 6. a; 7. c; 8. a, b, c; 9. c; 10. False; 11. True; 12. True

5

Reference Files

MacBook (13-inch) service manual (macbook_13in.pdf)

Mac Pro service manual (macpro.pdf)

Combined Tools List (Combined Tools List.pdf)

Notes on Multimeter Use (Notes on Multimeter Use.pdf)

Time

This lesson takes approximately 45 minutes to complete.

Goals

Identify the correct hardware tools to service specific Apple products

Identify specialized tools available to AASPs from Apple

Given a specific Apple product, identify all hardware tools needed to perform a particular module replacement

Hardware Tools

This lesson reviews the hand tools you need for troubleshooting and servicing Apple desktop and portable products. In addition, it explains how to correctly identify tools for servicing Apple products.

TIP See also Lesson 4, "Safe Working Procedures and General Maintenance," for essential safety equipment.

Using the Right Tools

Experienced technicians can easily spot a bad repair when they see:

▶ Stripped screws

▶ Missing screws

▶ Bent pins

▶ Broken connectors

▶ Improperly bent cables

Many of these problems occur because someone was in a hurry and "made do" with the tools that were immediately available.

Such problems make repairs more difficult and time consuming. They complicate isolating any one issue because one badly done repair may create additional problems.

You can avoid all of these problems by following some basic steps:

▶ Review the service manual before attempting a new procedure.

▶ Identify and have on hand the correct tools called out in the service manual. Avoid "making do" with incorrect tools.

▶ Keep careful track of screws and other small parts to avoid using the wrong screw in the wrong place.

▶ If a procedure involves removing multiple parts, make sure that you have sufficient static bags for storage and some means of keeping track of the screws or other small parts you take out of the system.

Apple Authorized Service Providers (AASPs) can order tools from Apple via Global Service Exchange (GSX). They are ordered in the same fashion as service parts. You can see the complete array of Apple tools by doing a service part search for *tool*.

> **TIP** ▶ For a consolidated shopping list of tools, refer to the Combined Tools List (**Combined Tools List.pdf**) on this book's companion website, www. peachpit.com/ats.deskport3.

Tools Common to Desktops and Portables

If you are planning to do repairs on a wide range of Apple desktop and portable systems, be sure to have the following tools on hand.

Most of these tools are available from a number of hardware stores and tool manufacturers; some are only available from Apple.

Phillips Screwdrivers

▶ Phillips #0 screwdriver (3- to 4-inch shaft is recommended for desktops)

▶ Phillips #00 screwdriver

▶ Phillips #1 screwdriver (10-inch shaft for desktops)

▶ Phillips #2 screwdriver (10-inch shaft for desktops)

▶ Phillips #2 screwdriver short (because a full size screwdriver does not always fit in a computer)

Make sure that the shafts of the #1 and #2 screwdrivers are at least 10 inches long to easily work on the heatsink of most Mac Pro systems.

Torx Screwdrivers

Torx screwdrivers have a six-pointed cross section and provide a precise fit to the matching screw. For this reason, you should never try to use the wrong size Torx screwdriver.

▶ T6 screwdriver

▶ T8 screwdriver

▶ T10 screwdriver

AASP technicians should get a T10 Torx screwdriver with an 8-inch shaft directly from Apple (part number 922-7083).

Nut Drivers

Nut drivers are used to work on six-sided bolts in some systems.

▶ 3 mm nut driver

▶ 4 mm nut driver

▶ 5 mm nut driver

Hex Drivers

Set of metric hex keys (including 1.5 mm, 2 mm, 2.5 mm)

Miscellaneous Tools

▶ Nylon probe tool (also known as a black stick, available from Apple, part number 922-5065)

▶ Magnetizer/demagnetizer

- ▶ Precision needlenose pliers (small tips)

- ▶ X-Acto knife or razor blade

- ▶ Electrostatic discharge (ESD)–safe plastic probe

- ▶ Plastic tweezers

- ▶ Paper clip (put one in your tool kit since you can never find one when you need it)

- ▶ Coin (another thing you can never find when you need it)

- ▶ Multimeter

- ▶ 12-partition (or more) ESD-safe screw box (paper cups also work)

- ▶ White cotton gloves

- ▶ Dental pick

- ▶ Flashlight

- ▶ Metal tweezers

A magnetizer/demagnetizer enables you to magnetize your screwdrivers and other tools. It also allows you to demagnetize them in situations where a magnetized tool will harm components.

A multimeter is an instrument for measuring several electrical elements. You need to measure voltage and resistance in MacBook (13-inch) systems and Mac Pro systems. A multimeter can be very useful in many other troubleshooting situations, and is specifically called for in various Apple service documents and Apple Knowledge Base articles.

> **MORE INFO** ▶ For more on how to use a multimeter, refer to Notes on Multimeter Use (**Notes on Multimeter Use.pdf**) on the companion website, www.peachpit.com/ats.deskport3.

Desktop Tools

If you are planning to do repairs on a wide range of Apple desktop systems, you'll need the following tools in addition to the common tools listed in the preceding sections.

Most of these tools are available from a number of hardware stores and tool manufacturers; some you will have to purchase directly from Apple.

Torx Screwdrivers

▶ T15 screwdriver

▶ T25 screwdriver

Hex Drivers

2.5 mm hex driver with a 10-inch shaft

Flat-Blade Screwdriver

Flat-blade jeweler's screwdriver

Miscellaneous Tools

▶ Alignment tool, display service (available from Apple, part number 922-3504)

▶ Processor alignment tool for Xserve (available from Apple, part number 922-5856)

▶ Thermal pads (available from Apple, part number 076-0925, 076-0950)

▶ Putty knife for opening Mac mini models (available from Apple, part number 922-6761)

NOTE ▸ The putty knife available from Apple has been specifically modified for separating the Mac mini housing. If you substitute a standard putty knife, be sure and modify it per the instructions in the applicable service manual.

▸ 3 mm flathead hex driver with 8-inch shaft (available from Apple, part number 922-7122)

▸ 4 mm ballhead hex driver with 8-inch shaft (available from Apple, part number 922-7082)

▸ Cathode ray tube (CRT) discharge tool

▸ Glue gun/glue sticks

▸ Cup ring

Portable Tools

If you are planning to do repairs on a wide range of Apple portable systems, you'll need the following tools in addition to the common tools listed in the preceding sections.

Most of these tools are available from a number of hardware stores and tool manufacturers; some you will have to purchase directly from Apple.

▸ Thermal grease, G751 (available from Apple, part number 922-6495)

▸ Display take apart tool (available from Apple, part number 922-6120)

▶ Thermal pads (available from Apple, part number 076-1053) for PowerBook G4, PowerBook G4 (12-inch 1.33 GHz), PowerBook (12-inch DVI)

▶ Access card (available from Apple, part number 922-7172)

▶ Kapton tape (available from Apple, part number 922-1731)

▶   1600-watt hair dryer

▶   Small soft cloth

Lesson Review

Using the Mac Pro service manual, answer the following questions:

1. You need to replace the processor. What tools do you need to do this?

2. Is it all right for the thermal grease on the heatsink to come in contact with the processor connector?

3. What two steps must you be sure to take when reinstalling the processor heatsink cover?

Using the MacBook (13-inch) service manual, answer the following questions:

4. You are replacing the optical drive. What size Phillips screwdriver do you need?

5. What tools do you need to remove the display bezel?

Answer Key

1. No tools are required for this procedure. However, you may find a flathead screwdriver helpful in releasing the processor holder latch; 2. No; 3. Make sure the heatsink cover slides below slot #1 on the PCI card guide, and align the four slots on the underside of the heatsink cover's left edge with the four tabs on the front fan; 4. Magnetic Phillips #0; 5. ESD wrist strap and mat, nylon probe tool, access card

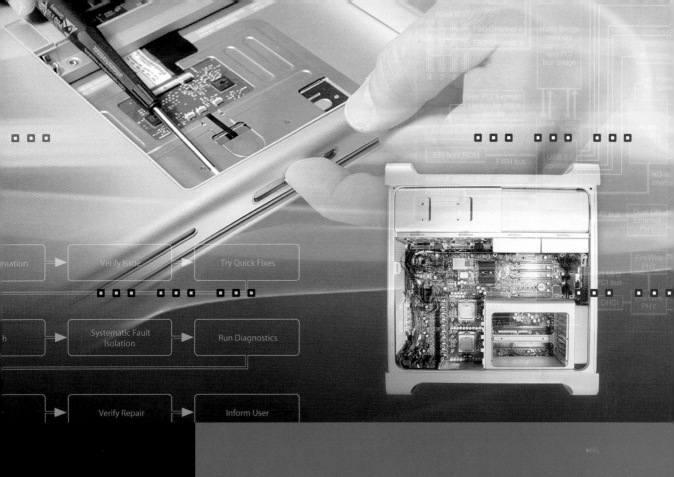

Common Hardware
and Technologies

6

Time This lesson takes approximately 1 hour to complete.

Goals Explain the different power and operating modes in Apple
systems

Describe power-saving techniques for Apple systems

Describe how to calibrate a portable system's main battery to
ensure optimal battery performance

Lesson 6
Power Management

Apple reduces a product's energy consumption in two ways: by using hardware components that require less power, and by using power management software to modulate the energy consumption of these components. The combination of hardware and software that control power supplied to the computer is referred to as "power management."

Power management in Apple computer products includes the PMU, the SMU or SMC, the battery, and the Energy Saver pane in System Preferences. The PMU, SMU, and SMC were covered in Lesson 5b, "Underlying Technologies" (which can be found on this book's companion website, www.peachpit.com/ats.deskport3), therefore this lesson focuses on other elements.

Although power management is present in both desktop and portable computers, energy consumption is most critical in the portable products because they can be run solely on batteries. Desktop computers also include power management preferences to comply with energy-saving regulatory rules.

This lesson focuses on power management issues that specifically pertain to portable computers, although most information applies to desktop models as well.

Power Management Components

All Apple portable computers (PowerBook, iBook, MacBook, and MacBook Pro models) may be powered either by a rechargeable lithium-ion battery or by an AC power adapter.

A variety of features programmed into the operating system enable the user to monitor the charge level of the battery and to control the computer's power usage. How the user configures these power management features and operates the computer while under battery power determines how long he or she can use the computer before recharging it. These same factors can also affect the battery's longevity—how long the battery lasts before it needs to be replaced.

Portable computers require a more complex power management software and hardware than desktop computers because they can be run off a battery. Portable power management must be able to activate and deactivate different components to save power, including the following:

▶ Hard disk drive

▶ Display backlight

▶ Any installed PC Card

▶ Chipsets not being used, such as sound circuitry

▶ Processor speed reduction

Power Modes

All computers have four power modes:

Power Mode	Definition	Power Use Implication
Awake	Computer is fully functional and ready to be used.	Full battery use.
Sleep	Computer is fully functional but in a resting state. The computer appears to be shut down but is actually operating at a reduced power level to conserve battery charge.	Reduced battery use.

Power Mode	Definition	Power Use Implication
Safe Sleep*	Safe Sleep writes the system memory contents to a file when the PowerBook goes to sleep. This protects data on the system in the event of the battery being drained.	Reduced battery use.
Shut down	Computer is powered off and must be restarted to become functional.	Minimal battery use.

*Safe Sleep is supported on all Apple portable computers beginning with the PowerBook G4 (Double-Layer SD) in October 2005 through the present MacBooks and MacBook Pros This does not include desktop models.

Of these four power modes, sleep and Safe Sleep modes require additional explanation.

There are several ways to put a portable computer into sleep mode:

▶ Choose Sleep from the Apple menu (Mac OS X).

▶ Press the power key for two seconds, and click Sleep in the dialog that appears (available on models with a power key).

▶ Close the portable case.

System software can attempt to place the computer into sleep mode automatically after a certain period of inactivity. You can specify this period of time in Energy Saver preferences (described later in this lesson). However, the computer will not go into sleep mode automatically if any of the following conditions are true:

▶ The computer is connected to a shared disk on the network.

▶ The computer's printer or modem port is in use.

▶ Sleep is set to Never in the Energy Saver preferences.

▶ DVD Player is the active application.

To wake a sleeping Mac, press any key except Caps Lock.

Safe Sleep mode is a new feature introduced with the PowerBook G4 (Double-Layer SD) and continuing through MacBook Pro. Prior to the system entering sleep, the current state of the computer is saved to the startup volume, including items such as desktop settings, open applications, and any work in progress. Safe Sleep also ensures that data stored in main memory will not be lost should the system shut down due to a loss of power or if the battery runs down during sleep mode. When a power adapter is connected or a freshly charged battery is installed, the computer can be restarted and it will automatically return to the desktop state that existed prior to entering sleep.

When the system is in Safe Sleep, the computer is completely powered off. You cannot wake a portable that is in Safe Sleep by simply pressing any key the way you would if in sleep mode only, because the keyboard is not monitored by the system when it's powered off. The only way to awaken a system in Safe Sleep is to press the power button, as this button alone is directly connected to the power management chip.

Upon restart, a progress bar indicates that the original state of the system is being restored.

Applications and files will remain exactly as they were prior to the system being put into Safe Sleep mode.

NOTE ▶ Before proceeding further in this lesson, fully review the following Knowledge Base documents: 25801, "Energy Saver: About sleep and idle modes in Mac OS X"; 302477, "Progress bar appears after waking from sleep"; and 303329, "How to swap the MacBook Pro battery."

Power Adapters

Each Apple portable model ships with a power adapter, which is used to power the computer and recharge its main battery.

Some power adapters may look identical, even down to their connectors, but they may have different wattage ratings. There are four types of white power adapters for Apple's current PowerBook G4, MacBook Pro, iBook G4, and MacBook models. Each has a different power rating: 45 watts (iBooks and some PowerBooks), 60 watts (MacBooks), 65 watts (some PowerBooks), and 85 watts (MacBook Pros). All current white square power adapters are clearly marked with their wattage. Older unlabeled white square power adapters are all 45-watt models.

45-watt adapters should not be used with computers that require 65-watt adapters, because doing so may affect the computer and its ability to charge the main battery. However, 65-watt adapters can be used with any of the computers that shipped with 45-watt adapters, because using the higher-wattage adapter will not affect the computer or battery performance. The 45-watt and 65-watt power adapters use the same type of connector, so make sure you read the wattage marking.

In addition, the 60-watt and 85-watt power adapters both use a MagSafe connector that is not compatible with the other two models. The same rule applies in that you may use an 85-watt adapter with a computer that requires a 60-watt adapter, but not vice-versa.

For best results, always use the power adapter that came with the computer.

45-watt power adapter

85-watt MagSafe connector

MORE INFO ▶ Refer to Knowledge Base documents 75448, "Apple Portables: Identifying the right power adapter and power cord," and 302461, "Troubleshooting iBook, PowerBook G4, and MacBook Pro power adapters" for more information on power adapters.

Batteries

All portable models ship with a main battery. Some models also have a backup battery. Apple maintains an informative website specifically for battery information: www.apple.com/batteries. This website contains useful information about the care and handling of Apple batteries and battery-operated products, such as PowerBooks, iBooks, and iPods.

Refer to the following Knowledge Base documents for information about specific battery-related issues:

▶ 86797, "PowerBook and iBook: Identifying the right battery"

▶ 10571, "About PowerBook and iBook Battery Storage Life"

- ▶ 86181, "Macintosh Family: Batteries and Part Numbers, Part 2"
- ▶ 106216, "Mac OS X, Portables: Batteries shouldn't be changed when computer is sleeping"
- ▶ 303785, "Intel-based Apple Notebooks: About the battery"
- ▶ 86284, "Calibrating your computer's battery for best performance"
- ▶ 30017, "PowerBook: Testing Backup Battery"
- ▶ 86440, "PowerBook, iBook: Battery Life"
- ▶ Apple battery website - www.apple.com/batteries

Lithium-Ion Batteries

Apple uses rechargeable lithium-ion (Li+ or Li-Ion) batteries in many of its recent portable computers. A lithium-ion battery should retain a minimal charge needed to operate a portable computer for one to two months. Lithium-ion (Li-Ion, or Li+) batteries are not subject to the memory effect and, therefore, have no need for periodic reconditioning. However, if the battery is not used for two to three months, you should recharge the battery. A lithium-ion battery stored for up to 12 months should still be able to accept a charge. Lithium-ion batteries are sensitive to heat and cold and may be permanently damaged by exposure to temperature extremes, so use and store these batteries only in reasonably temperate environments. Think about it this way: If the temperature feels uncomfortable to you, it's probably too hot or cold for your lithium-ion battery as well.

Lithium-ion batteries have battery level indicator lights that tell whether the battery is fully charged, three-fourths charged, one-half charged, one-fourth charged, or depleted. A blinking battery light indicates a problem with the battery. To check the battery status, press and hold the battery button until the indicator lights are on, to check the charge status of the battery.

With the introduction of the Intel-based MacBook and MacBook Pro, Apple included a new type of battery, the lithium polymer battery. Although the underside of the battery may state that it is "Li-Ion," it is using the lithium polymer implementation of this technology.

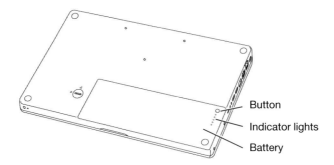

Button

Indicator lights

Battery

MORE INFO ▶ The memory effect, or lazy battery effect, was prevalent in older battery technologies, including nickel-cadmium rechargeable batteries. For additional information, visit www.answers.com/topic/memory-effect.

Battery Calibration

You can calibrate your iBook, PowerBook, MacBook, or MacBook Pro computer's lithium-ion battery for best performance.

The battery has an internal microprocessor that provides an estimate of the amount of energy in the battery as it charges and discharges. The PMU, SMU, or SMC in the computer reads this information from the battery and passes it along to Mac OS X for display to the user as either a time-based readout (such as 2:15 remaining) or percentage-based readout (such as 72%). Over time, after numerous repeated charge/discharge cycles, partial charge cycles, sleep/wake cycles, possible battery swaps, and other various interruptions, the battery microprocessor may no longer have an accurate estimate of the battery's energy range, which could result in an erroneous onscreen battery display. The battery needs to be recalibrated from time to time to ensure that the onscreen battery time and percent display remain accurate. With all iBooks and PowerBook G4 computers, except the aluminum PowerBook G4 (15-inch Double-Layer SD), you should perform this procedure when you first use your computer and then every few months thereafter. This calibration is also recommended in the newer Intel-based MacBook and MacBook Pro computers as well.

> **MORE INFO** ▶ To review battery calibration procedures, consult Knowledge Base document 86284: "Calibrating your computer's battery for best performance;" for Intel-based portables, visit http://docs.info.apple.com/article.html?path=Mac/10.4/en/mh2339.html.

Battery Storage

When storing batteries for a long period of time (for example, over the summer school break), a user should fully charge the battery and then use the computer until the battery has depleted 50 percent. The user may then shut down the computer, remove the battery, and store it in a cool, dry place.

> **NOTE** ▶ When the battery is inserted in the computer, it creates a closed circuit. So, even if the computer is shut down, the battery will eventually drain.

Low-Power Messages

When the battery charge drops to about 1 percent, the computer displays a low-power message. If you continue working until the computer goes to sleep automatically, you may not be able to wake it again until you plug the computer into AC power. If you are unable to plug in the AC power adapter immediately, the contents of RAM are preserved in sleep mode for at least two days. During this time, you should be able to wake the computer and resume work where you left off after it has been plugged in to the AC power adapter, provided the battery has not been removed in the interim.

TIP ▶ Recharge a depleted battery as soon as possible. Leaving a depleted battery in the computer for longer than two weeks (especially in a hot location, such as the trunk of a car) may damage the battery so that it can't be recharged. If your battery falls into a deep-discharge state, you must replace the battery.

Battery Recharge

To recharge a battery, simply plug in the AC power adapter. You do not need to shut down the computer before plugging in the adapter, but always connect the adapter to AC power before you attach the adapter to the computer.

TIP ▶ If you connect the AC power adapter to the computer before you connect the adapter to an electrical outlet, you run the risk of making the Power Manager software unusable. Symptoms of issues with the Power Manager software include startup problems and the inability to shut down the computer (the computer restarts spontaneously after shutdown). To resolve this issue, you need to reset the PMU. Procedures for resetting the PMU differ depending on the model; you can find them in the appropriate service manual and in Knowledge Base document 14449, "Resetting PowerBook and iBook Power Management Unit (PMU)."

You can continue to use the computer while the battery is recharging, but the battery will take longer to recharge if you do. Battery recharging time while the computer is in use depends on how often you use the hard drive, how bright the screen is, whether you are using an external monitor, how completely the battery is depleted, and other factors.

If you are using several power-consuming features such as an external monitor or a program that requires frequent hard drive access, and you are not using the features designed to conserve power (such as reduced processor speed), the battery may not recharge until you put the computer to sleep or shut it down. Simply put, the more power you consume during computer use, the less power is available to recharge the battery.

While the computer is shut down and the AC power adapter is plugged in, you can remove a charged battery from the computer and replace it with another battery you want to charge. If you do this, remember to reconnect the AC power adapter to recharge it.

Power Conservation

Two portable computer operations drain the battery the most—using the backlight on the screen and using the hard drive. To increase battery life, reduce the use of these components. Set the hard drive to spin down quickly and turn off or lower the brightness of the backlight. Using the slower processor speed also increases battery life. When not in use, put the computer to sleep.

To get the maximum amount of power duration from your portable's battery, you need to set the Energy Saver preferences properly and adhere to the following usage tips.

Energy Saver Preferences

The most important tools for managing power consumption on a portable are found in Energy Saver preferences. Choose System Preferences from the Apple menu, and then click Energy Saver.

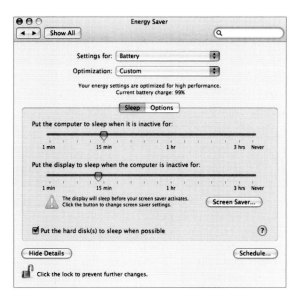

The Energy Saver preferences are used to specify when the screen dims and when the hard drive spins down. You can use the provided presets or customize preferences for battery use and power adapter use.

In the Sleep tab, you can specify a global setting (put system to sleep) or specify separate settings for the display and the hard drive. To save power, you can simply set the entire computer to go to sleep after a particular period of inactivity. You should get into the habit of putting the computer to sleep when not in use, because this conserves the most power, short of shutting the system down. Waking a computer from sleep takes only a few seconds, but if you find this delay unacceptable, consider at least turning off the display separately and putting the hard disk to sleep when possible. Note that Energy Saver preferences apply to all users of the computer, not just the user that is currently logged in. You must have administrator-level access to the computer to change Energy Saver preferences, which is why you see a lock icon in the lower-left corner of this system preference. A few other system preferences, such as Networking, also behave this way.

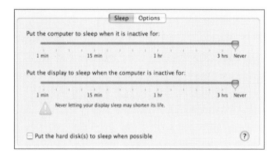

Note the warning when the computer and display are set to never sleep.

NOTE ▶ If you specify a separate sleep delay for the display, the Mac OS will automatically partially dim the backlighting at half that setting, and completely turn off backlighting when the full period of inactivity has elapsed.

The Schedule button enables you to set startup and shutdown times for your system.

On the Options tab, you can control the computer's waking on modem or network activity, restarting automatically after a power failure, display brightness, and the battery status icon.

Keep a close eye on the battery level. Select the "Show battery status in the menu bar" checkbox to add a battery icon in the menu bar that displays either the time remaining or the percent of battery power remaining. Keep in mind that these estimates are based on the battery's average consumption. If, for example, you begin using the optical drive to watch a DVD, you will notice the time remaining drop accordingly.

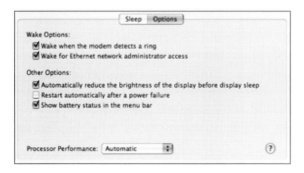

Deselect the "Wake when the modem detects a ring" checkbox unless you really use your computer's modem to accept incoming calls for faxes or remote access connections. Constantly checking the modem for incoming calls requires power.

On many portable and desktop models introduced since May 2001, users can elect to reduce processor speed, if they are running Mac OS X 10.1.5 or later. Simply choose Reduced from the Processor Performance pop-up menu. You may notice a perceptible slowdown, but you'll benefit from increased battery life. The slower the CPU runs, the less power it consumes, and the less heat the computer generates overall.

> **MORE INFO** ▶ For additional information about Energy Saver options, refer to "Mac OS X 10.4 Help: Setting Energy Saver options for your computer" (http://docs.info.apple.com/article.html?path=Mac/10.4/en/mh1669.html).

Power-Saving Techniques

Knowing how to manage a portable computer's energy is important. The number-one power-saving tip is to use the AC power adapter as often as possible. You can control many of the hidden areas of power consumption by following a few simple tips and techniques that can affect battery usage.

Settings and Controls

You can easily set the following operating-system settings to minimize power consumption:

▶ In Energy Saver preferences, select the option to put the display to sleep automatically.

▶ In Energy Saver preferences, select the option to put the hard disk to sleep automatically. (The default is on, so you will have to change it manually.)

▶ Turn off AirPort and Bluetooth when not in use.

▶ Watch your battery level carefully. Choose to show the battery in the menu bar, showing either time remaining or percent remaining. The displayed battery level is only an estimation based on the battery's current average consumption. For example, the menu bar could display 2 hours of remaining power, but the battery might last only 1.5 hours after the hard drive or optical drive starts spinning. The estimated time remaining will rise again if the hard drive goes back to sleep.

▶ Reduce processor speed by choosing Reduced from the Processor Performance pop-up menu in Energy Saver preferences. This reduced setting slows down the computer a little, but the battery life is increased. (This setting is not available in all models.)

▶ Reduce screen brightness (backlight). Dim the screen to the lowest comfortable level to achieve maximum battery life, since the screen is one of the largest power consumers in a portable. You may be able to dim the screen brightness considerably and still be able to work without any problems.

Application Software

Here are several tips for conserving battery power while using different applications:

▶ Under battery power, don't use applications or features (such as spell-checking or QuickTime) that require lots of hard drive access.

▶ Use applications suited to nomadic use. Don't use resource-consuming applications if you do not require their features. Use a light word processing application such as AppleWorks or TextEdit rather than Microsoft Word, which is processor-intensive. Games and graphics applications such as Adobe Photoshop keep the hard disk actively spinning, which drains the battery more quickly.

▶ Set up locations files optimized for different environments. Suggest prioritizing different network interfaces for each place that the user uses his or her computer. The customer may, for example, prefer internal modem when at home but AirPort when at work or school.

▶ Simultaneously open the files you want to work on so the disk spins up a single time.

▶ You may elect to run frequently used programs off a RAM disk, especially if they are disk-intensive.

▶ When near an AC outlet and planning to use battery power later, launch the applications and open data files with AC power, then put the computer to sleep. Your work will be in RAM when the computer is awakened from sleep.

Peripherals

Use the following tips to conserve battery power when using peripheral devices:

▶ As soon as the user is finished with the modem, quit any program that uses it.

▶ Turn off the "wake on ring" and "fax receive" options for modems.

▶ Disconnect the modem cable—a connected modem, even when not in use, drains power (remove the modem cable from the computer, but it may remain in the wall phone jack).

▶ Disconnect peripherals because some peripherals are not self-powered (USB mouse, or even a FireWire hard disk even removed from the desktop). Peripherals may draw power from the portable computer, even if they're not actively in use.

▶ Deactivate and remove any cables from unused ports, even if not in use.

▶ Use the disk drive as little as possible and eject any optical discs not in use.

▶ Use only low-power USB devices that are designed for portable computers.

▶ Remove any PC Cards from the PC Card expansion slot. Some cards draw power even when they are not in use.

Energy-Saving Standards

In addition to allowing users to work as long as possible unrestrained by cables, the power management system meets the following energy-saving standards:

▶ Energy Saver

▶ The U.S. Environmental Protection Agency (EPA) ENERGY STAR program, of which Apple was a founding member

▶ The California Energy Commission appliance efficiency regulations

▶ The U.S. Federal Energy Management Program (FEMP)

▶ The European Union Code of Conduct on Efficiency for External Power Supplies

▶ Blue Angel (Germany)

To meet these standards, the default configuration of the computer must draw less than 7 watts in sleep mode and less than 5 watts in off mode while plugged into the AC adapter and with the battery removed.

MORE INFO ▶ For further information regarding these standards, consult www.apple.com/environment/energyefficiency.

Troubleshooting

Troubleshooting the power system can be difficult. Power is potentially distributed over several boards and connectors. In addition, a number of settings and use patterns could contribute to the symptom. In portable computers, a main battery is added to this list of variables. Many interconnected points could individually or in some grouping cause the symptom you're trying to resolve.

If portable users complain that they do not seem to be getting the battery life they once did, check that proper power conservation settings have been set in Energy Saver preferences and, if necessary, reset the Power Manager. Also, check whether the portable's main battery has had an excessive number of charge cycles and is now depleted (worn out), requiring replacement. This is easily verified using System Profiler in Mac OS X v10.4 and later, and looking in the Power section under Cycle Count. Compare this to information in www.apple.com/batteries/notebooks.html to verify if the battery is depleted.

User Settings

After you verify the problem, you can start eliminating areas of potential causes, starting with user error or settings.

Start by considering the power-saving tips discussed in the previous section to see if you can return the computer to optimum performance. Ensure that no settings or running applications are preventing the portable from realizing energy savings.

Support Pages

The Apple Support site is another resource that can assist you in trouble-shooting power management issues. The support pages for iBooks, MacBooks, PowerBooks, and MacBook Pros have detailed advice on how to conserve power and investigate power-related issues.

Power Management Resets

In Lesson 5b, you were introduced to the PMU, SMU, and SMC. These system elements are often reset as part of investigating power management issues. Before attempting a reset, make sure that you have located the correct reset procedures for the model under repair.

The computer's power is managed by an integrated circuit (computer chip) located on the logic board. Depending on the model, it may be a PMU, SMU, or SMC. It is responsible for managing the computer's power, including hard disk spin down, sleep and wake, some charging aspects, fans, and how any devices attached to the computer affect sleep.

If the settings of this power management chip become corrupted over time, you may notice abnormal conditions such as your computer not turning on, not displaying video, or not waking from sleep. These situations may require you to perform a reset, but don't do so as a first resort.

Resetting the computer's power management returns the computer hardware, including NVRAM, to default settings and forces the computer to shut down. Performing a reset will not resolve a computer being unresponsive or sluggish. Only perform a reset if your computer hardware is believe to have failed or in situations where the power management system is suspect.

Before performing a reset, try restarting the computer. If you cannot perform a normal restart, you may need to Force Quit (Option-Command-Escape) the application you are using and/or Force Shutdown (press the power button for 10 seconds). If restarting the computer doesn't solve the problem, perform a reset. Again, reset procedures vary from system to system, so verify that you are using the correct procedure for your particular model.

Lesson Review

1. What power modes were discussed in this lesson?

    a. Awake, sleep, energy saver, shut down

    b. Awake, sleep, safe sleep, and shut down

    c. Awake, sleep, and shut down

2. Which power mode uses the least power?

    a. Sleep

    b. Safe Sleep

    c. Shut down

3. System software can attempt to place the computer into sleep mode, unless:

    a. Sleep is set to 15 minutes in the Energy Saver pane.

    b. The hard disk is sleeping.

    c. DVD Player is the active application.

    d. Battery status is set to display in the menu bar.

4. In which System Preferences pane do you set separate timing for display dimming?

    a. Energy Saver

    b. Displays

    c. Desktop & Screen Saver

5. True or false: While it is sleeping, a portable normally shuts down when the display is opened.

6. True or false: The power management reset is the first option you should use when diagnosing or repairing a sleep issue.

7. Which AC power adapters have a MagSafe connector?

    a. 45-watt and 65-watt

    b. 60-watt and 85-watt

    c. 60-watt and 65-watt

    d. All of the above

8. What action provides additional power savings on a portable?

    a. Reduce processor speed.

    b. Turn off International System Preferences.

    c. Turn on a screen saver.

9. Which of the following items is the most energy-consuming device in a portable?

    a. Modem

    b. PC Card

    c. Screen

10. True or false: Lithium-ion batteries must be reconditioned periodically to overcome the "memory effect," otherwise they lose their ability to hold a full charge.

Answer Key

1. b; 2. c; 3. c; 4. a; 5. False, a portable should reawaken when it is opened while sleeping; 6. False; 7. b; 8. a; 9. c; 10. False, lithium-ion batteries are not subject to the "memory effect" and will hold a full charge unless they remain drained for an extended period.

7

Reference Files

AirPort Extreme Technology Overview (PDF)
(L303115A_Airport_Extreme_TO.pdf)

Designing AirPort Networks v4.2
(Designing_AirPort_Networks_v4.2.pdf)

AirPort Extreme Base Station Setup Guide
(AirPortExtremeBaseStationSetupGuide.pdf)

Time

This lesson takes approximately 1 hour to complete.

Goals

Describe differences among IEEE 802.11 standards

Understand similarities and differences among different
models of AirPort Extreme Cards and AirPort Extreme
Base Stations

Learn how to configure an AirPort client

Establish a Computer-to-Computer connection

Discover sources of interference for AirPort networks

Understand basic security features of wireless networking

Learn how to add and sync up a Bluetooth device to your
computer and basic Bluetooth troubleshooting issues

Lesson 7
Wireless

Wireless networks transfer data between computers using radio frequency waves, similar to how a cordless telephone works. These networks are so popular that they can be found at hotels, airports, and coffee shops around the world. In fact, many cities use wireless technology to offer free or low-cost Internet connectivity to their residents.

Wireless networking is no more complicated than wired networking, and it accomplishes the same results; it just transmits the information over another medium. When you surf the World Wide Web, you are communicating via Transmission Control Protocol/Internet Protocol (TCP/IP), whether you are using Ethernet cables or radio waves.

In this lesson you'll learn to support and troubleshoot wireless networks built with Apple AirPort products. In addition, you will be introduced to the technical underpinnings of wireless networking.

Throughout this lesson we'll use the term *client* to refer to a computer that is connecting to a wireless network. Examples of wireless clients are Macintosh desktop and portable models that are configured with AirPort or AirPort Extreme Cards and appropriate AirPort software.

The term *base station* refers to any wireless network hardware that creates a wireless network and connects this wireless network to a wired Ethernet network. Base stations are also sometimes referred to as *wireless access points*.

Wireless networking has some advantages over wired networks:

▶   Installation is fast and easy.

▶   Radio waves can go places wires cannot.

▶   Adding new users or extending its range is easy.

But wireless also has some disadvantages:

▶   It's slower than 100Base-T Ethernet networks.

▶   It has a limit of ten simultaneously connected clients with the original AirPort Base Station (Graphite) and the AirPort Express, and a maximum of 50 clients with all other models.

▶   Because you are broadcasting your data through the air, security is easier to compromise than on a wired network.

Required Tools and Equipment

To practice creating and troubleshooting wireless networks, you will need the following:

▶   A Macintosh computer with Mac OS X and AirPort capability

▶   Access to an established 802.11b or 802.11g wireless network

▶   Access to a second AirPort-equipped Macintosh computer

▶   An AirPort, AirPort Express, or AirPort Extreme Base Station

▶   Internet access

> **NOTE** ▶ Macintosh computers are compatible with most third-party wireless networks. As part of your training, we will be focusing on Apple wireless products only.

Basic Terms

Before we continue much further into wireless networking, let's review some basic terms and concepts.

Radio Frequency

Radio frequency (RF), is a term that refers to electromagnetic waves that are used to transmit and receive information. Hertz (Hz) is the unit of measurement for frequency, which equals one cycle per second. One thousand cycles per second is one kilohertz (1 KHz). One million cycles per second is one megahertz (1 MHz). One billion cycles per second is one gigahertz (1 GHz).

A *band* is a range of frequencies that are used for a particular purpose. Many people don't realize that our world is filled with electromagnetic waves in many bands. The household electrical current in the U.S. has a frequency of 60 Hz (50 Hz in many other parts of the world). In the U.S., the AM radio band is transmitted between 530 KHz and 1.7 MHz, while the FM band is transmitted between 88 to 108 MHz.

Wireless networking uses several bands. The two most popular are 5 GHz and 2.4 GHz.

Bandwidth

In communications and computing, *bandwidth* refers to the amount of data that can be transmitted on a network over a given period of time. Bandwidth is measured in terms of *bit rate*, the number of bits of information that is transmitted per second. Wireless communications use bit rates in megabits per second (Mbps).

The 802.11 Standard

The Institute of Electrical and Electronics Engineers (IEEE) is an international professional organization dedicated to the advancement of technology that sets industrial standards for a number of industries. One set of standards provided by this organization, called IEEE 802.11, addresses wireless communication between computers and networks.

The IEEE 802.11 standards currently consist of six different protocols for wireless communication. The most commonly used versions of these protocols are:

▶ IEEE 802.11a: Uses the 5 GHz band to communicate and can transfer data at a maximum of 54 Mbps. Apple AirPort Extreme equipment can join such networks but cannot establish networks using this protocol. Currently, Apple does not support this standard.

▶ IEEE 802.11b: Used in the original Apple AirPort hardware and was the first widely accepted wireless standard. It has a maximum data transfer rate of 11 Mbps and uses the 2.4 GHz band.

▶ IEEE 802.11g: Used in current AirPort Extreme and AirPort Express hardware. It uses the 2.4 GHz band and has a maximum transfer rate of 54 Mbps.

▶ IEEE 802.11n: Will be implemented in the new AirPort Extreme Base Station announced at Macworld 2007. This technology, according to the IEEE draft specifications, will enable communications of up to 180 Mbps using the 2.4 GHz band. Most new Macintosh computers are already capable of using this standard, but will require 802.11n Enabler for Mac software.

Devices based on the 802.11b and 802.11g standards are compatible with one another, so older products can communicate with newer products but do so at their maximum transmission rate at 11 Mbps.

Wi-Fi

In 1999, industry leaders formed the Wi-Fi Alliance with the goal of adopting a single worldwide standard for high-speed wireless networking.

Wi-Fi is also used as a name for implementations of the IEEE 802.11 standards, and as another word for wireless connectivity. It is commonly used on Windows-based PCs and wireless routers.

Wi-Fi CERTIFIED™ devices have been tested for interoperability based on the Wi-Fi Alliance certification standards.

Apple AirPort systems are compatible with Wi-Fi networks, as they both use the IEEE 802.11 standard.

Bluetooth

Bluetooth is a standard for wireless personal area networks. It enables short-range wireless connections between desktop and notebook computers and peripherals such as handhelds, personal digital assistants (PDAs), mobile phones, camera phones, printers, digital cameras, headsets, video consoles, keyboards, and even computer mice. Bluetooth uses the 2.4 GHz band for communications.

Power over Ethernet (PoE)

This standard allows low-power network devices to receive DC power directly through the Ethernet cable, eliminating the need to connect a separate power supply to the device.

AirPort

AirPort, introduced into Apple products in July 1999, is the name for the Apple wireless networking technology products that are compliant with the IEEE 802.11b standard. AirPort is also known as AirMac in Japan. The original AirPort Card (M7600LL/E) works with almost all Macintosh models released from mid-1999 through 2002.

AirPort Extreme

AirPort Extreme is the Apple implementation of the IEEE 802.11g standard. It was announced in January 2003 and provides a higher maximum transfer rate of 54 Mbps. Starting with the January 2003 introduction of the PowerBook G4 (12-inch) and PowerBook G4 (17-inch), all new Apple computer models are compatible with AirPort Extreme.

MAC Address

A Media Access Control (MAC) address, also called AirPort ID number, is a unique code assigned to networking hardware. This designator also provides a small measure of security, as the number is unique to the device to which it is assigned and networks can be restricted to allow access only to devices with known MAC addresses.

AirPort Hardware Overview

The first Apple AirPort products, released in July 1999, implemented IEEE wireless standard 802.11b. The original AirPort products were the AirPort Card, AirPort Base Station (Graphite), and AirPort software. These products have a range of up to 150 feet at 11 Mbps.

Based on the 802.11g standard, AirPort Extreme was released in January 2003. This second-generation line from Apple consists of the AirPort Extreme Card, two models of the AirPort Extreme Base Station, and updated AirPort software. In April 2004, Apple introduced a third member of the AirPort Extreme Base Station family: the AirPort Extreme Base Station (PoE/UL 2043), which supports the new IEEE 802.3af Power over Ethernet specification.

In June 2004, Apple introduced the AirPort Express, a portable 802.11g device capable of acting as a base station and wirelessly streaming music from iTunes to standard stereo equipment.

AirPort Express and AirPort Extreme products introduced these key features:

► Maximum 54 Mbps transfer rate

► Compatibility with 802.11b networks and 802.11g networks

► Tight security

► Wireless printer sharing

► Specific tailoring for Mac OS X for optimal speed and performance

The following table details some specifications for Apple AirPort products.

Hardware	IEEE Standard	Maximum Transfer Rate	Maximum Range	Comments
AirPort Card				
	802.11b	11 Mbps	150 feet (11 Mbps) 300 feet (1 Mbps)	Original AirPort Card. Usually customer-installable.
AirPort Extreme Card				
	802.11g	54 Mbps	50 feet (54 Mbps) 240 feet (6 Mbps) 300 feet (1 Mbps)	Normally user-installable. Some newer Macintosh systems use a different AirPort Extreme Card that is not user-installable.

Hardware	IEEE Standard	Maximum Transfer Rate	Maximum Range	Comments
AirPort Base Station (Graphite)				
	802.11b	11 Mbps	150 feet (11 Mbps) 300 feet (1 Mbps)	Original AirPort Base Station. Has only one Ethernet connection (wide area network, or WAN) and is reset via pinhole on bottom of unit.
AirPort Base Station (Dual Ethernet)				
	802.11b	11 Mbps	150 feet (11 Mbps) 300 feet (1 Mbps)	Similar to Graphite model but has local area network (LAN) Ethernet connection as well as WAN, and reset button is between LAN Ethernet connection and power cable.
AirPort Extreme Base Station or AirPort Extreme Base Station (no modem) or AirPort Extreme Base Station (PoE/UL 2043)				
	802.11g	54 Mbps	50 feet (54 Mbps) 240 feet (6 Mbps) 300 feet (1 Mbps)	AirPort Extreme Base Station: First base station to offer IEEE 802.11g standard. Set to accept Kensington security locks.

Hardware	IEEE Standard	Maximum Transfer Rate	Maximum Range	Comments
AirPort Extreme Base Station (no modem)				
				(no modem): Same as AirPort Extreme Base Station but does not offer a modem connector or external antenna connector.
AirPort Extreme Base Station (PoE/UL 2043)				
				(PoE/UL 2043): Allows power to be supplied via the WAN Ethernet connection in compliance with the UL 2043 standard.
AirPort Express				
	802.11g	54 Mbps	50 feet (54 Mbps) 240 feet (6 Mbps) 300 feet (1 Mbps)	Offers IEEE 802.111g connections for up to 10 systems rather than the 50 provided by AirPort Extreme Base Stations.

AirPort Extreme Card

The AirPort Extreme Card allows you to connect to an AirPort Extreme Base Station at up to 54 Mbps. Even with this increased performance, the AirPort Extreme Card is compatible with all existing AirPort products as well as third-party Wi-Fi–certified 802.11b products.

The rear of the AirPort Extreme Card shows the card's MAC address and serial number.

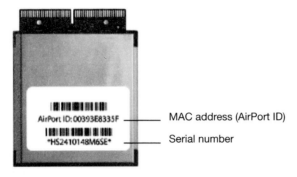

MAC address (AirPort ID)

Serial number

AirPort Extreme Card

All AirPort Extreme Cards require your computer to have an AirPort Extreme Card slot.

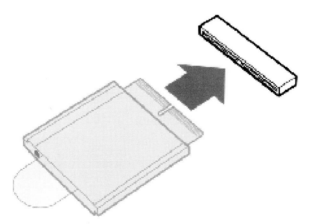

AirPort Extreme Card and slot

The AirPort Extreme Card requires a different slot from the original AirPort Card slot (an AirPort-only, modified low-voltage PCMCIA slot), which was not capable of handling the 54 Mbps data transfer speeds used by 802.11g connections.

Wireless Card Configurations

The AirPort Extreme Card is available in four configurations, containing one of four AirPort Extreme Cards supporting different ranges of channels required in different countries.

The four base kits are:

- ► Domestic (U.S.) AirPort Extreme Card kit
- ► Worldwide AirPort Extreme Card kit
- ► Japanese AirMac Extreme Card kit
- ► French AirPort Extreme Card kit

> **NOTE** ► In Japan, AirPort products are called AirMac products (for example, AirPort Extreme is called AirMac Extreme).

Many countries have other localized versions of these cards. For example, it's useful to know that Singapore may use the Domestic (U.S.) Card, but have all literature included in Chinese.

> **NOTE** ► When traveling, keep in mind that your AirPort product may be able to operate on channels that are not available in the country that you are visiting. To better understand wireless communications internationally, refer to Apple Knowledge Base document 58567, "Using AirPort Wireless Communication Internationally."

AirPort Extreme Cards in Later Products

Intel-based Macintosh systems and more recent Power Mac systems do not always use a standard AirPort Extreme Card. Instead, they are configured with internal AirPort Extreme Cards that are not user-installable. These cards are installed at the factory and are replaced as service parts when defective.

AirPort Extreme Base Station

The AirPort Extreme Base Station provides a wireless connection between Macintosh computers with AirPort or AirPort Extreme Cards and an Internet connection. It can be used in conjunction with an Ethernet connection (such as from a cable modem, DSL modem, or Ethernet network) through the integrated Ethernet port, or with a telephone line through a modem.

The AirPort Extreme Base Station introduces these features:

▶ Wireless bridging: Allows you to add up to four AirPort Extreme Base Stations to the one connected to your wired DSL, cable, or Ethernet network and wirelessly bridge a network backbone. This is another way to extend the range of your network and double the number of users you can support.

▶ Wireless printing: With Mac OS X, just plug in your printer and you can quickly and easily print. Use the base station's USB port to plug in an inkjet printer directly into the base station.

▶ Extended user capacity: Up to 50 users can now be connected to the Internet simultaneously up to 150 feet away from an Ethernet connection or a phone line.

▶ Transmission power control: You can reduce the size of your wireless network, down to just a single room for extra privacy, using AirPort Admin Utility. This is useful if you don't want to provide your neighbors with free Internet access.

▶ External antenna port: With the AirPort Extreme Base Station you can also manage the range of your wireless network. On the base station configuration with external antenna port, you can attach one of two types of antennas, an omnidirectional or a directional. With these antennas, which are discussed below, you can extend the range of the AirPort Extreme Base Station.

▶ Compatibility mode: You can configure the AirPort Extreme Base Station into one of three data rate modes:

802.11b only

802.11b/802.11g compatibility

802.11g only

NOTE ▶ When the base station is set to compatibility mode, a mixed environment consisting of 802.11b (AirPort) and 802.11g (AirPort Extreme) clients can connect to the AirPort Extreme Base Station at the appropriate data rate supported by that card.

The following image shows the front of an AirPort Extreme Base Station.

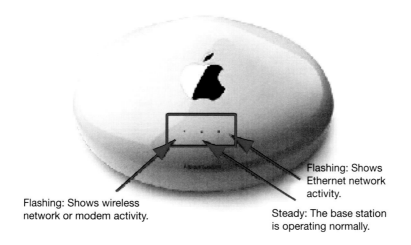

Flashing: Shows wireless network or modem activity.

Flashing: Shows Ethernet network activity.

Steady: The base station is operating normally.

The following image shows the back (I/O ports) of an AirPort Extreme Base Station.

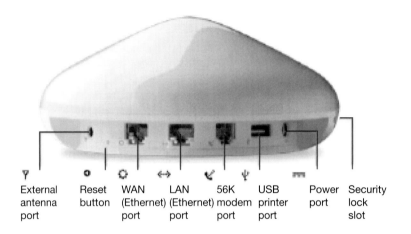

| External antenna port | Reset button | WAN (Ethernet) port | LAN (Ethernet) port | 56K modem port | USB printer port | Power port | Security lock slot |

AirPort Extreme Base Station (PoE/UL 2043)

Some models of the AirPort Extreme Base Station can receive power through the Ethernet WAN port when it is connected to 802.3af-compliant Power Sourcing Equipment (PSE) using plenum-rated category 5 (CAT 5) Ethernet cable. Powering the base station using a PSE is known as Power over Ethernet (PoE). A PSE is a line-powered Ethernet device, like a switch or a hub, which supplies power to Powered Devices (PDs).

PoE enables you to run both data and power through the same cable. If you are using PoE, all switches connecting directly to PoE-receiving base stations need to be 802.3af-compliant. You cannot mix 802.3af switches with non-802.3af switches, as the power current may damage their hardware. This feature makes it feasible and cost-effective to install low-power Ethernet network hardware (such as Wi-Fi routers or webcams) in locations where there is no AC power outlet nearby, such as in a ceiling crawl space.

Advantage of PoE

The advantage of PoE is that you no longer have to worry about locating or running special power lines and outlets to locations for the base station. When planning a wireless network, you have the added flexibility of placing the base station in locations that make the most sense for your coverage and usage patterns. For example, you can use the PoE to power the base station located in an air duct to provide wireless service in a location that may cost a large amount of money to wire for power.

The AirPort Extreme Base Station (PoE/UL 2043) uses the Ethernet WAN port to receive power. The LAN port does not support PoE.

The following image shows the back (I/O ports) of an AirPort Extreme Base Station (PoE/UL 2043).

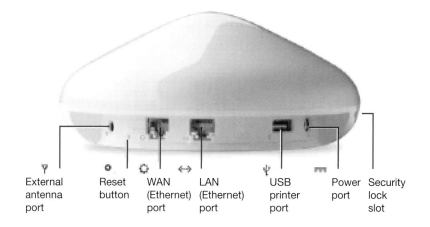

AirPort Express Base Station

The AirPort Express Base Station is a full-featured wireless access point that is smaller and more portable than other base station designs.

The AirPort Express Base Station:

► Is based on the IEEE 802.11g standard

► Has a data transfer speed of up to 54 Mbps

► Works with DSL or cable modems

► Enables up to ten simultaneous users to share a connection

► Enables wireless USB printing

► Protects your network with Wi-Fi Protected Access (WPA) or 128-bit Wired Equivalency Privacy (WEP)

► Has a built-in firewall

The following image shows the bottom of an AirPort Express Base Station (PoE/UL 2043).

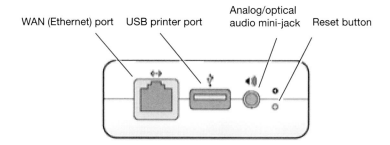

AirTunes

AirTunes allows an AirPort Express Base Station to play iTunes music on your stereo (or powered speakers) from just about any room in the house.

No need to connect cables from the computer to the stereo: You can play your iTunes music on an AirPort-equipped Macintosh or Wi-Fi compliant PC through your stereo, wirelessly.

The single audio port on the base station supports an analog or optical digital cable connection to your audio equipment.

Hardware Requirements

AirTunes has these hardware requirements:

▶   An AirPort Express Base Station

▶   Home audio equipment connected to the AirPort Express Base Station
     using either optical digital audio or analog audio cables

Macintosh Requirements

To use AirTunes with a Macintosh, you must have:

▶   A Macintosh computer with an AirPort or AirPort Extreme Card installed

▶   AirPort 4.0 or later

▶   Mac OS X 10.3 or later

▶   iTunes 4.6 or later (included on the AirPort Express CD)

Windows Requirements

To use AirTunes with a Windows PC, you must have the following:

▶   A Windows PC with 500 MHz (or faster) processor

▶   AirPort 4.0 Client Software for Windows

▶   Windows 2000 with Service Pack 4 (or later), or Windows XP Home or
     Professional

▶   iTunes 4.6 for Windows or later (included on the AirPort Express CD)

     NOTE ▶ A Macintosh or PC can access AirTunes speakers over both wire-
     less and Ethernet connections, so having a wireless card for either plat-
     form is not a strict requirement.

Setting Up a Wireless Client

Association is the process by which an AirPort client establishes a relationship with an AirPort Base Station or other wireless LANs. In password-protected AirPort networks, *authentication* is the beginning of the association process.

The association process is rather complex, but the following steps are a simplified version:

1. The client sends a probe (association request) spanning the entire wireless frequency band (all available channels) searching for in-range base stations.

2. The client receives an association response from the in-range base stations (only stations that authenticate the client will send an association response).

3. The client determines which of the association responses has the best communication quality (signal-to-noise ratio).

4. The client establishes an association with the base station that has the best communication quality and joins the network.

   NOTE ▶ Remember that a client can be associated with only one AirPort Base Station at a time.

AirPort clients use the Internet Connect application to access a wireless network. You can manually choose a network or have the computer automatically access an available one.

There are two steps to using Internet Connect to access a wireless network: choosing a base station and configuring your network preferences.

Step 1: Choosing a Base Station

The first step in manually connecting to a wireless network is to choose a base station. You can use the AirPort status icon in the menu bar, which acts as a shortcut to AirPort functions and the Internet Connect application, or you can use the Internet Connect application itself.

Using the AirPort Status Icon in the Menu Bar

The AirPort status icon gives you "one-stop shopping" access to most AirPort functions. The status icon appears on the menu even when other applications are launched. It's a functional replacement for the AirPort control strip module used in Mac OS 9.

With the AirPort status icon, you can:

▶ Turn AirPort on and off

▶ Choose from available networks, or manually enter a base station's TCP/IP address and password

▶ Create a Computer-to-Computer network

▶ Open the Internet Connect application

Using the AirPort status icon is the quickest method to choose a wireless network. Any wireless networks that are in range (and are not closed networks) are listed beneath the Turn AirPort Off command. Choosing a network places a checkmark next to its name.

In the image above, the wireless network Home Network is selected.

NOTE ► The AirPort status icon appears in the menu bar when an AirPort Card is installed and you have selected that it be shown using Network system preferences. While it can be manually removed by Command-dragging it away from the menu bar, it also removes itself when the AirPort Card is removed from the computer.

Using the Internet Connection Application

Internet Connect is used to make PPP and customized dial-up network connections, as well as connections to wireless networks. It functionally replaces the AirPort application used in Mac OS 9.

To use Internet Connect to connect to a wireless network:

1   Launch the Internet Connect application, located in the Applications directory.

2   Click the AirPort icon at the top of the Internet Connect window.

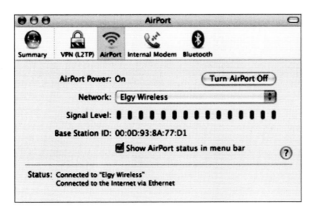

3 From the Network menu, choose the desired network.

Choosing a wireless network here will also show that same network the next time the AirPort status icon is selected. The converse is also true: When a network is selected in the AirPort status icon, that choice is also displayed in Internet Connect.

4 If you don't want to show the AirPort status icon on the menu bar, deselect the "Show AirPort status in menu bar" checkbox.

The Internet Connect application also shows useful information when trouble-shooting wireless client connections:

▶ AirPort Power: Indicates if the computer's AirPort circuitry is on or off.

▶ Signal Level: The signal is strongest when all or most of the blue bars are filled, and weakest when very are few filled.

▶ Base Station ID: This is the MAC address (AirPort ID) of the chosen base station.

Step 2: Configuring Network Preferences

After choosing the wireless network to which you want to connect, the next step is to make sure TCP/IP is configured correctly. Frequently, support issues are generated when users choose a base station, but have incorrect settings or missing information in the TCP/IP section of Network preferences.

This section shows some of the more common configurations used when connecting to a wireless network.

DHCP

The Dynamic Host Configuration Protocol (DHCP) configuration is the most common. With DHCP, the base station provides TCP/IP addresses across the wireless network for which it is responsible. With most DHCP configurations, no information needs to be entered into the TCP/IP preferences. A typical configuration looks like this:

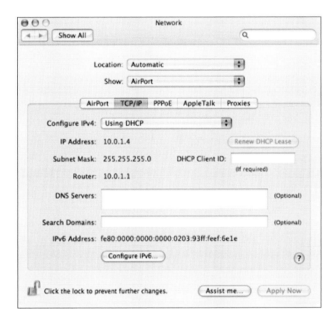

Although generally this configuration requires no user input, some network configurations may require you to enter the DHCP client ID, domain name server (IP), or search domains. When troubleshooting, you should always have the user check with their network administrator for additional TCP/IP configuration information.

The next tab to check is the AirPort tab, which provides another method to choose a wireless network as well as information providing the AirPort ID (also called the MAC or hardware address).

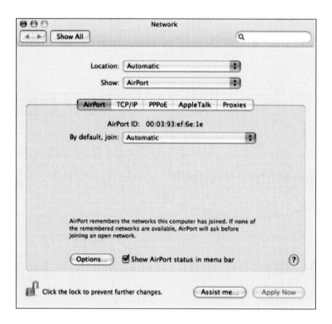

Other Protocols

It is possible that an ISP or your network administrator may distribute specific IP addresses for you to use and may require additional information about your computer, such as the MAC address. You may need to choose "Use DHCP with a manual address," "Manually," or "Using BootP" from the menu. The specific settings will depend on the information you are provided.

Regional Card Configurations

The 2.4 GHz band used by all 802.11 devices is broken down further into 14 channels. Please note that not all countries allow Wi-Fi devices to use all 14 channels. For instance, the FCC limits devices sold in the United States to channels 1 through 11. AirPort cards come in configurations that support different ranges of channels in use in different countries:

▶ Channels 1 through 11 for the United States, Canada, Latin America, and Taiwan

▶ Channels 1 through 14 for Japan

▶ Channels 1 through 13 for other countries ("worldwide" equivalent)

As an AirPort card user, you needn't concern yourself with channels. Your AirPort card adjusts itself automatically to connect to base stations as needed. The only potential problem would be when you are visiting an international destination where a base station has been set to a channel outside your card's range. In that case, the network administrator would have to change the base station's channel for you to gain wireless access to the network.

Creating a Computer-to-Computer Network

A Computer-to-Computer network is a wireless-only peer-to-peer network, also known as an Independent Basic Service Set (IBSS). The Computer-to-Computer network that you create is completely isolated. Think of Computer-to-Computer mode as the wireless equivalent of having an Ethernet hub and some Ethernet cables to connect two or more computers to each other, but to nothing else.

In an IBSS network, there is no central collection point or access point for wireless Ethernet packets to flow through. IBSS networks can be created at any time and by any wireless client computer that supports IBSS. Once one wireless client computer creates an IBSS, other wireless client computers in signal range may join. The IBSS will exist as long as at least one of the wireless client computers that created or joined the IBSS is still running and in signal range.

The main benefit of using Computer-to-Computer mode is that you do not need an AirPort Base Station or other wireless access point to establish basic wireless connectivity between two or more computers acting as AirPort clients. This means you can easily set up a temporary peer-to-peer wireless network to share files or play network games between multiple wireless computers. These may be a mix of Macintosh desktop or portable computers, as well as other wireless computers that support Wi-Fi and IBSS protocols.

This type of network is useful only for peer-to-peer basic wireless networking. It does not provide access to any other wired or wireless networks or the Internet.

To create an AirPort IBSS network other users can join:

1   In Network preferences, choose AirPort from the Show pop-up menu.

2   Click AirPort and make sure the "Allow this computer to create networks" checkbox is selected.

3   Open Internet Connect and click the AirPort icon in the toolbar.

4   From the Network pop-up menu, choose Create Network.

5   Give the network a name and click Options to give the network a password.

You can also use the AirPort status icon in the menu bar to create a Computer-to-Computer network.

Other AirPort-equipped computers within range can join the network you created by choosing it from their AirPort status menu or choosing it from the Network pop-up menu in Internet Connect.

Configuring Base Stations for Internet Access

Like your computer, the AirPort Extreme Base Station or AirPort Express must be set up with the appropriate hardware and Internet Protocol (IP) networking information to connect to the Internet.

To provide the Internet configuration information to your AirPort Extreme Base Station or AirPort Express, you can use the AirPort Setup Assistant. The AirPort Setup Assistant asks a series of questions to determine how the base station's Internet connection and other interfaces should be set up.

To set up more complex configurations, you use AirPort Admin Utility.

AirPort Setup Assistant

To connect to the Internet, use the AirPort Setup Assistant to enter the settings you received from your ISP for Ethernet, PPP over Ethernet (PPPoE), or the internal modem if your base station has one. You can also give your AirPort network a name and password. You can use the AirPort Setup Assistant to set up a base station as a wireless bridge and extend the range of an existing AirPort Extreme or AirPort Express network.

If you are using an AirPort Express, you can create a new wireless network or join an existing wireless network. If you connect AirPort Express to your stereo or powered speakers, you can set up your AirPort Express to play iTunes music using AirTunes.

To set up and configure your computer or base station to use AirPort for wireless networking and Internet access:

1 Open the AirPort Setup Assistant, located in Applications/Utilities.

2 Follow the onscreen instructions and enter the settings from your ISP or network administrator for the type of network you want to set up.

   When you have finished entering the settings, the AirPort Setup Assistant transfers the settings to your base station, and your base station shares its Internet connection with computers that join its AirPort network.

AirPort Admin Utility

AirPort Admin Utility is a convenient way to make quick adjustments to your base station configuration. Some of the AirPort Extreme Base Station and

AirPort Express advanced networking features can be configured only with AirPort Admin Utility. Use AirPort Admin Utility when:

▶ You want to provide Internet access to computers that connect to the base station using Ethernet

▶ You have already set up your base station, but you need to change one setting, such as your account credentials or the phone number for your ISP

▶ You need to configure advanced base station settings such as channel frequency, security options, closed networks, DHCP lease time, access control, WAN Privacy, power controls, or port mapping

To modify the base station configuration:

1 Open AirPort Admin Utility, located in Applications/Utilities.

2 Choose your base station and click Configure.

3 Enter the base station password, if necessary.

   The default base station password is *public*.

4 Make the necessary changes and click Update.

If you don't see your base station in the Select Base Station window:

1 Open the AirPort status menu in the menu bar and make sure that you have joined the AirPort network created by your base station.

2 Make sure your network and TCP/IP settings are configured properly:

   a Choose AirPort from the Show pop-up menu in Network preferences.

   b Choose Using DHCP from the Configure IPv4 pop-up menu in the TCP/IP pane.

If you can't open the base station's configuration:

1 Make sure your network and TCP/IP settings are configured properly:

    a Choose AirPort from the Show pop-up menu in Network preferences.

    b Choose Using DHCP from the Configure IPv4 pop-up menu in the TCP/IP pane.

2 Make sure you entered the AirPort Extreme Base Station or AirPort Express password correctly.

The default password is *public*.

TIP ▶ If you have forgotten the base station password, you can reset it to *public* by resetting the base station. To do so temporarily, press and hold the reset button for one second. To reset the base station back to its default settings, hold the reset button for five full seconds.

NOTE ▶ If you are on an Ethernet network that has other base stations, or you are using Ethernet to connect to the base station, AirPort Admin Utility scans the Ethernet network to create the list of base stations in the Select Base Station window. As a result, when you open AirPort Admin Utility, you may see base stations that you cannot configure.

MORE INFO ▶ For additional information about these management utilities and how to use them, refer to "AirPort Extreme Technology Overview" (PDF) and "Designing AirPort Networks v4.2" (PDF) available on this book's companion website, www.peachpit.com/ats.deskport3. Also read Knowledge Base documents 75422, "AirPort: Software compatibility table"; 93738, "AirPort: How to tell which AirPort software version is installed on a computer"; and 58568, "AirPort: Use the Same Software Version on All AirPort Devices."

Interference Sources

If an AirPort network is out of range or often interrupted, it may be due to interference. Interference may result in a decrease in the range of contact with the base station, as well as a decrease in the rate of data transfer.

The farther away the interference source, the less likely it is to cause an issue. The following items can cause interference with AirPort communication:

▶ Microwave ovens: Placing your computer or an AirPort Base Station near a microwave oven that is in use may cause interference.

▶ Direct Satellite Service (DSS) radio frequency (RF) leakage: The coax cable that came with certain types of satellite dishes may cause interference. Obtain newer cables if you suspect RF leakage.

▶ Certain electrical devices such as power lines, electrical railroad tracks, and power stations.

▶ 2.4 GHz telephones: A cordless telephone that operates in this range may cause interference with AirPort communication when used.

▶ Metal objects: If possible, move metal objects or change the placement of the base station so the path between your AirPort equipped-computer and the base station is free from metal objects that may cause interference.

▶ X-10 video transceivers (transmitters/receivers) that operate in the 2.4 GHz band.

▶ Any other devices that operate in the 2.4 GHz bandwidth (microwaves, cameras, baby monitors, security sensors, cordless telephones, etc).

NOTE ▶ Some devices may not overtly state that they operate in the 2.4 GHz band. The operations manual should indicate whether a particular device makes use of the 2.4 GHz band. Typically, these will be advertised as "dual-band" devices. For additional information on sources of interference, refer to Knowledge Base document 58543, "AirPort: Potential sources of interference."

Basic AirPort Security

With proper configuration, wireless networks can approach the level of security inherent in wired networks.

Wireless networks that use the AirPort Extreme Base Station have multiple security features. The first one in the following list is always in use; the other options can be used at the discretion of the administrator.

▶   The method of transmission, direct-sequence spread spectrum (DSSS), was developed by the U.S. military to prevent unauthorized access.

▶   WEP or WPA encryption can be enabled as part of the AirPort Extreme Base Station configuration.

▶   Wireless networks can be password protected.

▶   The network administrator can program AirPort Extreme Base Stations to allow entry only to authorized clients (through MAC address access control).

▶   AirPort Extreme Base Stations can be programmed as closed networks, not appearing in the list of available networks, thus requiring the client to know the name of the network.

▶   The AirPort Extreme Base Station also includes WAN Privacy.

MORE INFO ▶ Setting up a secure wireless network can be complicated. In addition to the previously mentioned PDFs on the companion website for this book, these resources will give you detailed information on the issues and procedures involved in creating and troubleshooting such a network:

▶   AirPort Support website (www.apple.com/support/airport)

▶   Knowledge Base document 106858, "AirPort troubleshooting guide"

▶   Knowledge Base document 303595, "AirPort Quick Assist"

▶   AirPort Extreme Base Station Setup Guide (PDF) available on the companion website, www.peachpit.com/ats.deskport3

Bluetooth

Bluetooth is a short-range wireless specification common in PDAs, cell phones, keyboards, mice, MP3 players, and computers. It is designed for easy connectivity with a range of devices. Bluetooth is intended as an alternative to infrared for linking wireless peripherals, rather than an AirPort competitor for creating wireless networks of computers.

Bluetooth operates over the same 2.4 GHz radio band as AirPort. Although they use different modulation schemes to communicate, there is a minor, yet real, possibility of interference.

Bluetooth devices can communicate from up to 30 feet away, and the signal can be boosted to extend its range to 300 feet. Bluetooth version 1.1 communication speeds run from 720 kilobits per second (Kbps) to 1 Mbps. More recently, the Bluetooth 2.0+ Enhanced Data Rate (EDR) specification has emerged, which offers a transmission speed up to three times faster (up to 3 Mbps) when used with other Bluetooth 2.0–compliant devices. It is backward-compatible with older Bluetooth 1.1 devices.

Pairing Bluetooth Devices

Before you can use your mobile phone to connect to the Internet or share contact information, share files with other devices, or use a Bluetooth keyboard or mouse, you need to set up the device to work with your computer. Once you've set up the device, it is "paired" with your computer, and you can see it in the Devices pane of Bluetooth preferences. Your computer and the device will remain paired until you delete the pairing.

To pair your computer and device:

1   Choose "Set up a Bluetooth device" from the Bluetooth status menu in the menu bar and follow the onscreen instructions for the type of device you want to set up.

2 If the Bluetooth status menu is not in the menu bar:

    a Open System Preferences and click Bluetooth.

    b Click Settings and select the "Show Bluetooth status in the menu bar" checkbox.

To delete a pairing with a device:

1 Open System Preferences and click Bluetooth.

2 Click Devices and select the device from the list.

3 Click Delete Pairing.

> **MORE INFO** ▶ For more information on Bluetooth use, refer to Knowledge Base document 86207, "Bluetooth: Macintosh Computers With Built-In Bluetooth," as well as the following websites:
>
> ▶ Apple Bluetooth Support (www.apple.com/support/bluetooth)
>
> ▶ Apple Wireless Keyboard and Mouse Support (www.apple.com/support/keyboard)
>
> ▶ Apple Bluetooth Technology (www.apple.com/bluetooth)
>
> ▶ The Bluetooth Technology (www.bluetooth.com)

Troubleshooting Bluetooth

Bluetooth is a powerful technology, yet simple to work with. Most issues arise from incorrect settings or out-of-date software.

Make Sure That You Have Bluetooth!

If you didn't physically connect a Bluetooth adapter to your computer, find out if you actually have a Bluetooth module installed in your computer. In Mac OS X 10.3 and later, open System Preferences and verify that Bluetooth appears in the Hardware section. If you're using a USB Bluetooth adapter, connect it directly to a USB port on your computer—not to a port on your keyboard, display, or other USB hub.

Check the Device's System Requirements

Make sure that your computer meets your Bluetooth device's system requirements; visit the device manufacturer's website for details. This also applies to a USB Bluetooth adapter, if that's what you're using to get Bluetooth capability.

Make Sure That Bluetooth and the Device Are Turned On

To check your computer's Bluetooth status, choose System Preferences from the Apple menu, then click Bluetooth. In the resulting Bluetooth preference pane, click the Settings tab. If the pane shows that Bluetooth power is off, click the corresponding Turn Bluetooth On button, or use the Bluetooth icon in the menu bar. Then check your device to make sure that it's also powered on.

If you're trying to pair a Bluetooth phone or PDA, make sure that Bluetooth is active and that the device is "discoverable." (Consult your product manual if you're unsure about how to change these settings on your device.)

Verify That You've Set Up the Device With Your Computer

If you're trying to pair a phone or handheld device with your computer, open System Preferences, click Bluetooth, and click the Devices tab. You should see your device listed. If not, follow the "Syncing Bluetooth Devices with Your Mac" instructions in Knowledge Base document 303591, "Bluetooth Quick Assist."

If you're trying to pair an Apple Wireless Keyboard and Mouse, open System Preferences, click Keyboard & Mouse, click the Bluetooth tab, and make sure that your keyboard and mouse appear in the pane. If not, click Set Up New Device to open the Bluetooth Setup Assistant. For versions prior to Mac OS X 10.3.4, you can access the Bluetooth Setup Assistant in the Utilities folder (Applications/ Utilities) to help with pairing issues.

Recharge or Replace the Bluetooth Device's Battery

If your Bluetooth device's battery is low, you may experience connection issues. Try charging the battery (if the device has a rechargeable battery), or replacing disposable batteries with fresh ones if that's the case.

Download and Install the Latest Software for the Device

Some Bluetooth devices (mainly Palm OS devices) require you to install software before you can use them with a Macintosh. Make sure that you did, and that you're using the latest software available for it on your computer. Check the device manufacturer's website for the latest updates and more information.

Check for a Bluetooth Update

To check for new software, choose Software Update from the Apple menu (make sure that your computer is connected to the Internet). If newer Apple Bluetooth software exists, Software Update will find it. To install an update, select the checkbox next to the software name and then click Install.

Check for Signal Spoilers

Because Bluetooth works by transmitting signals through the air, some things can interfere with connections. Avoid situations in which metal objects come between the device and the computer. Don't put your computer under a metal desk or locked away behind a metal cabinet. Keep cordless telephone base stations, microwave ovens, and other electrical devices that operate on a 2.4 GHz bandwidth away. And make sure that the device and the computer aren't more than 30 feet from each other.

Restart the Computer

Sometimes a simple restart—or two—is all it takes to get things running smoothly again. Try restarting your computer to see if that clears up the issue. If not, try shutting down, waiting a minute, and then restarting. You may also want to try resetting the computer's parameter random-access memory (PRAM) and nonvolatile memory (NVRAM).

Reset the Bluetooth Device

First try turning the device off and then on again. If that doesn't work, see if you can reset the device (refer to the device's documentation for instructions).

Lesson Review

1. What two standards are used in AirPort and AirPort Extreme networks?

    a. Wi-Fi and Bluetooth

    b. 802.11b and 802.11g

    c. 802.11a and 802.1b

2. What are the transmission rates of the two standards selected in question 1?

    a. 11 MHz and 54 MHz, respectively

    b. 11 and 54 cycles per second, respectively

    c. 54 Mbps and 11 Mbps, respectively

    d. None of the above

3. You see a sign in a coffee shop advertising a free Wi-Fi hotspot available for Internet access. Can your AirPort Extreme–equipped PowerBook connect to this network?

4. True or false: The AirPort Extreme Base Station has both WAN and LAN ports.

5. If you need to place base stations in air-handling spaces, which model must you use?

    a. AirPort Base Station Extreme Base Station (PoE/UL 2043)

    b. AirPort Base Station Extreme Base Station

    c. AirPort Base Station (Dual Ethernet)

6. True or false: The AirPort Express Base Station can connect to a USB printer.

7. True or false: AirTunes can be used with Macintosh systems using Mac OS X 10.3.

8. Which utility or application provides a convenient way to make quick adjustments to a base station configuration?

    a. Internet Connect

b.   AirPort Admin Utility

c.   Network Preferences

d.   AirPort status icon

9.   Which of the following are potential sources of AirPort signal interference?

a.   Microwave ovens

b.   Metal objects

c.   Cordless phones

d.   All of the above

10. True or false: Generally speaking, MAC addresses are unique to the equipment to which they are assigned.

11. Using the resources on the Apple Support site, locate and review the steps necessary to set up a Wireless Mighty Mouse. What utility do you use to set up this product?

12. If you have access to a Macintosh system with AirPort Extreme and an AirPort Extreme Base Station, do the following activities. Use the AirPort references cited in this lesson to assist you.

1.   Reset the base station to factory default.

2.   Set up the base station to join a WAN that provides Internet access.

3.   Create a closed network between the base station and the Macintosh system.

4.   Return the Macintosh and the base station to their original settings.

NOTE ▶ Do *not* use systems that contain any information you cannot afford to lose!

Answer Key

1. b; 2. c; 3. Yes; 4. True; 5. a; 6. True; 7. True; 8. b; 9. d; 10. True; 11. Bluetooth Setup Assistant

8

Reference Files

Apple General Troubleshooting Flowchart (AGTFwithNotes.pdf)

Questions Worksheet (Questions_Worksheet.pdf)

Cable Modem Reset (Cable_Modem_Reset.pdf)

Useful Links (TS_Links.html)

Time

This lesson takes approximately 2.5 hours to complete.

Goals

Given a troubleshooting scenario, identify the different components of a computer network in terms of nodes, links, and protocols

Given a description of a network problem and Apple references, isolate the problem to a hardware or software issue

Identify three useful tips to remember when using a base station–shared USB printer

Identify steps that demonstrate how to set up a basic wired network, including DSL, cable modem, IP, and Bonjour

Identify how to locate and fix trouble that prevents files from being shared between computers

Define common networking terms and how they relate to troubleshooting

Identify and explain networking error messages or faults

Network Troubleshooting

In this lesson, you will apply the general troubleshooting skills that you learned in Lesson 3, "General Troubleshooting Theory," specifically to network problems. This lesson begins by explaining how to identify the different parts of a network. Then it details the recommended troubleshooting steps and how to apply them to various problem scenarios.

Network Components

Generally speaking, the term *network* refers to a collection of related things that are interconnected.

A *computer network* is a communications system that interconnects computer systems and devices. Any computer, printer, or other electronic device connected to a network is called a *node*. The connection between these devices, called a *link,* is any data transmission medium (like wires, infrared waves, or radio waves) shared by a set of nodes and used for communication among the nodes. *Protocols* are rules (or languages) that govern how devices on a network communicate with each other.

A simple network could consist of two computers (nodes) interconnected by an Ethernet cable link and using Transmission Control Protocol/Internet Protocol (TCP/IP) as a protocol.

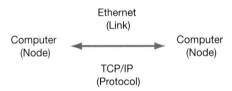

Networks can be quite simple or very complex. Here's a look at some examples of possible network components you may encounter:

Network	Node	Link	Protocol
LAN (local area network)	Computer	Ethernet cable	TCP/IP, Bonjour
WAN (wide area network)	Internal modem	Telephone wire	PPP (Point to Point)
LAN	Printer	Ethernet cable	TCP/IP, Bonjour
LAN	Ethernet switch	Ethernet cable	IEEE 802.3 Ethernet

Network	Node	Link	Protocol
LAN	Cable modem	Ethernet cable	TCP/IP
WAN	Cable modem	Coaxial TV cable	DOCSIS (Data Over Cable Service Interface Specification)
LAN	DSL modem	Ethernet cable	TCP/IP
WAN	DSL modem	Telephone wire	TCP/IP (for newer DSL modems) or PPPoE (Point-to-Point Protocol over Ethernet, for older DSL modems)
LAN	AirPort Extreme Base Station	Ethernet cable	TCP/IP, Bonjour
WAN	AirPort Extreme Base Station	Ethernet cable	TCP/IP, Bonjour
Wireless	AirPort Extreme Base Station	Radio waves	IEEE 802.11b, IEEE 802.11g, IEEE 802.11n

Some products combine a number of these nodes, links, and protocols into a single physical device. When troubleshooting, you may be tempted to think of a base station, a computer, or even a hub as only one node. Network troubleshooting is much easier if you think in terms of nodes instead of devices. An AirPort Extreme Base Station can act as an Ethernet switch, as a router, and as a Dynamic Host Configuration Protocol (DHCP) server, as well as providing wireless connectivity. Likewise, a PowerBook G4 can have multiple nodes, including a modem, Ethernet port, and AirPort port.

When you look at the Info tab of Network Utilities, notice the pop-up menu:

Each one of these interface names can be considered a separate node.

The interconnectivity of network components can make troubleshooting a bit more complex, and you must consider many variables: user and network errors as well as software and hardware problems. Making things more complicated is the fact that some types of errors may be related to network nodes and links you may not have control over, or even access to (such as Internet service provider, or ISP, equipment), so you may not always be able to locate and resolve all network issues without some help. Identifying all of the variables involved and isolating the issue are keys to resolving network issues.

Identifying Network Components

Now that you have a language with which to organize your understanding of a given network, try practicing with some customer scenarios.

A customer describes the following:

"I have an iBook G4 (Early 2004) with AirPort but when I'm in my classroom lab, I can't print to the lab inkjet printer, only to the laser printer."

In identifying all of the variables involved and isolating the issue, you might fill in the network components table like this:

Network	Node	Link	Protocol
LAN	iBook G4 (Early 2004)	Ethernet cable	TCP/IP, Bonjour
Wireless	AirPort Extreme Card (inside iBook G4)	Radio waves	IEEE 802.11b, 802.11g
LAN	Laser printer		
	Inkjet printer		

At this point, you can speculate that the inkjet printer must be physically connected to something, possibly another computer or a wireless base station. Likewise, the laser printer must be physically connected to something, probably an Ethernet switch or hub. This would be a good time to ask the customer a few more questions regarding the issue to identify all the variables involved.

A more complete network components table might look like this:

Network	Node	Link	Protocol
LAN	iBook G4 (Early 2004)	Ethernet cable	TCP/IP, Bonjour
Wireless	AirPort Extreme Card (inside iBook G4)	Radio waves	IEEE 802.11b, 802.11g
LAN	Laser printer	Ethernet cable	TCP/IP, Bonjour
	Inkjet printer (connected to AirPort Extreme Base Station via USB [Universal Serial Bus])	USB cable	USB
Wireless	Inkjet printer (connected to AirPort Extreme Base Station via USB)	Radio waves	IEEE 802.11b, 802.11g
Wireless	AirPort Extreme Base Station	Radio waves	IEEE 802.11b, 802.11g
LAN	AirPort Extreme Base Station	Ethernet cable	TCP/IP, Bonjour
LAN	Probably Ethernet switch	Ethernet cable	IEEE 802.3 Ethernet

When you're troubleshooting, you would query the customer to confirm the information in each of these boxes. Remember that the user is also a variable in isolating the issue, and examining the actual network setup yourself will help ensure you have the full picture.

Component Identification Exercise

For each of the following customer scenarios, fill out a network components table on a separate sheet of paper. Consider the possible components.

▶ Scenario A: "I keep getting a 'server not found' error when I try to view webpages. I'm running Safari on my Power Mac G5. The computer is hooked up to a DSL modem."

▶ Scenario B: "I bought an AirPort Express Base Station so I could hook it up to my cable modem and surf the Internet from wherever, but it's not working. I can't get onto the Internet."

▶ Scenario C: "I took my new PowerBook with me on a business trip last week. I usually use high-speed Internet, but this hotel had only dial-up connections in the room. I couldn't make it work."

NOTE ▶ The answers to this exercise are on the companion website, www.peachpit.com/ats.deskport3.

Troubleshooting Tools

Your first lines of defense in network troubleshooting are common applications, the Mac operating system, and bundled utilities.

Applications are the easiest methods of testing a connection. The utilities and diagnostics are more important in advanced troubleshooting of unresolved issues. Remember, one of the first things you must determine is whether your issue involves a single computer, multiple computers on your local network (your LAN), your ISP's equipment (WAN), or the Internet site you are trying to access. Because the Internet as a whole does not fail entirely, even large Internet-related problems are usually isolated to a single ISP, a small part of the overall Internet, or just a single website or server.

Applications

Use the following applications to help verify network problems and narrow your focus. These are part of the "try quick fixes" step of the troubleshooting chart.

Safari

You can use a browser, such as Safari, to determine if an Internet problem is isolated to a specific site or to your connection through the Internet to that site. If the browser displays an error when accessing one site, but not another, the problem is likely with just that site.

Using an alternative browser such as Firefox, OmniWeb, or Opera may reveal whether the problem is related to a specific browser's interaction with the site or a software preferences setting in a particular browser.

Browsers also create network activity when they attempt to access a remote webpage. This activity tasks the computer with acquiring an IP address via DHCP (if one has not already been assigned) to support that network activity, which you can use to both verify connectivity and to identify the particular network to which a computer is connected.

Mail

Attempting to send or receive mail can help you determine if you have an Internet connection.

If you can't get or send mail but can view uncached webpages, you have access to the Internet but have either a mail server issue or an ISP port blocking issue.

Or, if you can receive and send mail but can't load webpages, you have access to the Internet but have a Web-related (that is, HTTP) issue. If you use Mac OS X 10.4 Mail, you can try an additional tool called the Mail Connection Doctor (described in the "Utilities" section, later in this lesson). It checks all relevant functions of your incoming and outgoing mail servers for connectivity and validity, alerts you to any problems, and suggests troubleshooting techniques.

> **MORE INFO ▶** Port blocking by ISPs has become a common tool in fighting spam. Spamming is the unscrupulous business practice of sending unsolicited bulk electronic messages in junk email and other forms as an inexpensive way to reach consumers. Many ISPs block port 25 on their networks because it is a commonly abused port by spammers, leaving users to reconfigure their email client to use an alternate port or electing to use the ISP's mail services. To explore the topic of port blocking further, using a .Mac user as an example, consult Apple Knowledge Base document 151534, "I can't send mail because the connection to the server on port 25 timed out."

iChat

iChat instant messages can be transmitted over the Internet (WAN) via its connection with a valid messaging service such as AIM, ICQ, .Mac, Jabber, or an iChat service from a server using Mac OS X 10.4. iChat messages can also be sent locally over a wired or wireless LAN via the Bonjour protocol.

If you can send instant messages locally via Bonjour to another iChat client on your LAN but not to anyone else over the Internet via a known-good service you have used before, a WAN issue might be preventing this communication.

The Connection Doctor in iChat displays the audio and video stream throughput for both the local and remote sides of the chat. You can use this tool to help determine if any network bottlenecks may be preventing you from communicating via iChat.

iChat instant messaging and iChat AV use a series of ports that must be open for their use. If the network is using a firewall or if a firewall exists anywhere along the path of the network, the correct ports must be open.

MORE INFO ▶ For additional information on how to best configure a network for use with iChat AV, consult Knowledge Base document 93208, "Using iChatAV with a firewall or NAT router." For information on using Bonjour on your local network, read "iChat 3.0 Help: Chatting on your local network" (http://docs.info.apple.com/article.html?path=iChat/ 3.0/en/fz42.html).

Operating System

Use the following operating system functions to help you verify network problems as another "try quick fixes" step of the troubleshooting chart.

Network Preferences

Network preferences should be one of the first places to check when experiencing connectivity issues. Under Network Status, are the status indicators green, indicating a functioning Internet connection? Or are they yellow or red, indicating a more basic problem, such as a self-assigned IP address?

To check the IP address, choose the port you want to check from the Show pop-up menu, then click the TCP/IP button. When in doubt, click the Assist Me button to use the Network Assistant to create a new network location configuration, which will verify that all network preference settings are using default settings, while leaving the existing settings unchanged.

NOTE ▶ Addresses in the self-assigned range (169.x.x.x) are usually not routed for traffic on the public Internet. A 169 address typically indicates that your DHCP server is not assigning you a valid IP address or that you cannot connect to the network to receive the address. Though it is a very rare practice, be aware that your ISP or institutional network could choose to assign these addresses and route them within their private network.

Connect to Server

In the Finder, press Command-K or choose Connect to Server from the Go menu. After the window opens, click Browse, which may help you determine where a connection failure is occurring. After you click Browse, the system sends a broadcast message to the network, asking any servers to respond with their hostnames, which the Finder then displays in a window.

Do you see any other servers or shared Macintosh or Windows computers on your local network (LAN)? Were you able to browse and find a server, but were unable to connect to it? Were you expecting to see a large number of servers on the network and see none or only a few?

If you have never connected to a server before or if you have deleted your favorite server entries, the Connect to Server window will be empty. Mac OS X provides an auto-fill function that will display a previously typed information the next time you open the Connect to Server window and begin to type an IP address or server name in the Server Address field.

Once you click Connect, a Connecting to Server message appears.

Can you connect to a specific server to which you're sure you should have access? Can you connect to other computers using AppleTalk or the server IP address? If the server was not immediately found, an AFP Connection Status message may be displayed as the system attempts to resolve IP addresses to hostnames via DNS.

Such connection attempts may last as long as several minutes before timing out. If this happens, a dialog box informs users that the server to which they are trying to connect is not reachable at this time.

If you cannot connect to a particular server or have entered an incorrect IP address, the connection will fail. Are you using the correct IP address?

Answering questions such as these can help you isolate the issue before reaching for one of the utilities discussed in the next section.

MORE INFO ▶ For additional information on connecting to another computer or server using an IP address, read "Mac OS X 10.4 Help: Connecting to shared computers and servers using a network address" (http://docs.info.apple.com/article.html?path=Mac/10.4/en/mh1158.html).

Utilities
Use the following utilities to help during the "diagnostics, research, and/or repair" steps of the troubleshooting flowchart.

Apple Service Diagnostic

Service providers use Apple Service Diagnostic (ASD) to perform low-level tests of a number of Apple systems. Much like Apple Hardware Test (AHT), ASD does not rely on the system's Mac OS in order to check hardware components.

System Profiler

System Profiler is a Mac OS X utility that gathers and displays information about a computer. System Profiler can show you the internal components and external peripherals that the computer recognizes, as well as the operating system version, serial number, what versions of software have been installed, and more. Although System Profiler is not touted as a diagnostic utility, it can be valuable during troubleshooting to verify whether the operating system can recognize installed internal hardware components (such as random-access memory [RAM] or an AirPort Extreme Card) and external connections (such as network connections and even mounted server volumes).

Network Diagnostics

Network Diagnostics is a powerful troubleshooting utility first introduced in Mac OS X 10.4 Tiger. It automates many of the troubleshooting steps outlined later in this lesson, and provides context-sensitive, step-by-step instructions that can assist a user in isolating a specific networking issue. It works with built-in Ethernet, internal modem, or AirPort connections, and several Mac OS X 10.4 applications such as Finder, iChat, Mail, and Safari have been updated to take advantage of Network Diagnostics when a network connectivity issue arises. For more information, search Mac Help for "network diagnostics."

Network Utility

Network Utility is a very powerful collection of tools for gathering information and troubleshooting network connection issues in Mac OS X. One function of the Network Utility enables you to perform a simple network test, known as a *ping*, to verify network connectivity to a designated URL or IP address. Another function, called *traceroute*, literally traces the route of a packet through a TCP/IP network to a destination.

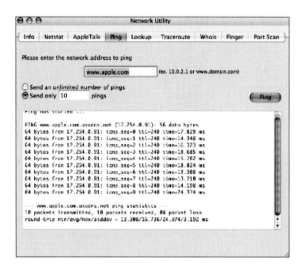

AirPort Admin Utility

The AirPort Setup Assistant and AirPort Express Assistant are great for setting up a base station, but AirPort Admin Utility allows you to make very specific changes that the assistant won't. AirPort Admin Utility enables you to open or restrict access to a base station and Internet connection, change the base station's frequency, or change the type of wireless security used on the network. You can administer AirPort, AirPort Extreme, and AirPort Express Base Stations from one interface.

Apple Hardware Test

AHT can detect problems with the computer's internal hardware components such as the logic board, memory, modem, video RAM (VRAM), and AirPort

Card. It does not check externally connected hardware components, nor does it check non-Apple devices such as PCI cards from other vendors. AHT can help eliminate a computer as a suspect during network troubleshooting.

AirPort Management Utility

Found on the software CD included with the AirPort Extreme Base Station (PoE/UL 2043), the AirPort Management Utility (AMU) enables you to configure, manage, and monitor all AirPort Base Stations on a network, all at once from a single location. You can view rolling event base station logs, group a number of base stations, individually confine their wireless range, and visually compare their configuration settings. This utility can also monitor and graph the wireless signal strength to each AirPort client node over a 5-minute period, which can be very useful in troubleshooting connectivity, base station placement, and interference issues.

Mail Connection Doctor

The Mail Connection Doctor checks the connection to the Internet and to each incoming and outgoing mail server. If it has trouble connecting to a particular server, a red dot will appear in the Status column. Next to each account name you see some additional information in the Details column.

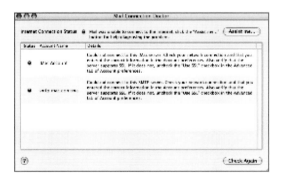

Console

Console is a Mac OS X utility that displays log files created by the computer to record error messages generated by applications and background processes. The main benefit of reading log files is that they can provide more information about an issue than an error message in a dialog. Log files may also contain messages that are never displayed to the user.

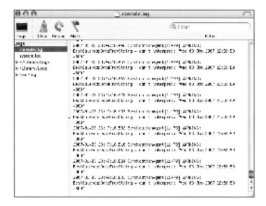

Each entry in a log file is time- and date-stamped, which can help you research past events or to help troubleshoot an issue that you can readily reproduce (like failing to connect to the Internet, for example).

Terminal

The foundation of Mac OS X is an implementation of the BSD version of the UNIX operating system called Darwin. Terminal is an advanced troubleshooting tool that allows you to issue UNIX commands in a command-line interface to accomplish tasks. Most customers will not be comfortable using UNIX commands and typically will never need to use Terminal. Some service and support technicians may prefer to use Terminal when troubleshooting various problems, such as network issues. The troubleshooting recommendations and steps in this book will not focus on UNIX Terminal commands, and instead will use graphical user interface (GUI) utilities wherever possible.

> **MORE INFO** ▶ If you are interested in learning more about BSD and Mac OS X, and consult Knowledge Base document 43139, "Mac OS X: What is BSD?"

Troubleshooting Steps

In Lesson 3 you learned about the Apple General Troubleshooting Flowchart, which documents the Apple recommended troubleshooting steps. A condensed version of this chart might look something like this:

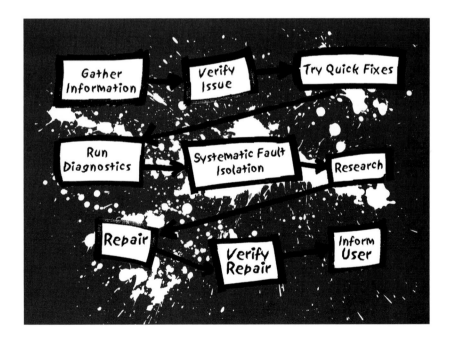

You might want to print the full flowchart (available on the book's companion website) to have it handy as you work through the following customer scenario (what you saw as Scenario A in the "Component Identification Exercise" section, earlier in this lesson):

"I keep getting a 'server not found' error when I try to view webpages. I'm running Safari on my Power Mac G5. The computer is hooked up to a DSL modem."

According to the flowchart, your next step is to gather information.

Gather Information

Gather information by asking good questions related specifically to the network issue at hand. Remember that the questions you ask during this step fall into two categories: open-ended questions and closed-ended questions. Here are some network-related examples of each:

Open-Ended Questions	Closed-Ended Questions
What is the issue?	What is the exact system configuration?
Can you describe your network for me?	• Exact system hardware
	• Macintosh OS version
What were you doing when the problem occurred?	• Amount of memory (RAM) installed
	• Other software involved, including versions
	• Exact type of network connectivity
	Have you recently added or removed any hardware or software?
	In which application does the problem occur?
	When did the problem start? Has the product ever worked properly? What was the last thing changed or added to the system?
	Do you have any peripherals attached to the system and have you changed anything about them recently?

TIP ▶ As you finish asking the customer questions, you might ask a simple but important one: "What else?" This very open-ended question can bring to light many details the customer may have overlooked, and it can provide a path for more specific questions as a follow-up. Once you have received a response, you may even ask it a second time. The customer will realize that you not only care about their situation, but that you are thorough and completely understand the problem at hand.

Your goal in asking these questions, in addition to gaining customer agreement that you understand the problem, is to be able to duplicate the issue. For network issues, you must understand the customer's network in terms of nodes, links, and protocols.

Nodes, Links, and Protocols

You already took a stab at describing this network in terms of nodes, links, and protocols a few pages back in the component identification exercise. Your table should look something like the following:

Network	Node	Link	Protocol
LAN	Power Mac G5	Ethernet cable	TCP/IP
WAN/Internet	DSL modem	Telephone wire, Ethernet cable	TCP/IP, T1/E1
	Telephone company equipment		
	ISP router		

Notice that this scenario includes two more nodes: the telephone company's equipment and the ISP's router that connects to the Internet. These additional nodes and links are typically very much a part of any scenario involving a customer's subscribed connection to the Internet, even though customers typically have no control or access to this equipment whatsoever. If this external equipment were to fail, the customer might not have any Internet access, and no amount of local troubleshooting will resolve these kinds of problems; generally, they are solely the ISP's responsibility. It's important to recognize that these kinds of problems can occur, and although it might be possible to isolate the issue to the ISP's equipment, it might also be impossible to resolve such issues without contacting and working with the ISP.

Taking this scenario a step further, to solve network problems, drawing a topological map is often very useful.

Topo Map

A topological map, or *topo map*, visually depicts the arrangement in which the nodes of a network are connected to each other with links. A map of this test scenario might look like the following:

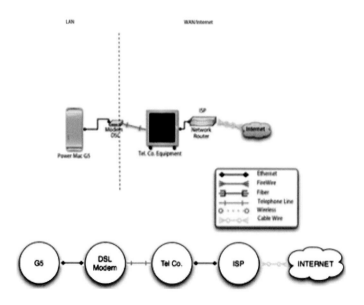

With the customer's answers to your questions, the network component table, and a map of the network's topology, you should now have the information you need to verify the problem.

Verify the Problem

Using the information you have gathered, set up the system and try to re-create the problem. If you're working with a customer over the phone, guide the customer through re-creating the problem as you would.

In network troubleshooting, you want to try to reach the network destination a few different ways. For example, if the customer is having trouble printing to a network printer, try accessing other nodes using the same protocol, like a LAN or WAN webpage (both nodes using TCP/IP). In this way, you are already starting to isolate the exact nature of the problem.

During this troubleshooting step, make detailed notes of any error messages that appear and note how long it takes for the message to appear. For example, getting a "server not found" error message could take up to a minute for a web server that's busy or on the far side of a malfunctioning router on a WAN. You will get the "server not found" message almost instantly if the problem is closer to the computer on the topo map (for example, if the Ethernet cable is not attached to the computer).

In this scenario, you first ask to specify a webpage the customer can't get to, and you both try accessing www.google.com. This is a good page to try to load because it's public, it's on the WAN/Internet, and normally it's quick to load.

After about 10 seconds, the customer describes the following error message:

On the topo map you drew of this network, how far do you think the network request is getting?

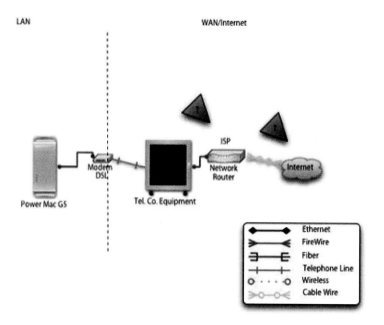

Use Network Diagnostics

Select the Network Diagnostics button.

Network Diagnostics is a new, powerful troubleshooting utility in Mac OS X 10.4 Tiger. It automates many of the manual troubleshooting steps outlined earlier in this lesson. If you are using Mac OS X 10.4 and a networking issue arises, the system may automatically guide you to use Network Diagnostics, which will check various settings and let you know what to check or do next, step by step.

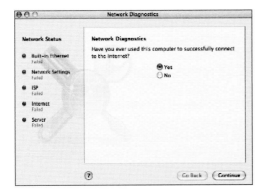

Once you have followed the steps that Network Diagnostics has provided, you should have sufficient information to verify the problem. It's time to try quick fixes.

Try Quick Fixes

Remember that a quick fix is a repair action that:

▶   Can be performed quickly

▶   Involves little or no risk of harm to the system

▶   Has little or no cost

Here are some network-specific quick fixes:

Consider First (Innocuous)	Consider Next (Less Invasive)	Consider Last (Invasive)
Check Top Support Questions if problem seems familiar	Attempt to obtain an IP address by opening a web browser	Perform a soft reset (AirPort—all base station models)
Verify with other users	Adjust user settings	Perform a hard reset (AirPort—all base station models)
Connect to another device or volume (locate other services, such as printers or file servers, on the network)	Check firewall settings	
	Check Active Ports settings	
	Reset modem	
Check for POP, IMAP, Exchange, or SMTP connection	Log in as test user	
	Change ports (such as Ethernet, USB)	
Connect to PPP test server (modem)	Restart the computer	
Open iChat	Update router firmware	
Browse Network icon in Finder window		
Use Connect to Server		
Check that cables are well-seated in proper ports		

MORE INFO ► Refer to "Creating and Connecting to Networks" at www.apple.com/support/panther/network (for Mac OS X 10.3) or www.apple.com/support/tiger/network (for Mac OS X 10.4). These pages list handy troubleshooting articles, organized by symptom or customer question.

When you're considering quick fixes, in addition to starting with the least invasive relevant options and working toward the more invasive options, it helps to think in terms of user-, software-, OS-, hardware-, and network-related fixes. Consider these possible causes of network-specific problems:

User-Related	Software-Related	OS-Related	Hardware-Related
Incorrect e-mail settings	Corrupt browser preferences	Out of date or corrupt protocol driver	Damaged or malfunctioning cables
Network system preferences set incorrectly			
Cables not plugged in correctly			
Network devices not powered on			

NOTE ► The RJ-11 connector on a telephone wire is very similar to the RJ-45 connector on an Ethernet cable. In fact, it is possible to plug the RJ-11 connector into most Ethernet ports, although Apple has made physical changes to these ports in recent computers to prevent this possibility. Keep this in mind when facing dial-up modem connection problems.

In this scenario, you'll need to check the settings for built-in Ethernet in Network preferences or direct the customer to do so.

Comparing what the customer tells you with what the customer's ISP recommends, you find that the customer has configured this port incorrectly for a manual IP address; the ISP requires that the built-in Ethernet be configured to accept IP addresses from a DHCP server.

Have the customer reconfigure Network preferences, then click Apply Now.

It may take a few moments for the change to take effect. From the Show pop-up menu, choose Network Status. The status indicator should be green for built-in Ethernet, indicating it has a valid IP address and is properly connected to the Internet.

You may consider trying these other quick fixes in the following order:

1   Have the customer inspect cables and verify that they are plugged in completely at both ends.

It's possible, for example, for an Ethernet cable to be in the port partially without being clicked in. In this case, the connection won't be formed.

2   Have the customer verify that the DSL modem has power.

3   Have the customer use Network Utility to verify that there is a valid, active link for the built-in Ethernet port (en0).

The Info pane in Network Utility should look something like this:

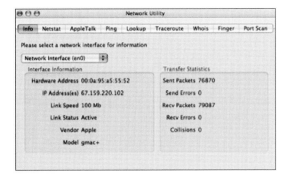

The Link Status is a software equivalent of a physical "link light" on a hub or switch. It simply reflects whether the Ethernet network interface card (NIC) circuitry is recognizing that the Ethernet cable is connected properly to live equipment at both ends.

4   Check network preferences settings against the recommendation of the customer's ISP.

If you map these four quick fixes to user settings–, software-, OS-, or hardware-related fixes, you get the following:

1. User settings-related: Check Network preferences…

2. Hardware-related: Have the customer inspect cables (this could a user-related issue as well, as cables can be damaged by user neglect)…

3. Hardware-related: Have the customer verify that the DSL modem…

4. Hardware-related: Have the customer use Network Utility…

Statistics show that over half of the problems seen in service are related to user settings or software/OS. Do you see how eliminating user settings first, then software-, then OS-, and then hardware-related potential problems, usually solves the problem faster?

As the name implies, a quick fix can—and often does—fix the problem. If that is the case, the next step on the flowchart is "repair/replace." Otherwise, you must use diagnostics and the subsequent flowchart steps to learn about network troubleshooting specifics.

Run Diagnostics

Diagnostic tools are software packages that enable you to check the performance of a system. You learned about these tools in Lesson 2, "Software Tools."

Some network troubleshooting diagnostic tools are:

▶ System Profiler

▶ Network Utility

▶ AHT

▶ ASD (for modem and AirPort Extreme Card)

> **NOTE** ▶ ASD is available to Apple Authorized Service Providers (AASPs) and Apple Technician Training (ATT) customers only.

Conduct Systematic Fault Isolation

The systematic fault isolation procedure (also known as split-half search), covered in Lesson 3, successively eliminates half the system as a possible trouble source. This is the one of the most efficient systematic search techniques. After you are left with a minimum of components, your chances of isolating the problem become more probable. Network troubleshooting examples using this technique include the following :

▶ Disconnect or eliminate third-party products (for example, USB or FireWire peripherals, PCI cards, and other third-party hardware): Is it an issue with an Apple product or non-Apple product?

▶ Compare WAN, LAN, and wireless connectivity: Is it an issue with local connectivity or in the network?

▶ Test within and outside subnet: Is it an IP issue?

▶ Disconnect all external devices: Is it an issue within the computer or with a peripheral?

Research the Problem

If you have completed the steps described so far on the flowchart and still can't determine the source of the problem, check these additional resources for network troubleshooting:

▶ Internet Connect's connection log

▶ AirPort Management Utility

▶ Console logs (specifically DirectoryService.error.log and DirectoryService.server.log, located in Library/Logs/DirectoryService)

▶ Verbose logging

▶ Apple Knowledge Base

▶ Developer Technical Publications (http://developer.apple.com/documentation/index.html)

▶   Service manual

▶   Users Guide

The Directory Service log reports authentication errors, date, and time.

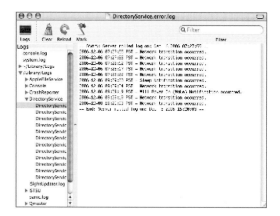

Escalate the Problem

If you still cannot solve a problem despite your best efforts, you may need to escalate the issue to Apple. How you conduct this escalation will depend on where you are located and the practices and policies of your business or agency. Escalation is not a troubleshooting step per se and therefore is not on the flowchart.

Repair or Replace

After determining the source of a problem, you need to repair or replace the faulty item. In Lesson 3 you learned the steps you must take before starting to replace software or hardware. When resolving network-related issues in Mac OS X, creating a new location in Network preferences or with the Network Assistant is a good idea. In this way, you will be able to adjust various settings during the repair without altering the customer's existing network settings.

Some troubleshooting steps involved during network-related repairs include the following:

Consider First (Innocuous)	Consider Next (Less Invasive)	Consider Last (Invasive)
Run AirPort Admin utility	Adjust user controls	Use AirPort Management utility
Run Directory Access	Reset PRAM	Use Terminal

Remember that you may have already implemented a repair as part of your "try quick fixes" step in the flowchart.

In your scenario, once you had the customer describe the Network preferences settings and change them to what the ISP requires, you implemented the repair. Your next step is to verify the repair.

Verify the Repair

To ensure a positive customer experience, thoroughly test every product you repair before telling the customer it is fixed.

Network troubleshooting-specific verifications include the following:

If the original problem involved...	Verify by...
Reaching the Internet or otherwise using TCP/IP	Viewing a webpage with Safari and/or another browser
SMTP, POP, IMAP, Exchange	Using Mail or another email client
Seeing other computers on the network menu in the Finder	Choosing Connect to Server from the Go menu in the Finder

TIP ▶ Throughout this book you will see references to several browsers that can be used for troubleshooting natively in Mac OS X. Safari is the browser of choice, but you need to have a reliable second browser tool as well. Many browsers are on the market, among them Firefox, OmniWeb, Opera, and Internet Explorer. Microsoft no longer supports Internet Explorer 5 for Mac.

Try to duplicate the original problem the customer described. If you can't, and you've satisfied the other recommendations in the "verify repair" section of the Apple General Troubleshooting Flowchart, move on to the next step in the flowchart and inform the user of what you've done to repair the system.

Recall that in the "verify the problem" step, the customer couldn't view the Google webpage. You have the customer try this again, and the page loads almost instantly. You can now move on to the Inform User step on the flowchart.

Inform User

Once you have returned the computer to normal operation (or escalated the problem), inform the customer of what you did to repair the system. Some specific communication tools you have for network-related troubleshooting include the following:

▶   Screen shots from Network Utility

▶   Screen shots from Network preferences

▶   References to appropriate Knowledge Base documents

Now that you've helped the customer configure the IP settings correctly, you might suggest that the customer print or save a screen shot of the settings. By educating the customer in a very courteous way, you will be providing them good customer service and may gain a loyal customer long-term.

Complete Administrative Tasks

You may have to complete administrative tasks after troubleshooting an Apple product. This will depend on where you are located and the internal policies of your business or agency. There are no administrative tasks specific to network troubleshooting.

After closing the conversation with the customer, complete whatever administrative tasks your organization requires.

It shouldn't take you more than 10 minutes to troubleshoot a problem like the one in this scenario, from gathering information to completing administrative tasks.

Practice

Now that you've stepped through Scenario A, you can practice the whole process yourself. Read the scenarios, follow the troubleshooting steps, and document what you did:

▶ "I bought an AirPort Express Base Station so I could hook it up to my cable modem and surf the Internet from wherever, but it's not working. I can't get onto the Internet."

In your conversation with the customer, you discover that the network consists of an AirPort Express Base Station and a cable modem linked to the Internet. The customer's operating system is Mac OS X 10.3.5. This is a recent issue as the system had been working flawlessly. The customer has tried both Safari and another browser, with the same result: can't load any outside pages.

▶ "I have two computers at home but I can get onto the Internet only from one."

The customer describes his network as two computers, an Ethernet hub, and a cable modem. The customer had been able to use the Internet before.

This morning his daughter was up before he was, and was already on the computer surfing the Internet. He could not access the Internet on his system. The IP address on the Power Mac G5 is 169.254.204.166, and the iMac address is 67.159.220.37. Both computers are configured for DHCP. The customer pays for two addresses at his location from the ISP.

▶ "I can't get onto the Internet using my wireless connection. I have to hook my PowerBook up to the Ethernet switch to get to the WAN/Internet."

Discussing the issue with the customer, you are informed that their network consists of a PowerBook G4 (15-inch) using Mac OS X 10.4, a laser printer, Ethernet switch, AirPort Extreme Base Station, and DSL modem. The customer has never been able to get the wireless connection to work. When plugged into the Ethernet switch, you are able to retrieve a webpage instantly, as well as to verify that the customer is using a manual IP address provided by the ISP.

NOTE ▶ Answers to this exercise are on the companion website, www.peachpit.com/ats.deskport3.

Lesson Review

1. The three components of a network are:

   a. Nodes, links, and protocols

   b. LANs, WANs, and the Internet

   c. Hardware, software, and the OS

   d. Computers, cables, and TCP/IP

2. Which of the following is a node?

   a. Telephone wire

   b. TCP/IP

   c. The Internet

   d. A printer

Questions 3 through 9 refer to the following scenario and network component table. Fill in the numbered blank cells.

"I bought an AirPort Express Base Station so I could hook it up to my cable modem and surf the Internet from wherever."

Network	Node	Link	Protocol
Wireless	3	4	802.11g
WAN/Internet	Cable modem	5	6
LAN	7	8	9

3. What is the node for the wireless network?

    a. AirPort Express Base Station

    b. Cable modem

    c. Computer

    d. Printer

4. What is the link for the wireless network?

    a. Radio waves

    b. Ethernet cable

    c. a and b

    d. None of the above

5. What WAN link does the cable modem use?

    a. Coaxial TV cable

    b. Ethernet cable

    c. a and b

    d. None of the above

6. What protocol does the cable modem use?

   a. 802.11g

   b. TCP/IP

   c. DOCSIS

   d. PPP

7. What is the node for the LAN?

   a. AirPort Express Base Station

   b. Cable modem

   c. Computer

   d. Printer

8. What link does the LAN node use?

   a. Ethernet cable

   b. Telephone wire

   c. a and b

   d. None of the above

9. What protocol does the LAN node use?

   a. 802.11g

   b. TCP/IP

   c. T1

   d. PPP

10. Given the following scenario, what network component is missing from the topo map?

"I took my new PowerBook on a business trip last week. I usually use high-speed Internet, but the hotel had only dial-up connections in the room. I couldn't make it work."

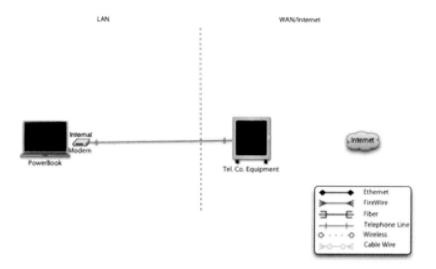

a. Ethernet port

b. ISP's network router

c. Wireless port

d. DSL modem

11. Which of the following is not usually a relevant question when gathering information for a network problem?

a. What is the exact system configuration?

b. Have you recently added or removed any hardware or software?

c. How much free space is available on the hard disk?

d. Do you have any peripherals attached to the system? Have you changed anything about them recently?

12. Which of the following is a network-specific quick fix?

    a. Check the active port configurations in Network preferences.

    b. Check Startup Disk preferences.

    c. Force quit.

    d. Reset permissions.

13. Given a network problem scenario, which of the following would you eliminate last?

    a. Network preferences set incorrectly

    b. Cables not plugged in correctly

    c. Network devices not powered on

    d. Damaged or malfunctioning cables

14. Which of the following is not useful for diagnosing network problems?

    a. Disk Utility

    b. System Profiler

    c. Network Utility

    d. Apple Hardware Test

15. Which of the following is a troubleshooting step that might be taken during a network-related repair?

    a. Run AirPort Admin Utility.

    b. Run Network Utility.

    c. Check cable connections.

    d. Reset PRAM.

    e. All of the above

    f. None of the above

Answer Key

1. a; 2. d; 3. a; 4. a; 5. a; 6. c; 7. b; 8. a; 9. b; 10. b; 11. c; 12. a; 13. d; 14. a; 15. e

Verify Issue → Try Quick Fixes

Systematic Fault Isolation → Run Diagnostics

Verify Repair → Inform User

Desktops

9

Time

Goals

This lesson takes approximately 1 hour to complete.

State the key features and benefits of a specified Macintosh system

Describe distinguishing visual features of a specified Macintosh system

Describe how to locate the AppleCare name for a product

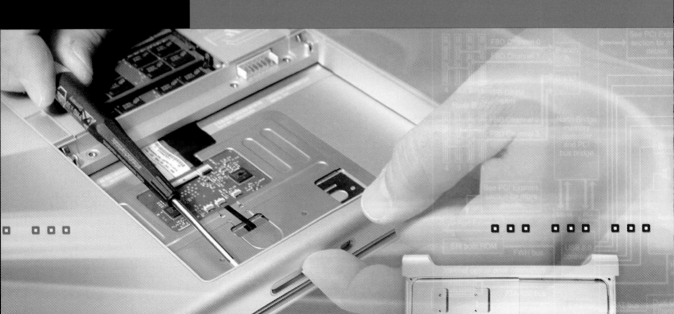

Lesson 9
About iMac Models

In January 2002, Apple introduced a new iMac design, featuring a PowerPC G4 microprocessor and a 15-inch flat-panel display at the end of a fully adjustable metal neck. Subsequent flat-panel iMac models sported larger displays and faster processors. The iMac is aimed at the consumer market, so it is usually designed to almost automatically connect to the Internet (for example) and is less expandable than the professional line of computers.

In August 2004, Apple replaced the dome base flat-panel iMac line with iMac G5 models that were just two inches thick and were mounted on a metal foot to let the display tilt back and forth. In May 2005, the iMac G5 models received a processor speed bump, plus AirPort Extreme and Bluetooth 2.0 capabilities. In January 2006, Apple introduced the iMac with Intel processors.

This lesson outlines the major technical differences among the iMac models. You can use the following charts to distinguish between various models and to determine the capabilities of each.

MORE INFO ▶ For more information on identifying various models based upon their distinguishing physical characteristics and capabilities, refer to Knowledge Base document 301724, "How to identify your iMac."

The iMac G4 Models

	iMac (17-inch 1 GHz)	iMac (USB 2.0)	iMac (20-inch Flat Panel)
Introduced	February 2003	September 2003	November 2003
Mac OS (minimum)	Mac OS X 10.2.3	Mac OS X 10.2.7	Mac OS X 10.3
Processor	1 GHz G4*	1 GHz G4 1.25 GHz G4*	1.25 GHz G4
Cache	256 KB on-chip L2	256 KB on-chip L2	256 KB on-chip L2
Memory	1 PC100 or PC2100* SO-DIMM slot and 1 PC2100 DIMM slot	1 PC2700 SO-DIMM slot and 1 PC2700 DIMM slot	1 PC2700 SO-DIMM slot and 1 PC2700 DIMM slot
Hard disk	60 GB Ultra ATA/66 80 GB Ultra ATA/100*	80 GB Ultra ATA/100	80 GB Ultra ATA/100

	iMac (17-inch 1 GHz)	iMac (USB 2.0)	iMac (20-inch Flat Panel)
Optical drive	SuperDrive* Combo	SuperDrive* Combo	SuperDrive
Graphics	NVIDIA GeForce4 MX with 32 MB and 2x AGP support NVIDIA GeForce4 MZ with 64 MB and 4x AGP support*	NVIDIA GeForce4 MX with 32 MB and 4x AGP support NVIDIA GeForce FX 5200 Ultra with 64 MB and 4x AGP support*	NVIDIA GeForce FX 5200 Ultra with 64 MB and 4x AGP support
Display	15-inch or 17-inch TFT LCD	15-inch or 17-inch TFT LCD	20-inch TFT LCD
Expansion	3 USB 1.1 2 FireWire 400 10/100Base-T Ethernet 56K V.92 modem AirPort Extreme*	3 USB 2.0 2 FireWire 400 10/100Base-T Ethernet 56K V.92 modem AirPort Extreme Bluetooth	3 USB 2.0 2 FireWire 400 10/100Base-T Ethernet 56K V.92 modem AirPort Extreme Bluetooth
Video connectors	Mini-VGA Composite* S-video*	Mini-VGA Composite S-video	Mini-VGA Composite S-video

*17-inch model

The iMac G5/Intel Models

	iMac G5 (17-inch)	iMac G5 (20-inch)	iMac G5 17-inch (Ambient Light Sensor)	iMac G5 20-inch (Ambient Light Sensor)
Introduced	September 2004	September 2004	May 2005	May 2005
Mac OS (minimum)	Mac OS X 10.3.5	Mac OS X 10.3.5	Mac OS X 10.4	Mac OS X 10.4
Technical specifications	support.apple.com/specs/imac/iMac_G5.html	support.apple.com/specs/imac/iMac_G5.html	support.apple.com/specs/imac/iMac_G5_Ambient_Light_Sensor.html	support.apple.com/specs/imac/iMac_G5_Ambient_Light_Sensor.html
Processor	1.6 GHz G5 1.8 GHz G5	1.8 GHz G5	1.8 GHz G5 2.0 GHz G5	2.0 GHz G5
Cache	512 KB on-chip L2	512 KB on-chip L2	512 KB on-chip L2	512 KB on-chip L2
Memory	2 PC3200 DIMM slots	2 PC3200 DIMM slots	2 PC3200 DIMM slots	2 PC3200 DIMM slots
Hard disk	80 GB or 160 GB Serial ATA	160 GB Serial ATA	160 GB Serial ATA	250 GB Serial ATA
Optical drive	SuperDrive or Combo	SuperDrive	SuperDrive Combo	SuperDrive

	iMac G5 (17-inch)	iMac G5 (20-inch)	iMac G5 17-inch (Ambient Light Sensor)	iMac G5 20-inch (Ambient Light Sensor)
Graphics	NVIDIA GeForce FX 5200 Ultra with 64 MB and 8x AGP support	NVIDIA GeForce FX 5200 Ultra with 64 MB and 8x AGP support	ATI Radeon 9600 with 128 MB and 8x AGP support	ATI Radeon 9600 with 128 MB and 8x AGP support
Display	17-inch TFT LCD	20-inch TFT LCD	17-inch TFT LCD	20-inch TFT LCD
Expansion	3 USB 2.0 2 FireWire 400 10/100Base-T Ethernet 56K V.92 modem AirPort Extreme Bluetooth	3 USB 2.0 2 FireWire 400 10/100Base-T Ethernet 56K V.92 modem AirPort Extreme Bluetooth	3 USB 2.0 2 FireWire 400 1000Base-T Ethernet 56K V.92 USB modem AirPort Extreme Bluetooth 2.0+EDR	3 USB 2.0 2 FireWire 400 1000Base-T Ethernet 56K V.92 USB modem AirPort Extreme Bluetooth 2.0+EDR
Video connectors	Mini-VGA Composite S-video	Mini-VGA Composite S-video	Mini-VGA Composite S-video	Mini-VGA Composite S-video

	iMac G5 (iSight)	iMac (Early 2006)	iMac (Mid 2006 17-inch)	iMac (Late 2006)
Introduced	October 2005	January 2006	July 2006	September 2006
Mac OS (minimum)	Mac OS X 10.4 Tiger	Mac OS X 10.4 Tiger	Mac OS X 10.4 Tiger	Mac OS X 10.4 Tiger
Technical specifications	support.apple.com/specs/imac/iMac_G5_iSight.html	support.apple.com/specs/imac/iMac_Early_2006.html	www.apple.com/imac/specs.htm	www.apple.com/imac/specs.html
Processor	1.9 GHz G5 2.1 GHz G5	1.83 GHz or 2.0 GHz Intel Core Duo	1.83 GHz Intel Core Duo	1.83 GHz, 2.0 GHz, 2.16 GHz, or 2.33 GHz Intel Core 2 Duo
Cache	512 KB on-chip L2	2 MB shared	2 MB shared	2 MB or 4 MB shared
Memory	1 PC2-4200 DIMM slot	2 PC2-5300 DIMM slots	2 PC2-5300 DIMM slots	2 PC2-5300S DIMM slots
Hard disk	160 GB or 250 GB Serial ATA	160 GB or 250 GB Serial ATA	80 GB Serial ATA	160 GB or 250 GB Serial ATA
Optical drive	SuperDrive	SuperDrive	Combo	Combo SuperDrive

NOTE ▶ The iMac (Mid 2006 17-inch) is an education-only configuration introduced July 5, 2006. The service manuals list shows this product, but not all official AppleCare models appear on the Product Specifications page. In such cases, readers must search the Knowledge Base.

	iMac G5 (iSight)	iMac (Early 2006)	iMac (Mid 2006 17-inch)	iMac (Late 2006)
Graphics	ATI Radeon X600 Pro with 128 MB ATI Radeon X600 XT with 128 MB	ATI Radeon X1600 with 128MB	Integrated Intel GMA 950	Integrated Intel GMA 950 ATI Radeon X1600 NVIDIA GeForce 7300 or 7600 GT
Display	17-inch or 20-inch TFT LCD	17-inch or 20-inch TFT LCD	17-inch TFT LCD	17-inch, 20-inch, or 24-inch TFT LCD
Expansion	3 USB 2.0 2 USB 1.1 2 FireWire 400 10/100/1000 Base-T Ethernet AirPort Extreme Bluetooth	3 USB 2.0 2 USB 1.1 2 FireWire 400 10/100/1000 Base-T Ethernet AirPort Extreme Bluetooth	3 USB 2.0 2 USB 1.1 2 FireWire 400 10/100/1000 Base-T Ethernet AirPort Extreme	3 USB 2.0 2 USB 1.1 2 FireWire 400/1 FireWire 800 & 1 FireWire 400 10/100/1000 Base-T Ethernet AirPort Extreme Bluetooth 2.0 (some models)
Video connectors	Mini-VGA Composite S-video	Mini-DVI Mini-VGA Composite S-video	Mini-DVI	Mini-DVI

Identifying the AppleCare Model Name

Use your knowledge of iMac computers and references to find the AppleCare model name of the iMac on your workbench (or any sample to which you have access).

1   In the following table, note the serial number, processor, and amount of RAM using About This Mac.

NOTE ▶ If the computer has had its motherboard repaired or replaced, the serial number may not be available in About This Mac, or it may be inconsistent with the serial number printed on the computer. If there is a discrepancy, use the serial number printed on the computer.

2   Go to GSX (if you have access) or Apple Support (www.apple.com/support/).

3   Enter the serial number in the appropriate text field and click Coverage Check or Go.

4   Complete the table:

Serial Number:

Processor:

RAM:

AppleCare Name:

Comparing Product Specifications

To familiarize yourself with each of the products, compare the product specifications so you get a sense of how the products differ from each other. Follow these steps:

1   In your Web browser, go to the Service Source home page.

2   On the right side, under Quick Links, click Product Specifications.

3   Starting on the last page of specs, work back to fill out the comparison table for the products listed in the following table. Draw or paste a thumbnail of the computer.

Component	eMac (USB 2.0)	iMac (20-inch Flat Panel)	iMac (Mid 2006 17-inch)	Mac mini
Thumbnail				
Processor				
Memory				
Hard drive				
Optical drive				
USB				
FireWire				
Networking				
AirPort				
Bluetooth				
Mac OS				

Lesson Review

1. Which of the following is not a dimension of an LCD iMac?

    a. 15 inches

    b. 16 inches

    c. 17 inches

2. True or false: All iMac models come with 10/100Base-T Ethernet.

3. True or false: All LCD iMacs have PowerPC G4 microprocessors.

4. True or false: All LCD iMacs have one SO-DIMM slot and one DIMM slot.

5. True or false: All iMac G5 models support optional internal Bluetooth.

6. True or false: The iMac G5 (17-inch) was the first model equipped with FireWire 800.

7. Which processor does the iMac (Late 2006) use?

    a. Intel Dual-Core

    b. Intel Core Duo

    c. Intel Core Solo

    d. Intel Core 2 Duo

8. Which iMac (Late 2006) configuration comes with an Intel Core 2 Duo processor with 2 MB of shared L2 cache?

    a. iMac (17-inch Late 2006 CD)

    b. iMac (17-inch Late 2006)

    c. iMac (20-inch Late 2006)

    d. iMac (24-inch)

9. What is the base memory configuration of the iMac (Late 2006) 17-inch
    Combo model?

    a. 256 MB

    b. 512 MB

    c. 1 GB

    d. 1.5 GB

    e. 2 GB

10. True or false: To obtain the most benefit from the maximum RAM
    installation on an iMac (20-inch Late 2006), you should install one 2 GB
    SO-DIMM and one 1 GB SO-DIMM.

11. True or false: Apple recommends that any memory upgrades for the iMac
    (17-inch Late 2006 CD) use matched pairs of SO-DIMMs for improved
    graphics performance.

12. True or false: All iMac (Late 2006) configurations have support for AirPort
    Extreme and Bluetooth 2.0 + EDR preinstalled.

13. What is the maximum amount of RAM supported in the iMac (Mid 2006
    17-inch)?

    a. 1 GB

    b. 1.5 GB

    c. 2 GB

    d. 2.5 GB

    e. 4 GB

14. How many USB 2.0 ports does the iMac (Mid 2006 17-inch) have?

    a. One

    b. Two

    c. Three

    d. Four

15. True or false: The iMac (Mid 2006 17-inch) computer has two SO-DIMM slots.

16. True or false: The iMac (Mid 2006 17-inch) ships with an Apple mini-DVI to VGA adapter.

17. Which processor does the iMac (Early 2006) use?

    a. PowerPC G5

    b. Intel Core Duo

    c. Intel Dual-Core

    d. PowerPC G5 Dual-Core

18. What is the base memory configuration of the iMac (Early 2006)?

    a. 256 MB

    b. 512 MB

    c. 1 GB

    d. 1.5 GB

    e. 2 GB

19. True or false: The iMac (Early 2006) has two SO-DIMM slots.

20. True or false: The AirPort Extreme and Bluetooth functions reside on the same combo card in the iMac (Early 2006).

21. True or false: You can order an external Apple USB modem for use with the iMac G5 (iSight).

Answer Key

1. b; 2. True; 3. False; 4. False; 5. False; 6. False; 7. d; 8. a; 9. b; 10. True; 11. True; 12. False; 13. c; 14. c; 15. True; 16. False; 17. b; 18. b; 19. True; 20. False; 21. True

10

Reference Files Mac (Late 2006) service manual
(iMac_Intel-based_Late2006.pdf)

Time This lesson takes approximately 1 hour to complete.

Goals Given an iMac (24-inch) and Apple resources, locate any DIY
(Do-It-Yourself) service options on the Apple Support site

Identify any requirements to perform the upgrade or use the
system

Given User Guide instructions, practice performing a memory
installation on the system

Increase your understanding of Apple resources

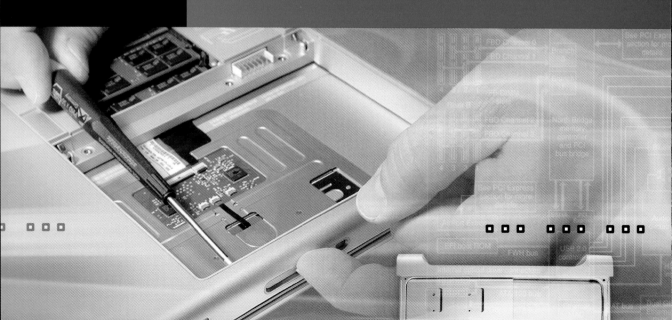

Upgrading an iMac

Although the ever-popular iMac line of consumer desktop computers may not be as expandable as the Mac Pro line, users can perform worthwhile upgrades to increase the performance of an iMac.

This lesson begins by exploring Apple resources, focusing on those available for the iMac (24-inch). After locating the Do-It-Yourself (DIY) section of the Apple Support site, you will then investigate if any DIY service options are available for this model. Finally, you will practice upgrading RAM on the iMac using the DIY references you have located, taking note of any requirements to use the system and perform the upgrade.

Identifying the System

Apple maintains many resources in support of its products. As part of learning to become a proficient technician, you will need to identify the most relevant Apple references for any particular procedure. One of the keys to Apple's success is in creating interfaces that are extremely intuitive. Whether it is their latest operating system or in the design of Apple online references, you will find that there are usually two or more paths to locate what you are looking for. Everyone learns in a different way, and Apple has incorporated this concept in their products. Learn the different ways to locate information on the Apple Support website, www.apple.com/support.

> **MORE INFO** ▶ Refer to Lesson 1, "Reference Materials," for more on finding support information.

> **NOTE** ▶ Screenshots in this lesson reflect the appearance of various resources at the time this material was written. As you go through the lesson and do its lesson review, you may find that some online resources differ in appearance from what is shown in this text.

To find all relevant support material for an iMac (24-inch):

1   Go to www.apple.com/support. In the Get Help section, select Computer + Server.

2   Peruse the different iMac support areas and become familiar with the types of information available.

In this list, the iMac (24-inch) is not listed specifically, and you do not currently know if the system is a G5 (iSight), a G4 (Flat-Panel), or any of the other iMac families listed.

3   If you have a serial number available, you can retrieve detailed information from the Find By Serial Number search field on http://support.apple.com/specs.

To locate your product's serial number, consult Apple Knowledge Base document 303372, "How to find the serial number of your Apple Hardware."

4   Return to the Apple Support main page and perform a search using the search tool for the iMac (24-inch).

The Search Results page lists memory specifications for this system, which indicate many important memory criteria. It also offers several documents, such as "How to identify your iMac," (Late 2006) - Technical Specifications," and "Mac (Late 2006): Memory Specifications." You now know that the iMac (Late 2006) was produced in four models: two 17-inch screen versions, a 20-inch screen version, and a 24-inch screen version, known as the iMac (24-inch). The model you will repair, according to "Technical Specifications for the iMac (Late 2006)," has a 2.16 GHz Intel-based, Core Duo processor. You now have additional information regarding the computer you are about to upgrade.

5   Return to the Apple Support main page and visit the Do-It-Yourself (DIY) section (www.apple.com/support/diy) to prepare for the next section.

Do-It-Yourself (DIY)

Apple maintains an extensive online collection of instructions and videos for each Macintosh model. Some models have replaceable Do-It-Yourself (DIY) service parts. Users can install these replacement parts and upgrades; they require only a moderate amount of technical ability and common tools.

Apple DIY parts include everything you need to complete many replacement tasks. Each DIY package includes genuine Apple-certified parts, simple step-by-step instructions, a list of tools you'll need to have on-hand, and the estimated time that it'll take for you to complete the installation.

Keep in mind that not every part found in an Apple system or product is available through DIY. Some typical parts that you can order include replacement keyboards, mice, power cables, modem cables, ear buds, and internal batteries. Apple doesn't offer parts that are generally difficult to access or replace by users. Available upgrades vary by model.

Under the section Installing DIY Parts, use the pull-down menu to explore the models available. As you have discovered, the iMac (24-inch) is not listed as an option. Choose iMac (Core Duo) from the pull-down menu to explore DIY. The DIY parts page for the iMac (Core Duo) lists several options to consider.

Want to order or find out more about DIY parts? Tell us what you'd like to do:

- Replace a part in my Intel-based iMac
- Upgrade my Intel-based iMac with more memory
- Find out more information in the DIY FAQ
- Go back to the Intel-based iMac Support page

Before proceeding, select "Replace a part in my Intel-based iMac" and investigate the DIY repair options available for this model.

Although you will not be replacing a part for this lesson, Apple recommends that, before you order a part, you first try to determine if a DIY part is the right solution for the issue. Many problems that seem to be hardware-related are actually software issues. Updating the software or simply changing its configuration can often quickly resolve the issue.

By reading all relevant troubleshooting documents on the Apple Support page, Knowledge Base, and the discussion forums, you may also resolve the problem at hand.

The DIY options available for this model include many customer installable parts that are simple to replace. The Ordering DIY Parts page also provides several resources and links about memory installation.

> • iMac User Guides for memory installation instructions
> • Read this article for additional memory installation help

Select iMac User Guides and find the correct User Guide for the iMac (Late 2006).

TIP ▶ Never use non-Apple resources as a guide for performing procedures. Although informational, these resources may not be reliable and could cause damage to the computer under repair or to the technician themselves.

Required Tools and Equipment

To complete this lesson, you need the following:

▶   Soft cloth

▶   Phillips #2 screwdriver

▶   667 MHz, PC2-5300, DDR2-compliant memory module (also referred to as DDR2 667)

Upgrading RAM on an iMac

Whether you are adding memory or repairing your system, your first step should be to carefully read the reference materials you will be using. Pay particular attention to safety precautions and any hardware or software requirements to use the system or perform the upgrade.

NOTE ▶ Be sure to follow the ESD guidelines spelled out in Lesson 4, "Safe Working Procedures and General Maintenance." Remember, Apple recommends to its customers that they use an Apple-certified technician—which would be you, once certified—to install memory. If you attempt to install memory and damage the equipment, that damage isn't covered by the limited warranty.

The iMac (24-inch) comes with at least 1 GB of Double Data Rate 2 (DDR2) Synchronous Dynamic Random Access (SDRAM) memory installed. You can add 1 GB or 2 GB memory modules for a maximum of 3 GB of memory. Memory modules must meet the following specifications:

▶ Small Outline Dual Inline Memory Module (SO-DIMM) format

▶ 667 MHz, PC2-5300, DDR2-compliant (also referred to as DDR2 667)

▶ Unbuffered and unregistered

The iMac (Late 2006) has two memory slots. You can add a memory module to the bottom slot and remove the memory module in the top slot to replace the installed memory.

To practice upgrading the memory, find the "Installing Memory" chapter of the User Guide or follow along here. To install or replace memory:

1 Turn the iMac off by choosing Apple > Shut Down.

2   Disconnect all cables and the power cord from the iMac.

   NOTE ▶ You must unplug the AC power cord to prevent the iMac from
   turning on during the upgrade procedure.

3   Place a soft, clean towel or cloth on your work surface. Hold the sides of
   the iMac and lay it down so that the screen is against the surface and the
   bottom is facing you.

   NOTE ▶ Always discharge static electricity before you touch any parts or
   components inside the computer. To avoid generating static electricity, do
   not walk around the room or allow others to make contact with you until
   you have finished installing the part and closed the computer.

4   Raise the stand and use a Phillips #2 screwdriver to loosen the two captive
   screws on the memory access door by turning them counterclockwise.

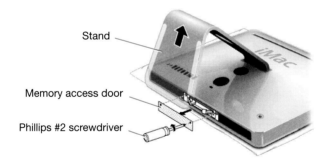

Stand

Memory access door

Phillips #2 screwdriver

5   Remove the memory access door and set it aside.

   TIP ▶ Successful technicians use a light touch with sensitive parts. Never
   force a memory module in place. Ensure that the memory module is facing
   the correct way and apply pressure evenly when inserting the module.
   Memory slot levers can also break if you don't take proper care. Never use
   the levers to seat the memory in the compartment.

6   Pull the two levers in the memory compartment to eject any installed
   memory modules you want to replace.

7   Remove the memory modules from the iMac.

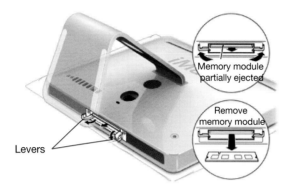

8   Insert the new memory modules into the slots, with the notches facing left, as shown in the illustration.

9   Press the memory modules firmly and evenly into the compartment. You'll hear a slight click when the memory modules are seated correctly.

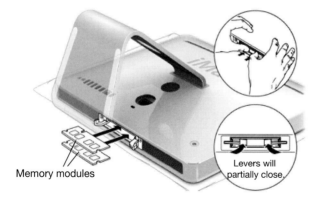

10 Push the levers toward the center of the compartment until they are fully closed.

11 Replace the memory access door and use a Phillips #2 screwdriver to tighten the screws.

The iMac will not function properly without the memory access door.

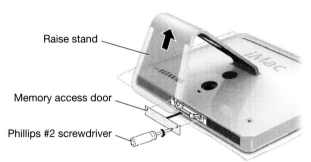

Raise stand

Memory access door

Phillips #2 screwdriver

12 Holding each side of the iMac, turn it right-side up and then reconnect and power cord.

13 Press the power button on the back of the iMac to turn it on.

You will need to verify that the iMac recognizes the new memory.

1 Start up the iMac.

2 When you see the Mac OS desktop, choose Apple > About This Mac.

You'll see the total amount of memory installed in the iMac. For additional details regarding the memory installed, open System Profiler by clicking More Info.

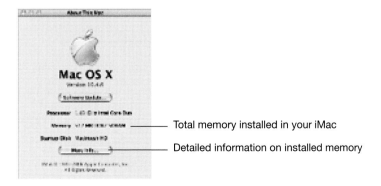

Total memory installed in your iMac

Detailed information on installed memory

MORE INFO ► For additional information on Apple System Profiler, consult www.apple.com/support and perform a search using keywords *khelp ksp*.

Lesson Review

1. True or false: Users may filter Apple Support search results to narrow the results returned.

2. What tool do you need to open the memory access door on an iMac (24-inch)?

    a.   Phillips #2 screwdriver

    b.   Flat-blade screwdriver

    c.   2.5 mm hex

    d.   None of the above

3. What memory module may be installed in an iMac (24-inch)?

    a.   667 MHz, PC2-5300, DDR2-compliant, buffered and unregistered

    b.   667 MHz, PC2-3500, DDR2-compliant, unbuffered and unregistered

    c.   667 MHz, PC2-5300, DDR2-compliant, unbuffered and unregistered

    d.   Any of the above

4. What type of memory slots are in an iMac (24-inch)?

    a.   VRAM

    b.   SO-DIMM

    c.   DIMM

5. True or false: The iMac (24-inch) can use either PC3200 or PC5300 memory modules.

6. True or false: Up to a 3 GB memory module may be installed in the iMac (24-inch).

7. True or false: Do-It-Yourself service options are simple upgrades and repairs that may be performed by users.

8. Which way does a memory module insert into the memory compartment in an iMac (24-inch) in the procedure as described?

   a. Notches to the right.

   b. Notches to the left.

   c. It doesn't matter because the memory is SO-DIMM.

9. True or false: The memory replacement procedure requires ESD precautions.

10. True or false: For *detailed* information about the memory installed on an iMac, users should use "About This Mac."

Answer Key

1. True; 2. a; 3. c; 4. b; 5. False, only PC5300 modules work; 6. False, a combination of 1 GB and 2 GB modules can be installed for a total of 3 GB of memory; 7. True; 8. b; 9. True; 10. False, System Profiler provides detailed memory information.

11

Lesson 11

Taking Apart an iMac (24-inch)

In the previous lesson, you learned how to install memory in an iMac (24-inch). Now we will dig even deeper into the iMac to remove a liquid crystal display (LCD) panel. This panel, including backlights and inverter, are responsible for displaying the video signal coming from the system.

> **NOTE ▶** The iMac (24-inch) Service Source manual refers to the monitor as an LCD Display Panel. For the purposes of this book, however, we will simply refer to it as an LCD or LCD panel.

On this book's companion website (www. peachpit.com/ats.deskport3) you will find a complete service manual for this system, including reassembly instructions. Use the Apple Service Source manual as your guide and this text to accompany it.

If you are not an AppleCare Desktop Technician (ACDT) with an up-to-date certification, *do not* attempt this Take Apart procedure, as it may void the warranty on the system. This lesson and the service manual on the companion website will demonstrate the Take Apart procedure for you.

If you are currently certified as an ACDT and have access to an iMac (24-inch) for this lesson, become familiar with the Take Apart procedure until you are confident in your skills and can perform the procedure efficiently. If you are performing this procedure as an authorized repair, be sure to follow electrostatic discharge (ESD) procedures as required, and return the components to Apple in the packaging provided, taking into account any instructions that accompany the service part.

For this scenario, your lead technician has diagnosed the video issue to the LCD panel.

Required Tools and Equipment

You will need a wrist strap and a grounded ESD-safe workstation and mat. Follow the ESD guidelines discussed in Lesson 4, "Safe Working Procedures and General Maintenance."

In addition, you will need the following tools and equipment:

▶ Soft, clean towel or cloth (to protect the display and removed parts from scratches)

▶ Nylon probe tool (also referred to as a Black Stick; may also use another nonconductive nylon or plastic flat-blade tool)

▶ Phillips #2 screwdriver

▶ Torx T6 screwdriver (magnetized)

▶ Torx T8 screwdriver (magnetized)

▶ Torx T10 screwdriver (magnetized)

▶ Screw tray

▶ Apple Hardware Test (AHT) diagnostic disc for the iMac (24-inch) model

Taking Apart the iMac (24-inch)

At each stage of the Take Apart procedure, we'll let you know if there are special notes and information; otherwise, we'll proceed component to component, from the outside in.

Service Manual

Open the service manual for this unit, which you will find on the companion website for this book, www.peachpit.com/ats.deskport3.

The manual is roughly divided into four sections: Take Apart, Additional Procedures, Troubleshooting, and Views. Become familiar with these different sections and the types of information they contain. We will be using the Take Apart section throughout this lesson.

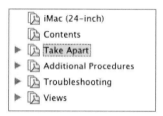

The Take Apart section contains general information and Take Apart procedures to help you replace each part in the unit. The General Information pages contain important safety information, as well as other useful information to ensure the repair is performed properly and using the correct tools.

Pay particular attention to the precautions, as they may be different for each model and may have been updated since the last time you read them. This model, for example, contains the following warning in the General Information section: "When the computer is under power, be aware that the power supply contains high voltages that pose a potential hazard to your personal safety. Never work on or near the power supply with the unit powered on; and as a further precaution, always make sure the unit is unplugged when working on it with the front bezel removed."

In the service manual, go to page 51, where Take Apart material on the LCD panel begins. Notice that this procedure begins by listing the tools required, as well as any preliminary steps required, and the part location.

After ensuring that you have the correct tools, proceed to the section that covers the first preliminary step: the access door. As with the LCD panel section, the Access Door section lists required tools, preliminary steps, and part location.

As covered in Lesson 4, in addition to following the safety precautions for this unit, don't wear jewelry, watches, necklaces, or other metallic articles that could present a risk if they accidentally make contact with the power supply circuitry. Although you won't be working on a powered-on unit during this lesson, make it a rule to take off any jewelry before doing technical work.

For this lesson we will assume that you have followed these steps:

► Read the General Information section, which contains the safety precautions.

► Set up a grounded ESD workstation and mat, and put on your ESD wrist strap.

► Unplug the unit from the wall outlet and the computer itself.

► Properly ground yourself.

For most steps, the unit should be placed screen-side up, with the bottom facing toward you. Now we can review the procedures themselves in detail.

Access Door

Begin by reading the steps outlined in the procedure, reviewing all pictures, precautions, and notes. You should be somewhat familiar with this procedure from Lesson 10, "Upgrading an iMac," during the memory upgrade procedures for this unit.

This procedure begins with a preliminary step: Place the computer face down so that the bottom is facing you. To remove the access door, raise the stand and loosen the two captive access door screws.

Now you can remove the door, revealing the memory compartment. You do not need to remove the memory modules for this procedure, and the dual inline memory module (SO-DIMM) levers must remain closed, as you will see later in the procedure.

Notice the location of the serial number for this unit. The serial number should be visible on the bottom of the stand, as shown below.

Moving on to the next preliminary step, we'll remove the front bezel.

Front Bezel

Read the procedure in full detail on page 17 of the service manual, ensuring that you have the correct tools and understand any safety precautions involved.

The first two steps position the computer for you so that you can easily locate and remove the screws.

You may encounter many types of screws during a repair. It is a best practice to use a screw tray. It will keep your screws organized in order of removal, which you replace in reverse order to reassemble the unit.

NOTE ▶ The iMac (24-inch) does not require a special access card, as other models do. Eventually you will need to obtain an access card to perform procedures on other models. The design of the iMac (24-inch) incorporates the use of screws for the above step instead.

In step 3 of the service manual, you hold the memory card levers and start tilting up the lower end of the bezel. Grasp the levers delicately.

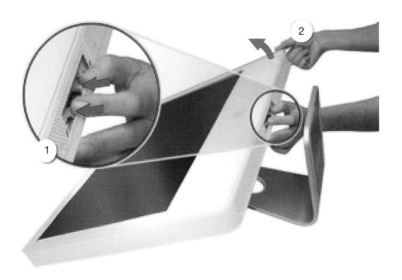

Now that the lower corners are loosened, you can lift the bezel partially to reveal the microphone and camera cables. Take particular care to avoid damaging the face of the LCD panel. Disconnect the camera cable from the camera board and the microphone cable from the cable extension.

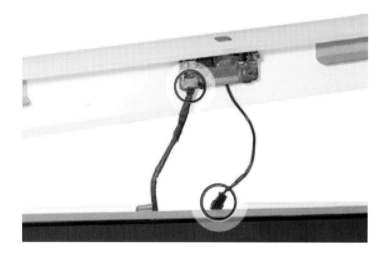

You can now remove the front bezel from the unit and move on to the LCD panel itself.

LCD Panel

You have completed the preliminary steps of removing the access door and the front bezel. Now return to the removal procedure on page 51 of the service manual.

After placing the computer face up, remove the low voltage differential signaling (LVDS) connector and inverter cable in steps 2 and 3.

Once you have removed the eight screws from the panel frame sides in step 4, place them in the screw tray. Notice that these are 8-millimeter (mm) screws and the front bezel screws were 6 mm screws.

In step 5, you peel up the strip of tape at the lower corners of the LCD panel on both sides. This tape forms part of the electromagnetic interference (EMI) shield. To follow Federal Communication Commission (FCC) guidelines (as well as guidelines from many other regulating agencies worldwide), the computer's EMI shield reduces spurious radio emissions emanating from the computer.

Later you must place the tape (pictured below) in its original position to ensure the integrity of this shielding.

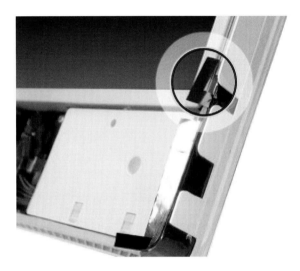

Carefully grasp the LCD panel at the bottom edge and tilt up the panel to remove it from the computer assembly. Do not press on the screen panel itself in any way.

NOTE ▶ If you are replacing the LCD panel as part of an authorized repair, disconnect the LVDS cable from the panel and the inverter cable from the inverter board before returning the module to Apple. Transfer the two cables to the replacement panel. A replacement panel includes the inverter board, both display panel mounting brackets, the EMI strip surrounding the panel, and the foam strip and gaskets.

▶ **Component Identification**

Now that you have removed the LCD panel, you will have a clear view of some of the components in the upper part of the unit. We will not be removing these components in this lesson, but are taking the opportunity to highlight them along the way to increase your familiarity with the components.

Hard Drive

The hard drive is located in the center of the unit. Locate the hard drive temperature sensor cable, power, and data cables. The temperature sensor itself is located on the side of the hard drive. The sensor location would need to be marked if you were replacing the hard drive in order to act as a reference for you during reassembly. Squeezing the black plastic clip allows the hard drive to be removed.

Optical Drive

Locate the optical drive, optical sensor cable, and optical drive fan. Like the hard drive, the optical drive's temperature is also monitored by the system. The temperature sensor itself will not be visible at this stage. Keep in mind that the optical drive's internal mechanisms are very sensitive, and for this reason, the drive should be handled by the edges only as to not damage its internal components. Should you replace this unit as part of an authorized repair, remember the placement of the EMI mesh tape. If this tape is not returned to its original position, it may interfere with the insertion of optical media into the drive upon reassembly.

Continues on next page

▶ **Component Identification** *(continued)*

Power Supply

In the above picture, the power supply is located to the right of the hard drive. This component remains energized whenever the system is plugged in. It is secured in place by several screws and a locking cable. Special precautions must be taken when working with this component as it is a high voltage source.

Other Components

Locate the following components in the Take Apart or Views sections of the service manual: Bluetooth card, AirPort Extreme Card, and logic board.

When You Are Finished

If you are performing this procedure as part of an authorized repair, return the faulty LCD panel to Apple in the packaging provided, taking into account any special instructions that were enclosed in the part box. Consult the service manual for the replacement procedures.

Verify that the system works correctly by starting up the system, running AHT, and doing a few user tasks such as printing a file or viewing graphics.

Account for all of your tools and clean up your workstation if needed.

Next Steps

Each iMac model design has a unique set of Take Apart procedures, challenges, and precautions. It is important to review the latest service manual for the model you will be repairing. Once certified and working for an approved service provider, you will be able to access additional iMac service manuals. Let's look at some differences between the models as an example.

The iMac (Flat Panel) presented a number of challenges for heat dissipation. The design incorporates the use of a heat pipe and fan to conduct heat away from the microprocessor to the metal base of the unit. The use of Thermal Pads and Thermal Grease to ensure heat conductivity between heat producing components and those that dissipate heat is crucial to the unit. This unit also requires 17 inch-pounds of torque to reattach the bottom housing. Given its unique design, special tools and a service stand are required to service this unit.

The iMac G5 has two different types of design and layout within very similar shells, and it's important to select the correct service manual. The iMac G5 was produced with and without an optical drive initially, which meant that two different midplane boards were produced, followed by a third for the 1.8 GHz model. The different models have different inverter installations procedures and neck assembly procedures.

The Intel-based iMac models all have different layouts, and all except the iMac (24-inch) require a special access card.

Lesson Summary

▶ Each iMac model has different Take Apart procedures that are explained in detail in that model's service manual. The information presented in this lesson applies to the iMac (24-inch) only.

▶ Gaining access to a particular component often requires the removal of other components first.

▶ Whenever you work on the internal components of an iMac, it's imperative to follow proper ESD procedures.

▶ You must unplug the AC power cord to prevent the iMac from turning on during the Take Apart procedure.

12

Reference Files	iMac (24-inch) service manual (c15_imac_24in.pdf)
Time	This lesson takes approximately 45 minutes to complete.
Goals	Identify the Intel-based Mac startup key combinations
	Identify changes made to the startup management screens
	Locate and describe known issues and solutions for the system
	Given the symptom of "No Video," return the product to normal operation
	Describe the types of symptoms that resetting the SMC would likely resolve
	Identify the diagnostic LED used to determine a "No Power" condition
	Identify the diagnostic LED used to determine a "No Video" condition

Lesson **12**

Troubleshooting an iMac (24-inch)

In this lesson, we'll review general troubleshooting procedures and symptom charts, providing an overview that will help you better trouble-shoot and repair iMac computers. Developing an understanding about the iMac computer's underlying operations can help you recognize problems more easily.

Trying to track down and resolve technical problems on a computer can be a challenge. By following the troubleshooting procedures step by step, you will more efficiently reach a cure and save a great deal of time. These procedures are designed to focus on simple solutions first, progressing to more complex and invasive cures if required.

It is important to remember that there are slight differences between the iMac models presented in this lesson and other iMac models. When working with a particular model, always refer to the most specific resource material available before proceeding.

The troubleshooting procedures will serve as a demonstration to accompany the service manual. Only AppleCare Desktop Technicians (ACDTs) should perform any of the outlined procedures.

Our scenario in Lesson 11, "Taking Apart an iMac (24-inch)," focused on the "No Video" symptom for an iMac (24-inch). Keep this symptom in mind as you go through the lesson to better understand what led to your replacing the LCD panel. We will explore several symptoms while learning about troubleshooting an iMac (24-inch).

Startup Key Combinations

These are startup key combinations you can use to modify startup on all Intel-based Macs. It's important to know them well, as they will be used frequently throughout the book.

Press During Startup	Description
C	Start up from a bootable CD or DVD, such as the Mac OS X Install disc that came with the computer.
D	Start up in Apple Hardware Test (AHT) if the Install DVD 1 is in the computer.
Option-Command-P-R (until you hear two beeps)	Reset nonvolatile memory (NVRAM).
Option	Start into Startup Manager, where you can select a Mac OS X volume from which to start.
Eject, F12, or mouse/trackpad button	Eject any removable media, such as an optical disc.
N	Attempt to start up from a compatible network server (NetBoot).
T	Start up in FireWire Target Disk mode.
Shift	Start up in Safe Boot mode and temporarily disable login items.

Press During Startup	Description
Command-V	Start up in verbose mode.
Command-S	Start up in single-user mode.
Option-N	Start from a NetBoot server using the default boot image.

Diagnostic LEDs

The iMac (24-inch) has four internal diagnostic LEDs and one external LED on the main logic board that can help you to troubleshoot the computer. The internal LEDs are located to the right of the memory slot, under the front bezel. The external LED is in front, located in an opening at the center of the right speaker.

Accessing the Internal LEDs

To access the internal LEDs:

1   Follow the Take Apart instructions in the service manual to remove the memory access door and front bezel.

2   The four internal diagnostic LEDs—1, 2, 3, and 4 (numbered bottom to top)—are in a column located to the right of the memory slot. Peel back the tape to view the LEDs.

Interpreting the LEDs

To interpret the LED indications, refer to the following table:

LED	Indication	On	Off
1	Main logic board detects trickle voltage from the power supply.	iMac (24-inch) is connected to a working AC power source. The LED will remain on even when the computer has been shut down or put to sleep.	AC power source is disconnected or power supply is faulty.
2	Main logic board detects proper power from the power supply when the computer is turned on.	Computer is turned on and power supply is working correctly.	LED 2 will be off when the computer is turned off or the power supply is working incorrectly.
3	Communication exists between computer and video card.	Computer is communicating properly with video card.	If LEDs 1 and 2 are on and you heard the startup sound, but LED 3 is off, video card may either be installed incorrectly or need replacement.

LED	Indication	On	Off
4	Communication exists between computer and LCD panel.	Computer is turned on and video signal is being generated. If LED 4 is on and there is no display on panel, panel or inverter may either be installed incorrectly or need replacement.	LED 4 will be off if the computer is turned off or if no video signal is being generated.
Front	Computer has power but no video signal.	Computer is starting up or display has entered sleep mode, turning off the video signal.	The front LED will pulse when the entire system has entered Energy Saver mode.

SMC Reset

If the computer shows symptoms of power-related issues, resetting the system management controller (SMC) may solve the problem. The SMC controls several functions, including:

▶ Telling the computer when to turn on, turn off, sleep, wake, idle, and so forth

▶ Handling system resets from various commands

▶ Controlling the fans

Unlike the iMac G5, the iMac (24-inch) does not have a button on the main logic board for resetting the SMC. This eliminates the need to remove the computer's cover to reset it (as required for some other models).

To reset the SMC on an iMac (24-inch):

1   From the Apple menu, choose Shut Down (or, if the computer is not responding, hold the power button until it turns off).

2   Unplug all cables from the computer, including the power cord.

3   Wait at least 15 seconds.

4   Plug the power cord back in, making sure to not press the power button at the time.

5   Reconnect the keyboard and mouse to the computer.

6   Press the power button to start up the computer.

> **NOTE ▶** Resetting the SMC does not reset the parameter random-access memory (PRAM), nor does it help when the computer is unresponsive. In these cases, restarting the computer may resolve the issue. To do so, either perform a force quit (Option-Command-Esc [Escape]) to exit the unresponsive application, restart the computer (Control-Command-power), or a manual shutdown (press and hold the power button for 10 seconds).

Symptom Charts

The symptom charts included in the accompanying Apple Service Source manual will help you diagnose specific symptoms and follow the guidelines set forth in the Apple General Troubleshooting Flowchart. Not all sections are contained in this lesson. Because cures are listed on the charts in the order of most likely solution to least likely, try the cures in the order presented. Verify whether or not the product continues to exhibit the symptom. If the symptom persists, try the next cure.

You'll learn to diagnose more accurately as you go. Over time, you will be able to diagnose the issue quickly and efficiently, select the correct part the first time (if a part is needed), and be sure the computer won't return for the same issue. Meeting these goals, coupled with outstanding customer service on your part, will likely result in very happy and loyal customers.

> **NOTE** ▶ If a cure instructs you to replace a module, and the symptom persists with the new module, reinstall the original module before you proceed to the next cure.

No Power

The computer will not turn on. The display remains black and there are no sounds from the fans or drives. Let's review the chart. You may use the service manual on the companion website (www.peachpit.com/ats.deskport3) along with this text.

1   Verify the power outlet is good. Plug a different device into the socket to ensure there is power, or plug the iMac into another outlet. Does the iMac power on now?

    Yes: Resolved. Bad outlet.

    No: Go to step 2.

2   Check the power cord. Use a known-good power cord. Does the iMac power on now?

    Yes: The power cord has failed. Replace the AC power cord.

    No: Go to step 3.

3   Check the connection of the power cord on both ends. Verify that the power cord is securely plugged into both the AC outlet and back of the computer. Does the iMac power on now?

    Yes: You may have a loose fit to the power cord. Replace the AC power cord and test.

    No: Go to step 4.

4   Follow instructions in the General Information section in the service manual to reset the SMC. Does the iMac power on now?

Yes: Issue resolved.

No: Go to step 5.

5   Remove the memory access door and front bezel to gain access to the four diagnostic LEDs. (See "Diagnostic LEDs" in this lesson.)

6   Plug the power cord into the iMac and an AC outlet. Is LED 1 on or off?

On: The power supply is getting good power from the AC outlet. Go to step 7.

Off: The computer is not detecting AC power. If both the AC outlet and the power cord are good, replace the power supply. If the issue persists, replace the AC line filter.

7   Press the power button. Does LED 2 come on, come on momentarily, or stay off?

On: The power supply is functioning. Go to step 8.

Momentarily on or stays off: Replace the power supply.

8   At this point in the power-on process, you should hear a boot chime and see that LEDs 1 and 2 are on. Do you hear a boot chime?

Yes: The power systems of the computer are working correctly. See "No Video, Boot Chime Heard," later in this lesson.

No: The logic board is not passing the power-on self test (POST). Replace the synchronous dynamic random-access memory (SDRAM) with known-good memory and test. If the issue persists with known-good SDRAM, replace the logic board.

POST

Intel-based Macintosh computers such as the iMac (24-inch) rely on a combination of tones and blinking LEDs to display POST error codes.

If the computer detects no RAM or the RAM installed does not meet the appropriate specifications, the screen will remain black but the power LED on the front of the computer will blink once per second to signal the error. This error condition may be due to physically damaged RAM as well.

Some RAM may appear to pass the POST but still cannot be used by the operating system. In this case, the computer will display a gray screen, sound three tones, blink the power LED on the front of the computer three times, pause, and repeat the blinking until the computer is turned off.

The solution to both of these situations is to reseat the memory and test again. If the memory fails the POST test again, try known-good memory or order new memory.

Video

It's pretty easy to tell when the issue you're facing is associated with the video on your computer. Here are the initial clues you will get and some steps for troubleshooting.

No Video, No Boot Chime

The computer will turn on (indicated by the front LED being on), but there is no boot chime and no video on the display. The faint sound of the fans, hard drive, and optical drive may also be heard.

1   Follow instructions in the General Information section in the service manual to reset the SMC. Does the computer display video after successfully resetting the SMC?

    Yes: Problem solved.

    No: Go to step 2.

2   Verify that only supported SDRAM memory has been installed and that it has been installed correctly. Unsupported and/or defective memory can prevent the computer from booting. It may be necessary to install known-good memory for testing purposes and replace any unsupported or defective small outline dual inline memory modules (SO-DIMMs) identified during this process. Does the computer display video after verifying and/or replacing the memory with known-good memory?

Yes: Problem solved. Verify full system functionality before returning the system to the customer.

No: Replace the logic board.

No Video, Boot Chime Heard

The computer will turn on, the boot chime can be heard, the front LED is on, and sounds from the fan or drive activity are audible, but the display has no picture or color.

1   Check if the computer is sleeping. Press the spacebar to wake the computer from sleep mode. Did the computer wake from sleep?

Yes: Put the computer to sleep from the Apple menu and wake the computer again to test. Check Energy Saver settings to see when the computer has been designated to sleep.

No: Go to step 2.

2   Reset the PRAM.

   a   If the iMac is on, turn it off by holding the power button until it powers off. The fans should go quiet.

   b   Hold down the Command-Option-P-R keys and press the power button. When you hear the computer's start up chime for the second time, you can release the keys.

   c   If you didn't hear at least two startup chimes, go to the top of this section and begin again. It's important that you hear two startup chimes when performing this procedure. This indicates that you have successfully reset the computer's PRAM.

Does the computer display video after successfully resetting the computer's PRAM?

Yes: Restart the computer from the Apple menu and make sure the computer is now working correctly.

No: Go to step 3.

3   Turn off the computer. Remove the access door and front bezel to access the diagnostic LEDs. Plug in and start up the computer to observe the diagnostic LEDs. At this point in the power-on process, you should hear a boot chime, and LEDs 1 and 2 are on. Is LED 3 on or off?

On: The video card and logic board are communicating properly. Go to step 4.

Off: The video card and logic board are not communicating. Replace the video card. If the issue persists, replace the main logic board.

4   LED 4 should be on when the video card and LCD display have communicated properly to produce a video image. Is LED 4 on or off?

On: The video card has communicated properly with the LCD panel. In this case, there is a problem with the backlights in the panel or the inverter. Replace the LCD panel, which replaces both the backlights and the inverter.

NOTE ▶ This is the cure for our scenario. In Lesson 11 you learned how to replace an LCD panel. The above symptom chart step would have directed your lead technician to ask you to replace the module indicated.

Off: The video card and logic board are unable to communicate to generate video. Replace the video card. If the issue persists, replace the LCD panel. Does the system function now?

Yes: Test the system and return the computer to the customer.

No: Go on to step 5.

5 Unplug the iMac and remove the SDRAM. Replace with known-good SDRAM. Plug the iMac back in and power on the unit. Does the front LED go off after a few moments?

Yes: Replace the original SDRAM and test again. If the front LED does not go off with only the original SDRAM installed, replace the SDRAM. If the LED is now reliably going off after a moment, but you still do not have any video, go to step 6.

No: If the LED remained on, the main logic board is not communicating with the LCD panel to generate video. Replace the main logic board.

6 If video is displayed normally on an external display but not on the iMac internal display panel, replace the LCD.

Display Is Tinted Another Color

1 Reset the PRAM. Press and hold the Command-Option-P-R keys and press the power button. After you hear the second startup chime, release the keys.

Does the computer display properly tinted video after successfully resetting the computer's PRAM?

Yes: Problem resolved. Restart the computer from the Apple menu and make sure the computer display is no longer tinted another color.

No: Go to step 2.

2 Connect an external monitor to the mini-DVI port. Does the external display exhibit the same color tinting?

Yes: Replace the video card.

No: Go to step 3.

3 Check the low voltage differential signaling (LVDS) cable connections. If connected properly and the same color tinting persists, replace the LVDS cable. Does color tinting persist after changing the LVDS cable?

Yes: Replace the LCD panel.

No: Problem solved. Restart the computer from the Apple menu and make sure the computer display is no longer tinted another color.

Hard Drive

If you suspect that the hard drive is to blame, here are a number of scenarios you might need to work through in order to solve the issue.

Hard Drive Failure

In a hard drive failure, the computer fails to start up to the desktop and may display a flashing question mark, or an alternating question mark and Mac OS (face or a folder).

> **NOTE ▶** Before troubleshooting hard drive problems, it is a good idea to back up any important data. Some troubleshooting steps may require erasing the contents of the hard drive.

1 Boot from the Install DVD that came with the computer and open Disk Utility. Does the hard drive show in Disk Utility?

Yes: Run Repair Disk and Repair Permissions to correct any directory and permissions issues. Go to step 2.

No: Go to step 4.

2 Did Disk Utility successfully repair directory or permissions?

Yes: Restart the computer, booting from the hard drive. Go to step 3.

No: Go to step 4.

3   Did the computer successfully start to the internal hard drive?

Yes: Run Apple Hardware Test version 3A108 or later for this machine and return to the customer if it passes.

No: Go to step 4.

4   Boot the machine to AHT, version 3A108 or later, or to Apple Service Diagnostic (ASD) for iMac (Mid-2006), version 3S106 or later. Did the machine successfully boot to AHT or the diagnostic?

Yes: Run the test suites.

No: Make sure you're using the correct version of the diagnostic and that the disc is able to boot another machine that it supports. If so, then try booting from an external optical drive. If this is successful, you should replace the optical drive and retest the machine booting to the diagnostic disc.

5   Did the tests pass?

Yes: Reinstall the system software that came with the computer and test.

No: Replace the component(s) that the test results indicate.

To ensure Intel-based and Power-PC (PPC) Macintosh drive compatibility, drives to be used in booting Intel-based Macintosh hardware should be formatted and partitioned with an Intel-based Macintosh disk utility running on Intel-based Macintosh hardware. That should ensure you get the correct default partition map and structure for reliable booting. Intel-based Macintosh CPUs in target disk mode will mount only on PPC machines running Mac OS X 10.4 or later, and may show one contiguous partition rather than separate partitions on the host machine. Always make sure to use the OS that came with the machine if you need to reinstall software (ask the customer for the discs if necessary) and the diagnostics designated specifically for that hardware.

System Hangs During Normal Startup Process

1   Boot from the Install DVD that came with the computer. Use Disk Utility to verify the hard drive.

2   Using Disk Utility, reformat the hard drive.

3   Check all cable connections to and from the hard drive.

4   Replace the hard drive.

5   Replace the main logic board.

Optical Drive

If the issue you're facing has to do with the optical drive, you might encounter one of the following clues.

CDs or DVDs Do Not Show Up on the Desktop

1   Choose Preferences from the Finder menu. Make sure the checkbox to show CDs, DVDs, and iPods is selected in the General window.

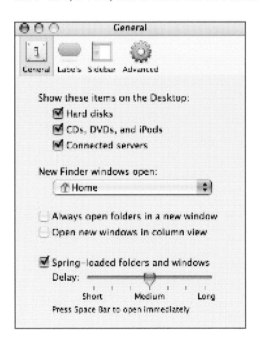

2   Choose System Preferences from the Apple menu and open the CDs & DVDs preferences window. Make sure that audio CDs are set to launch iTunes and movie DVDs set to launch DVD Player when those media are inserted.

3   Check that the drive can read discs normally. Insert an audio CD and check whether it shows up on the desktop or launches iTunes. Does the audio CD mount on the desktop or in iTunes?

Yes: The drive seems to read CD discs well. Go to step 4.

No: Make sure that other computers can read the disc. Try other CD discs. If none mounts or no audio CDs launch iTunes, replace the optical drive.

4   Eject the audio CD and insert the iMac Software Install and Restore DVD that came with the customer's computer, or insert a DVD movie. Does this disc show up on the desktop, or does the movie launch DVD Player?

Yes: The computer is reading CD and DVD media. This may be related to a specific disc or discs the customer is using; you should examine those discs.

No: The optical disc is reading CD media, but not DVD media. Try other DVD discs. If none mounts or movie DVDs do not launch DVD Player, replace the optical drive adapter board.

5   If after replacing the optical drive adapter board the drive still won't mount any optical media, replace the optical drive. If the issue persists, replace the logic board.

Computer Will Not Burn Discs

1 Check whether the drive can read CDs and DVDs normally. Perform the steps in the preceding section, "CDs or DVDs Do Not Show Up on the Desktop."

2 Try a test burn by creating a Burn folder:

   a In the Finder, choose File > New Burn Folder.

   b Open the Burn folder, drag an item into it for testing, and click Burn in the upper-right corner of the window.

3 If the disc fails to burn with an error, check for these error messages.

   ▶ Unknown Error -2147352480. See Apple Knowledge Base documents 25480, "Mac OS X: 'Unknown Error -2147352480'" when burning CD-R, CD-RW, or DVD-R media," and 25750, "You see a 'buffer underrun' error when burning a disc in Finder or iTunes," for more information.

   ▶ Buffer underrun error. See Knowledge Base documents 25480 and 25750 for more information.

   ▶ Unknown Error. See Knowledge Base document 152224, "Mac OS X 10.3 Help: I got an 'unknown error' message while burning a CD or DVD disc," for more information.

4 If the blank disc is ejected, try another blank disc. If the issue persists, try another brand and speed of blank media; if you're using blank CD media, see if this happens with blank DVD media. If the drive consistently rejects all blank media, or rejects only blank CD media while accepting blank

DVD media or vice versa, replace the optical drive adapter board and test. Does the drive successfully burn to disc after replacing the optical drive adapter board?

Yes: Problem solved.

No: Go to step 5.

5   Replace the optical drive. Does the new optical drive burn correctly?

Yes: Problem solved.

No: Replace the logic board.

Discs Won't Insert

1   Is there a disc already in the drive?

Yes: Eject the disc before inserting another. Refer to Knowledge Base document 51008, "iMac: If You Can't Eject a CD or DVD, or Open the Drive Tray." If none of these options ejects the disc, you may have to disassemble the drive to recover the disc. See Knowledge Base document 86382, "Macintosh: How to Remove a Stuck Disc from a Slot-Loading Drive."

No: Reseat the optical drive. Perform the optical drive procedure in Take Apart to reseat the drive in the mounting aperture and reconnect the optical drive to the logic board.

2   After reinstalling the optical drive, can you now insert a disc?

Yes: Issue resolved. Run diagnostics and return the system to the customer.

No: Replace the optical drive adapter board.

3   After replacing the optical drive adapter board, can you insert a disc now?

Yes: Issue resolved. Run diagnostics and return the system to the customer.

No: Replace the optical drive.

TIP ▸ When you become more experienced as a technician, you will see customers present some interesting issues. Take the opportunity to kindly educate customers and help them be more knowledgeable users. Keep your eyes open for cases where the customer has attempted to use the unit in a manner for which it was not intended. For example, you might find multiple discs inserted at the same time or loose change inside the optical drive. These cases are easily solved.

Optical Disc Constantly Ejects

1   Disconnect all peripheral devices, especially the mouse in cases where the disc is constantly ejecting. Retest. If the issue is resolved, reconnect peripherals one at a time until you identify the faulty peripheral.

2   Try cleaning the disc. If the disc is dirty or scratched, it may not mount. Is the issue resolved?

Yes: Problem solved.

No: Try a different disc. If the issue persists, go to step 3.

3   Boot from AHT (hold down the D key at startup). If you can boot to this volume, run the Quick and Extended tests. Does the unit pass the tests?

Yes: Restart to the internal hard drive and test again.

No: Replace the component(s) that the test results indicated. If you cannot boot to AHT because it ejects, go to step 4.

4   Boot from the Install DVD (to use Startup Manager, hold down the Option key at startup). If you can boot from this volume, perform an Archive and Install with the Install DVD that came with the computer and test. Is the issue resolved?

Yes: Problem solved.

No: If you cannot boot to AHT or to the Install DVD because they eject, reseat the optical drive adapter board to the logic board and retest.

5 Replace the optical drive adapter board.

6 Replace the optical drive.

7 Replace the logic board.

Fans and Noise

When the customer complains of whirring fans or other noises, these are the troubleshooting steps you should take.

Fans Running at Full Speed After Computer Turns On

The customer may have entered the computer into a diagnostic mode that causes the fans to run at full speed. Restarting the system will not restore normal fan operation. To solve the problem, the user or technician should do the following:

1 Shut down the system.

2 Disconnect the power cord and wait 15 seconds.

3 Reconnect the power cord and wait 5 seconds.

4 Power on the system.

> **NOTE ▶** Customers reporting this symptom should be told to press the power button *after* the power cord has been fully inserted. Inserting the power cord while pressing the power button will cause the fans to run at full speed.

Loud Fan Noise

The iMac (24-inch) has a trio of fans that circulate air throughout the system. It also includes temperature sensors and advanced thermal software that spins the fans fast or slowly, as needed. As the system usage increases, the fans will adjust their speed to meet the cooling needs of the system.

Under normal conditions, rotating fans will make a slight hum that varies in relationship with rotational speed and the amount of air that they are moving. In addition, the normal functioning of the hard drive and optical drive will generate additional whirring and scratching sounds that may be audible. All of these sounds are normal and do not indicate a computer failure.

To begin troubleshooting a possible fan issue, you need to qualify the sound that you're experiencing.

1   Does the sound occur only under specific light or heavy usage conditions?

Yes: CPU-intensive applications such as iTunes, GarageBand, and DVD Player—or having two or more applications open at once—will cause the fans to run at an increased rate, making them more noticeable. If the sound occurs only when one or more of these applications is running, this is normal.

No: If the sound isn't affected by CPU-intensive application, it may be due to other factors. Go to step 2.

2   Is the sound always present, or does the sound vary?

The sound is always present: The normal functioning of the hard drive and optical drive will generate additional whirring and scratching noises that may be audible. Check whether this sound is related to one of the components. Go to step 4.

The sound varies: Under normal conditions, rotating blowers will make a slight hum that varies in relationship with their rotational speed and the amount of air that they are moving. To see if this is indeed the case, go to step 3.

3   Are the fans making a normal humming sound that increases or decreases in relation to processor usage as to cool the system?

Launch the Activity Monitor application included with Mac OS X in the Utilities folder to determine whether the noise corresponds with heavy usage of the CPU. Does fan activity increase and decrease with the CPU

Usage graph in Activity Monitor? Check by running CPU-intensive applications such as iTunes.

NOTE ▶ In the "old" days, a good lead technician might run Graphing Calculator to place a "load" on a system in OS 9. Along the same lines, playing music in iTunes with Visualizer on is a good method. Intensive applications with graphics and sound will increase CPU usage and the need for fan cooling.

Yes: This is normal operation and none of the fans requires replacement.

No: If the fan activity does not coincide with CPU usage, the sound you're hearing may not be fan activity. Go to step 4.

4   The normal functioning of the hard drive and optical drive will generate additional whirring and scratching noises that may be audible. You can isolate these noises by booting the computer to the Install DVD.

   a   Place the disc in the drive and restart the machine while holding down the C key.

   b   At the Installer window, choose Open Disk Utility from the Installer menu.

   c   Once Disk Utility is open, select the system's hard drive and click Unmount on the toolbar. If the drive has multiple partitions, unmount each of these partitions.

This will spin down the hard drive. The optical drive will also be busy at this time; wait a moment for the optical drive to spin down also and then listen to the machine. Is the sound still present?

Yes: With the hard drive and optical drive inactive, all you should be hearing are the fans in the machine. While booted to the DVD, these fans should be running at a lower level since CPU activity is low with both drives inactive. Fan sound that includes objectionable ticking, whistling, or squealing may require further investigation and/or replacement of the particular fan. Go to step 5.

No: The normal functioning of the hard drive and optical drive will generate additional whirring and scratching sounds that may be audible. All of these sounds are normal and do not indicate a failure with the machine. If you want to check the health of the hard drive, see Knowledge Base document 152349, "Replacing a disk before it fails."

5 Shut down the computer, remove the power cord and any other connected cables, and remove the access door, front bezel, and EMI shield. Stand up the computer, plug it in, and start it up by pressing the external power button.

As the machine starts up, listen carefully to each of the three fans, and see if you can locate the fan from which the objectionable ticking, whistling, or squealing sound is coming. The CPU fan is the left-most fan, the hard drive fan is in the center, and the optical fan is on the right.

Can you pinpoint the fan making the sound?

Yes: Replace the noisy fan.

No: If you can hear an objectionable ticking, whistling, or squealing sound, but you cannot identify the source of the sound, contact Apple Technical Support.

Audible Buzzing, Whining, or Ticking Noise

The iMac (24-inch) contains several mechanical devices such as motors and fans that may make audible buzzing, ticking, or whining noises when they are operating in a normal manner. The sounds will vary depending on how the system is used.

To troubleshoot abnormal noises:

1 Follow the previous steps to eject any media in the optical drive and quit all applications and test the computer again.

The optical drive will make a variety of normal sounds when accessing optical media. Processor-intensive applications may cause the fans to run at a higher speed and therefore be more audible.

2 Boot to the latest version of ASD for iMac (24-inch) and select the Extended Firmware Interface (EFI) test suite by holding down the D key during startup. The diagnostic tests fan speeds and thermal sensor functionality. Should tests fail, replace any parts that the diagnostic indicates.

3   Reboot the computer and check the computer again. If the noise persists and is unusually loud, contact Apple Technical Support.

> **TIP** ▶ Verify that the computer is running a supported version of the Mac OS X operating system. If an earlier version of the operating system has been installed, the fans may run at excessive speeds.

> **TIP** ▶ Determine that the noise you hear is related to the computer by removing and shutting down all other devices in the vicinity that could be causing a sound.

Fans Running at a Constant High Speed

If the fans on the system are running at a constant high speed, or ramp very quickly to high speed and do not vary once this speed is reached, the fans are most likely receiving incorrect thermal input. Follow these steps:

1   Reset the SMC and then test to see if the fans still exhibit the issue.

2   Boot to the EFI tests of the latest version of ASD for iMac (24-inch). This will test the fans and thermal input of the sensors. If the tests fail, replace the component(s) that the test indicates.

AirPort

If the issue relates to the AirPort, here are some troubleshooting scenarios you may encounter.

Computer Cannot Connect Wirelessly with AirPort

1   From the Apple menu, choose About this Mac.

2   Click More Info to open System Profiler.

3   In the left column of System Profiler, under Network, select AirPort Card. Does the section to the right say "No Information Found"?

Yes: The computer does not realize it has an AirPort Card installed. Go to step 4.

No: The iMac recognizes that it has an AirPort Card installed. Go to step 5.

4   Remove the access door, front bezel, right speaker, and two card mounting screws, and reseat the AirPort Card. Reinstall the two card mounting screws and check System Profiler again. Does to the computer see the AirPort Card now?

Yes: Problem solved. Replace the lower EMI shield and front bezel, and retest the system to verify that the original symptom is resolved.

No: Replace the AirPort Card. Refer to the Take Apart section for AirPort Card. If the issue persists, replace the logic board.

5   Check the antenna cables. If the antennas are not plugged in all the way, you may have a very short AirPort range. Remove the access door, front bezel, right speaker, and two card mounting screws. Disconnect the card and reconnect the antenna cable connectors to it. Make sure the antenna connectors are firmly seated. Reconnect the card and other components, and retest.

6   If the antennas are plugged in properly and the AirPort Card is recognized but the problem persists, there are a number of other things that could cause issues with wireless networking. Refer to Knowledge Base document 106858, "AirPort troubleshooting guide," for more networking information.

7   Replace the AirPort Card.

8   Replace the AirPort antennas.

9   Replace the logic board.

Bluetooth

If you believe that the issue relates to the Bluetooth device, follow these clues and solutions.

Bluetooth Devices Won't Sync with Computer

1   Make sure the computer has a Bluetooth board installed. Open System Preferences, then verify that Bluetooth appears in the Hardware section of the window.

2   Locate the Bluetooth board inside the computer. Reseat the Bluetooth board and the Bluetooth antenna.

3   Turn on Bluetooth. In System Preferences, click Bluetooth and then click the Settings tab. If you don't see "Bluetooth Power: On," click the Turn Bluetooth On button. Make sure that you also enable Bluetooth on your device (refer to your device's documentation for instructions).

4   Set up a new device. To set up a Bluetooth cellular phone or PDA, click the Devices tab in Bluetooth preferences and then click Set Up New Device to open the Bluetooth Setup Assistant. Follow the onscreen instructions to set up the device. To set up an Apple Wireless Keyboard and Mouse, open System Preferences, click Keyboard & Mouse, click the Bluetooth tab, and then click Set Up New Device to open the Bluetooth Setup Assistant. Follow the onscreen instructions to set up the keyboard and mouse.

5 Recharge or replace the Bluetooth device's battery. If the battery is low, you may experience connection issues.

6 Download and install the latest software for the device.

7 Check for a Bluetooth update. Choose Software Update from the Apple menu (make sure the computer is connected to the Internet). If newer Apple Bluetooth software exists, Software Update will find it.

8 Check for signal spoilers. Avoid situations in which metal objects come between the device and the computer. Don't put the computer under a metal desk or locked away behind a metal cabinet. Keep away cordless telephone base stations, microwave ovens, and other electrical devices that operate on a 2.4 GHz bandwidth. Make sure that the device and the computer aren't more than 30 feet apart from each other.

9 Restart the computer. Try resetting the computer's PRAM and NVRAM.

10 Turn the Bluetooth device off and then on again. If that doesn't work, see if you can reset the device.

11 Replace the Bluetooth board and test the computer again.

12 Refer to the Bluetooth Support site, www.apple.com/support/bluetooth.

13 Replace the logic board.

Speakers

If the customer complains about a lack of sound coming from the speakers, first you'll need to figure out exactly where the sound is *not* coming from. There are basically just two possibilities.

Sound Does Not Come from the Speakers

1   Disconnect any external microphones, speakers, or headphones.

2   Open System Preferences, then click Sound. In the Sound window, click
     Output and make sure the internal speakers are selected as the device for
     sound output, the output volume is adequate, and that Mute is not
     selected. Do you have sound now?

     Yes: Problem resolved.

     No: Go to step 3.

3   Reset PRAM. Hold down Command-Option-P-R and press the power
     button. Listen for two startup chimes and then release the keys. Do you
     have sound now?

     Yes: Problem resolved.

     No: Go to step 4.

4   Plug headphones or external speakers into the line out/headphone port.
     Do you have sound through these devices when plugged in?

     Yes: Go to step 5.

     No: Replace the logic board.

5   Verify that the speaker cable connector is securely attached to the logic
     board. Do you have sound now?

     Yes: Problem resolved.

     No: Replace the speakers.

Sound Comes from Only One Speaker

1   Disconnect any external microphones, speakers, or headphones. Do you hear audio from both of the built-in speakers on the iMac?

    Yes: It looks like the built-in speakers are working properly. This may be an issue with the microphone, speakers, or headphones that were plugged into your iMac. Work with the manufacturer to troubleshoot this issue.

    No: Go to step 2.

2   Check the speaker balance. From the Apple menu, open System Preferences. Click the sound icon and then the Output tab. Make sure the balance setting is in the middle. After adjusting the audio balance, does audio come from both speakers?

    Yes: It looks like balance was not set properly.

    No: Replace the speakers.

3   If the new speakers did not solve the problem, replace the logic board.

Mouse

When the issue seems to be related to the mouse, you can follow through these troubleshooting scenarios.

Mouse Does Not Work at All

1   Turn over the mouse. Is the red LED on the underside of the mouse lit?

    Yes: The mouse has power. Try using the mouse on another surface. Nonreflective, opaque surfaces without repetitive patterns work best. The surface should be clean but not shiny. Optical mice won't work on glass, mirrored surfaces, glossy materials, or mousepads with pictures.

    No: The mouse does not have power. Try plugging the mouse into one of the USB ports on the machine. If the mouse won't power on from any

USB port, try it on a known-good machine. If the mouse fails to power on with a known-good machine, replace the mouse. If the mouse will power on with a known-good machine, replace the main logic board.

2   If the underside LED is lit, the surface is good, and the mouse still does not track, try plugging the mouse into another USB port on the machine. Does the mouse track now?

Yes: Issue resolved. Try the other USB ports on the system to make sure you don't have a bad port, which would require the logic board to be replaced.

No: Try using a known-good mouse. If a known-good mouse resolves the issue, replace the mouse. If a known-good mouse does not resolve the issue, replace the main logic board.

Mouse Works Intermittently (Cursor Stops Responding Randomly) or Responds Slowly

1   Try using the mouse on another surface. Nonreflective, opaque surfaces without repetitive patterns work best. The surface should be clean but not shiny. Optical mice won't work on glass, mirrored surfaces, glossy materials, or mousepads with pictures. Does the mouse track on a proper surface?

Yes: Issue resolved.

No: Check the Mouse Tracking setting in the Mouse window of Keyboard & Mouse preferences.

2   Boot to another volume (like the Install DVD). Does the mouse track properly now?

Yes: Reinstall the system software that came with the computer and test.

No: Try using a known-good mouse. If a known-good mouse resolves the issue, replace the mouse. If the issue persists with a known-good mouse, replace the main logic board.

Apple Wireless Mouse Is Slow or Not Tracking Smoothly

Refer to Knowledge Base document 93369, "Apple Wireless Mouse is slow or not tracking smoothly."

Keyboard

If the customer's complaint has to do with the keyboard, follow these clues and solutions.

None or Only Some of the Keys Function

1   Unplug all devices from the computer, including the mouse, keyboard, printer, scanner, external hard drives, and hubs.

> **NOTE ▶** Some devices such as external storage devices may require you to perform steps before it is safe to unplug them.

2   Plug the keyboard, then the mouse, into the back of the computer firmly and securely. Take special care to make sure the connectors are completely in the sockets. Does your keyboard work now?

Yes: Problem solved.

No: Go to step 3.

3   Unplug the keyboard and plug it into another USB slot on the back of the computer. Does it work now?

Yes: This means that the ports are not functioning and the mouse and keyboard are known-good, so you must replace the logic board.

No: Go to step 4.

4 Unplug the keyboard and plug the mouse into the port the keyboard just occupied. Does the mouse work now?

Yes: Replace the keyboard.

No: Replace the logic board.

Keys Are Sticky or Slow to Respond

1 Try a known-good keyboard.

2 Open System Preferences, click Keyboard & Mouse, and adjust the Key Repeat Speed and Delay Until Repeat rates.

3 Replace the keyboard.

Unfamiliar Characters Appear on the Screen When Typing

Depending on the iMac settings, a simple keystroke can change a keyboard from English to Japanese. This can result in unfamiliar characters showing up when you type. To switch to the US keyboard:

1 Open System Preferences.

2 Click the International icon.

3 Click the Input tab.

4 Scroll down the list and deselect any non-US keyboard layouts.

5 Close System Preferences and type a few characters. Did this solve the problem?

Yes: Problem solved.

No: Replace the keyboard.

USB Port on the Keyboard Doesn't Work

1 Unplug all devices from the keyboard.

2 Plug the Apple mouse into the left USB port on the keyboard. Does the mouse work?

Yes: Go to step 3.

No: Try a known-good mouse or keyboard and go to step 3.

3 Plug the mouse into the right port. Does it work?

Yes: Try a known-good keyboard.

No: Try a known-good mouse to rule out the mouse. Go to step 4.

4 Unplug the keyboard from the USB port on the back of the iMac, and plug the mouse into the port the keyboard had been in. Does the mouse work now?

Yes: Replace the keyboard.

No: It appears that the USB port on the iMac isn't functioning properly. Replace the logic board.

Apple Wireless Keyboard Is Not Responding Correctly

Refer to Knowledge Base document 86496, "Apple Wireless Keyboard and Mouse: Troubleshooting Connection Issues."

Lesson Review

1. How many LEDs that can be used for troubleshooting are present on the iMac (24-inch)?

   a. Two

   b. Three

   c. Four

   d. Five

2. True or false: The diagnostic LEDs can indicate that the optical drive is malfunctioning.

3. True or false: The diagnostic LEDs can help you troubleshoot a faulty power supply.

4. LED 4 is off: What is the cause?

    a. Power is off.

    b. No video is being generated.

    c. Both of the above.

5. True or false: If LED 1 is on, the power supply is getting good power from the AC outlet.

6. If you reset the SMC, which of the following is not affected?

    a. Sleep issues

    b. Fans

    c. PRAM

7. True or false: Apple System Profiler is the first tool used to troubleshoot an AirPort Card.

Answer Key

1. d (four hidden LEDs and one on front); 2. False; 3. True; 4. c; 5. True; 6. c; 7. True

13

Time   This lesson takes approximately 1 hour to complete.

Goals   Describe the key features of the Mac mini models

Explain the differences in the Mac mini models

Locate technical specifications for the Mac mini models

About Mac mini Models

On January 11, 2005, Apple unveiled the Mac mini, a new desktop computer designed specifically for the consumer and education switcher markets. Mac mini features a radically different form factor and an aggressive pricing structure. Additionally, a keyboard and mouse are not included with the system; they must be purchased separately.

Visually, the Mac mini is comparable to the Power Mac G4 Cube because, most notably, it ships without a display and is small. The Mac mini footprint is an impressive 6.5 inches square by 2 inches tall, and it weighs only 2.9 pounds. (In contrast, the Power Mac G4 Cube was quite a bit larger, coming in at a whopping 8 inches square by 10 inches tall and weighing 14 pounds.)

The following chart outlines the major technical differences among the Mac mini models. Use this chart to distinguish between various models and to determine the capabilities of each.

Mac mini

	Mac mini	Mac mini (Early 2006)	Mac mini (Late 2006)
Introduced	January 2005	February 2006	September 2006
Mac OS (minimum)	Mac OS X 10.4	Mac OS X 10.4	Mac OS X 10.4
Technical specifications	http://support.apple.com/specs/macmini		
Processor	1.25 GHz G4 1.42 GHz G4	1.5 GHz Intel Core Solo 1.66 GHz Intel Core Duo	1.66 GHz Intel Core Duo 1.83 GHz Intel Core Duo
L2 cache*	512 KB on-chip L2 cache	2 MB on-chip L2 cache	2 MB on-chip L2 cache
Memory	512 MB DDR SDRAM	512 MB DDR SDRAM	512 MB DDR SDRAM

	Mac mini	Mac mini (Early 2006)	Mac mini (Late 2006)
Hard disk	40 GB Ultra ATA (1.25 GHz) 80 GB Ultra ATA (1.42 GHz)	60 GB Ultra ATA (1.5 GHz) 80 GB Serial ATA (1.66 GHz)	60 GB Ultra ATA (1.66 GHz) 80 GB Serial ATA (1.83 GHz)
Optical drive	Combo (1.25 GHz) Combo/SuperDrive (1.42 GHz)	Combo (1.5 GHz) SuperDrive (1.66 GHz)	Combo (1.66 GHz) SuperDrive (1.83 GHz)
Graphics	ATI Radeon 9200 with 32 MB and AGP 4x support	Intel GMA 950 graphics processor	Intel GMA 950 graphics processor
Expansion	2 USB 2.0 ports 1 FireWire 400 port 10/100Base-T Ethernet AirPort Extreme Bluetooth (1.42 GHz)	4 USB 2.0 ports 1 FireWire 400 port 10/100/ 1000Base-T Ethernet AirPort Extreme Bluetooth 2.0	4 USB 2.0 ports 1 FireWire 400 port 10/100/ 1000Base-T Ethernet AirPort Extreme Bluetooth 2.0
Video connectors	DVI VGA	DVI VGA	DVI VGA

*The Mac mini is the first Apple desktop computer to officially support both DVD-R and DVD+R discs with its optional SuperDrive.

Lesson Review

1. What is the lowest speed of the CPU in any Mac mini introduced before September 2006?

    a.   1.0 GHz

    b.   1.25 GHz

    c.   1.42 GHz

2. How large is the L2 cache in the Mac mini (January 2005)?

    a.   128 KB

    b.   256 KB

    c.   512 KB

3. True or false: The Mac mini comes with Gigabit Ethernet (1000 Base-T).

4. What type of optical drive comes in the "Best" Mac mini (Late 2006)?

    a.   CD-ROM

    b.   Combo

    c.   SuperDrive

5. What brand of graphics controller is used in the Mac mini?

    a.   ATI

    b.   NVIDIA

    c.   AGP

6. Which Mac mini model first featured the Intel Core Duo processor?

7. This figure shows the back of the Mac mini (Early 2006). Name as many I/O ports as you can. Use the Answer Key to fill in any you may have missed.

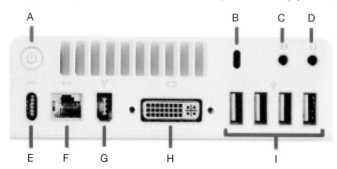

Answer Key

1. b; 2. c; 3. False—the Mac Mini comes with 10/100Base-T Ethernet, but the Mac mini (Early 2006) and the Mac mini (Late 2006) both come with Gigabit Ethernet (1000Base-T). 4. c; 5. a; 6. Mac mini (Early 2006) 1.66 GHz; 7. A. Power button; B. Security slot; C. Audio-in/optical audio-in port; D. Headphone-out/optical audio-out port; E. Power port; F. 10/100/1000Base-T Ethernet port; G. FireWire 400 port; H. DVI video-out port; I. USB 2.0 ports

14

Reference Files	Mac mini Service Manual (mac_mini_early_late_06.pdf)
Time	This lesson takes approximately 1 hour to complete.
Goals	Install a hard drive in a Mac mini

Upgrading a Mac mini

The Mac mini line of consumer desktop computers is not designed to be modified by end users. Additional random-access memory (RAM) and any other options or upgrades must be either ordered as configure-to-order (CTO) options at the time of purchase, or installed by an Apple Authorized Service Provider (AASP) or Apple retail store after purchase.

This lesson demonstrates how Apple-certified service technicians can open the Intel-based Mac mini (Early 2006) to upgrade the memory and hard drive. Open the Apple Service Source manual, review the General Information section, and locate the necessary steps in the manual to perform the procedure. Use this lesson to accompany the service manual steps.

> **NOTE ▶** These procedures are intended to be followed by certified technicians only. If you are not certified, use these procedures as a demonstration only. If an end user opens a Mac mini and any damage to the unit results, the repair of such damage will not be covered under the Apple warranty or the AppleCare Protection Plan.

Required Tools and Equipment

In addition to the standard electrostatic discharge (ESD) workstation, wrist strap, and mat—which you should always use, following the guidelines discussed in Lesson 4, "Safe Working Procedures and General Maintenance"— you will need the following tools and equipment:

▶ Jeweler's Phillips #0 screwdriver

▶ Phillips #1 screwdriver

▶ Nylon probe tool (or Black Stick), or other nonconductive nylon or plastic tool

▶ Soft cloth (to protect removed parts from scratches)

▶ Screw tray

▶ Putty knife, 1.5 inch (38 mm), flexible blade

Opening a Mac mini

Before we begin, let's take a look at the preliminary steps to replace a hard drive.

Preliminary Steps

Before you begin, remove
- Top housing
- Internal frame
- Disconnect the AirPort antenna

As you may have discovered by now, each procedure in the service manual lists preliminary steps, which in turn may list additional preliminary steps. Follow each of the preliminary steps in the order given. For example, when you read the procedures, you'll find that a preliminary step to removing the internal frame is to disconnect the AirPort antenna. Therefore, you'll actually complete that step before removing the frame.

And before anything else, be sure to protect yourself from electrical shock and to protect the unit from ESD.

1   Shut down the computer.

> **WARNING** ▶ Always shut down the computer before opening it to avoid damaging its internal components or the components you are installing. Do not open the computer or attempt to install items inside it while it is on.

2   Unplug all external cables from the computer except the power cord.

3   Touch the metal case to discharge any static electricity from your body.

> **NOTE** ▶ Always discharge static before you touch any parts or install any components inside the computer. To avoid generating static electricity, do not walk around the room until you have finished working and closed the computer.

4   Unplug the power cord.

5   Put on an ESD wrist strap.

> **NOTE** ▶ The following procedure demonstrates the case-opening on the previous Mac mini model. The top housing removal procedure is the same for the Mac mini (Early 2006) computer.

Top Housing

Whether you are adding memory or providing a hard drive upgrade to a Mac mini, the first step is to remove the top housing of the computer.

1 Place the computer on a clean, flat surface.

2 Turn the computer over so the ports are facing you and the bottom of the computer (gray color) is facing up.

3 To avoid scratching or denting the case, use caution when using the putty knife. Hold the putty knife with the beveled edge facing the bottom housing. Find the gap on the left side of the computer where the metal housing and bottom assembly come together. Insert the putty knife 0.25-inch (6.35-mm) into the gap.

NOTE ▶ If the tool is inserted too deep, it could damage the EMI foam on the inside of the top housing.

4 Gently release the internal latches by prying the tool away from the computer. You will hear little popping sounds as the latches release and the bottom separates from the top housing, creating a gap at the top of the input/output (I/O) panel.

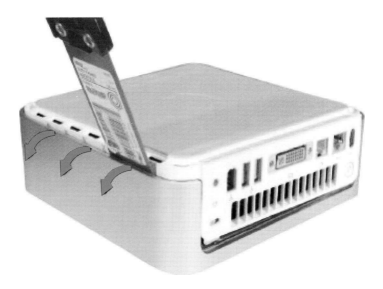

5   Repeat the procedure on the right side of the computer.

6   Push the I/O panel upward until the top housing is removed. The popping
    sounds will continue as you push the I/O panel; this is normal.

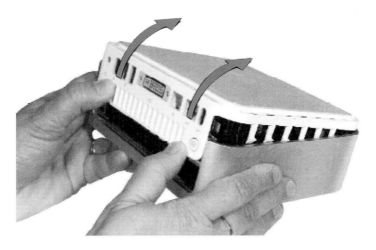

7   Set aside the top housing.

AirPort Antenna

Now that you have removed the top housing, proceed in the service manual to the next preliminary step before removing the hard drive.

In the internal frame preliminary steps, notice that you are to disconnect the AirPort antenna only from the spring and black posts to which it is attached. Do not disconnect the antenna from the AirPort Extreme Card.

Proceed to the section of the service manual that addresses the AirPort antenna.

On the internal frame, locate the spring and black plastic posts to which the AirPort antenna is attached. With your fingers, squeeze the black posts to release the AirPort antenna.

The other steps are more invasive than necessary.

Internal Frame

Now return to the Internal Frame section to perform the procedures listed.

1   Turn the Mac mini so the speaker at the front of the computer is facing
you. With a pair of tweezers, disconnect the hard drive sensor cable from
the logic board.

2   Near the I/O ports, disconnect the flexible cable on the audio board from
the connector on the interconnect board.

3 With a jeweler's Phillips #0 screwdriver, remove the four screws on the internal frame (one screw in each corner). The bottom-left screw is longer than the other three screws; be sure to keep this in mind during reassembly.

4 Lift the internal frame straight up and off the bottom housing.

A number of parts are connected to the internal frame. There is no need to disconnect them. Proceed to the hard drive removal steps in the Service Source manual.

Removing the Hard Drive

Before proceeding to the hard drive removal steps, be sure you have a static-proof bag so that after you remove the drive, you can place it in the bag. Avoid touching any hard drive circuitry by holding the drive by the edges.

1 Flip over the internal frame to expose the hard drive. Using a Phillip's #1 screwdriver, remove the four hard drive screws.

2 With a nylon probe tool or other nonconductive tool, pry the hard drive off the connector on the interconnect board. Pull the hard drive in the direction of the speaker.

> **TIP** ▶ It is a generally accepted practice to perform the steps we have taken in reverse order to reassemble the unit, but in doing so you would bypass the service manual reassembly instructions and any special notes to ensure the proper reassembly of the unit. Instead, take a few extra moments to read the directions. Your extra efforts will provide better customer satisfaction and save some time on your part.

Before reassembling the unit, let's look at the procedure for performing a memory upgrade.

Installing RAM

Older Mac mini models come with a single dual inline memory module (DIMM) slot. This unit has two internal small outline DIMM (SO-DIMM) RAM slots.

This model ships from the factory with at least 512 MB of PC2-5300 DDR2 synchronous dynamic RAM (SDRAM), consisting of two 256 MB modules. More memory may be installed if the unit was custom configured when ordered (two 512 MB or 1 GB modules) to a maximum of 2 GB total.

> **MORE INFO** ▶ For more information on Mac mini memory specifications for this model, refer to Apple Knowledge Base document 303378, "Mac Mini (Early 2006): Memory Specifications and Upgrades."

The following installation process assumes you have already grounded yourself, removed the Mac mini computer's top housing, disconnected the AirPort antenna, and removed the internal frame. Locate the memory module(s).

1   Press the metal latches outward to release the memory DIMMs. The DIMM will pop up slightly.

2   Pull the DIMM from the slot on the logic board.

3 Locate the memory module replacement procedure in the service manual and install the memory modules.

During the replacement procedure, pay particular attention when lining up the notch on the RAM with the notch on the slot. Take care not to force the memory modules into place.

Do not use the metal latches on the slot while inserting the memory modules. Return to the hard drive replacement procedure in the manual and reassemble the unit as directed.

There are a few steps remaining. Given that you have installed a new hard drive, you will need to restore the operating system and applications, and ensure that the memory is functioning properly.

Lesson Review

1. True or false: There are no user-installable parts for the Mac mini.

2. What tool do you need to open the top housing on the Mac mini?

    a. Phillips #1 screwdriver

    b. Flat-blade screwdriver

    c. Modified putty knife

3. What optional component, if present, must be removed when upgrading RAM in a Mac mini?

    a. AirPort antenna

    b. Bluetooth antenna

    c. Power supply

4. What type of memory slot is in a Mac mini (Early 2006)?

    a. VRAM

    b. SO-DIMM

    c. DIMM

5. True or false: The Mac mini requires PC3200 memory modules.

6. True or false: The hard drive removal for the Mac mini (Early 2006) requires removal of the AirPort Card and antenna.

Answer Key

1. True; 2. c; 3. a; 4. b; 5. False, the Mac mini (Early 2006) takes PC2-5300 memory modules; 6. False, you need to disconnect the AirPort antenna only from the internal frame.

15

Reference Files	Mac mini Service Source manual (mac_mini_early_late_06.pdf)
Time	This lesson takes approximately 45 minutes to complete.
Goals	Remove a logic board from a Mac mini

Taking Apart a Mac mini

In Lesson 14, "Upgrading a Mac mini," you learned how to install memory and a hard drive in a Mac mini. In this lesson, you're going to dig deeper into the Intel-based Mac mini (Early 2006) to remove a faulty logic board—one of several possible reasons a Mac mini won't turn on, has no startup chime, has no drive or fan sound, or has an unlit power-on LED (see Lesson 16, "Troubleshooting a Mac mini").

Use this text along with the service manual included on this book's companion website (www.peachpit.com/ats.deskport3) to follow step-by-step Take Apart instructions. (Apple Authorized Service Providers [AASPs] should download and refer to the latest service manual from AppleCare Service Source before servicing any Apple product.) You'll begin by opening the service manual to the General Information pages in the Take Apart section.

At each stage of the Take Apart procedure, we'll let you know about special notes and information; otherwise, we proceed component to component, from the outside in. Several of the steps required for removing the logic board are the same for upgrading the Mac mini and were covered in detail in Lesson 14.

> **NOTE ▶** The Mac mini is not designed with any Do-It-Yourself (DIY) parts for repair by users. If anyone other than an AASP opens a Mac mini for any reason, and any damage to the unit results, the repair of such damage will not be covered under the Apple warranty or the AppleCare Protection Plan.

Required Tools and Equipment

In addition to the standard electrostatic discharge (ESD) wrist strap and mat— which you should always use, following the guidelines discussed in Lesson 4, "Safe Working Procedures and General Maintenance"—you will need the following tools and equipment:

▶ Soft cloth

▶ Torx T10 screwdriver

▶ Tweezers

▶ Nylon probe tool, also called a Black Stick (or other nonconductive nylon or plastic tool)

▶ Putty knife, 1.5 inch (38 mm), flexible blade

▶ Phillips #0 screwdriver

▶ Apple Hardware Test (AHT) diagnostic disc for the Mac mini model

Preliminary Steps

Review the preliminary steps you will need to follow in order to remove a logic board. You will find these instructions on page 16 of the service manual.

Top Housing

The first step in replacing any internal component is to remove the top housing of the computer.

1   Perform preliminary steps 1 through 5 on page 16 of the service manual.

    For the protection of you and the computer, always remember the following:

    ▶   Shut off the computer and unplug it from its power source before attempting to open the unit.

    ▶   Follow ESD procedures at all times.

2 Perform removal procedures 1 through 7, beginning on page 17 of the service manual.

Use caution when using the putty knife. Be extremely careful not to scratch or dent the top or bottom housing when inserting the tool. If you insert the tool too deep, it could damage the EMI foam on the inside of the top housing.

3 Set aside the top housing. As always, make sure that your work area is clean and that the top housing is protected from being scratched.

AirPort Antenna

Proceed to page 23 of the service manual to disconnect the AirPort antenna.

1 On the internal frame, locate the spring and black plastic posts to which the AirPort antenna is attached. With your fingers, squeeze the black posts to release the AirPort antenna.

2 Pay particular attention to avoid bending the antenna.

Internal Frame

Gaining access to the logic board requires first removing the black plastic internal frame, to which various other components are attached.

1 Perform removal procedure steps 1 through 5 on page 29 of the service manual.

2 After you have removed the internal frame from the bottom housing, take a moment to examine several parts that are connected to the internal frame.

The Bluetooth antenna is paired with the AirPort antenna, and vice versa. Should you need to replace either in the future, keep in mind that you will need to replace both. Do not mix different vendors' antennas; they may interfere with each other.

When taking apart a Mac mini, note how cables are routed before removing any parts. When you reassemble the system, place the cables in the same positions they were in before Take Apart. There is very little room to spare inside of these systems, and cables can be damaged unless they are replaced exactly to specifications.

Keep in mind that the Mac mini has a large number of components packed very tightly into a small space. It's important that the Mac mini is placed on a hard, flat surface when running to maximize airflow into the base of the computer. Also, keep other materials and equipment away from the Mac mini.

Be sure the fan connector is connected during reassembly. If it is disconnected when you turn on the computer, the Mac mini will quickly flash the LED and then shut off to protect itself from thermal damage.

Now that the top housing is put aside, the AirPort antenna is disconnected, and the internal frame is removed, you can remove the logic board.

▶ AirPort and Bluetooth Components

The AirPort and Bluetooth components can be difficult to envision when already installed. The graphic below depicts these components removed from the computer.

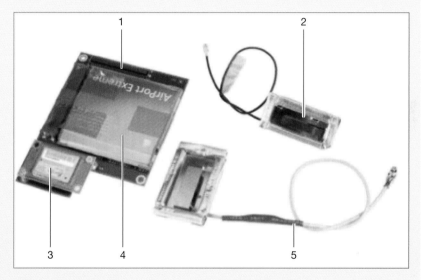

1 Mezzanine board
2 Bluetooth antenna
3 Bluetooth card
4 AirPort Extreme Card
5 AirPort Extreme antenna components

In Lesson 14 we examined the hard drive and hard drive sensor cable. The optical drive is fairly easy to spot as well, right next to the Bluetooth card. Find the main components of this computer in your service manual and become familiar with their locations.

Continues on next page

▶ **AirPort and Bluetooth Components** *(continued)*

Crucial to the Mac mini's operation, the fan maintains a steady flow of air to cool the unit.

Fan (Highlighted grey object at top corner)

Continues on next page

▶ **AirPort and Bluetooth Components** *(continued)*

Locate the system management controller (SMC) reset switch. We will review this switch in more detail during Lesson 16. Do not press the SMC reset switch at this time.

SMC reset switch (circled in blue)

The IR (infrared) board, speakers, and interconnect board are also visible. Using the service manual, identify each of these parts.

Logic Board

The logic board contains the microprocessor and SMC, and it manages both the hard drive sensor and fan. First, review the steps in the service manual beginning on page 106:

1 Perform step 1 of the removal procedure to disconnect the power button cable.

2 Perform step 2 on page 107, where you will disconnect both the hard drive sensor and the power-on LED.

Hard drive sensor (right blue circle)
Power-on LED (left blue circle)

3 Perform step 3 on page 108 to remove the standoff screw. The standoff screw will require the use of a Torx T10 screwdriver. As you remove the standoff, use as little pressure as necessary, and keep a steady hand. When you replace the standoff screw later, do not over tighten or strip it. As your skills grow as a technician, you will develop a light touch when working with small parts.

Standoff (circled in blue)

4 Perform step 4 on page 108 to lift the logic board. As you are lifting it, do not force the logic board by bending it. If you feel that the logic board is still tightly attached, do not force it; review all of the proceeding steps to ensure that you did not skip any.

NOTE ▶ The logic board contains thousands of metal traces that carry signals to all of its components. Stressing these traces can cause damage.

5 Perform steps 5 and 6 on page 109 of the service manual.

When You Are Finished

1 Return the faulty logic board to Apple in the packaging provided.

2 Install the replacement logic board following the instructions in the service manual on page 110.

3   Follow the internal frame reassembly steps in the service manual, beginning on page 32.

4   Verify that the system works correctly by starting up the system, running AHT, and doing a few common user tasks, such as launching a browser, opening applications, or launching Mail.

When replacing a logic board or bottom housing, put in a new thermal pad as well. Of course, any time you find the pad is torn, withered, or damaged, replace it. The thermal pad transfers heat from the microprocessor and logic board to the bottom housing to cool the unit.

TIP Wear gloves to ensure that the oil in your skin does not degrade the pad's ability to conduct heat properly.

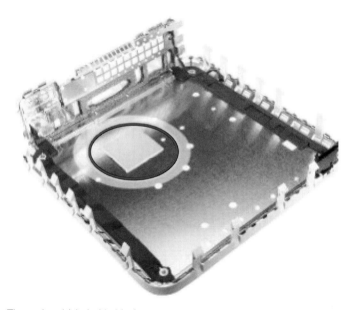

Thermal pad (circled in blue)

Lesson Summary

- ► There are no DIY parts in a Mac mini. If anyone other than an AASP opens a Mac mini for any reason, and any damage to the unit results, the repair of such damage will not be covered under the Apple warranty or the AppleCare Protection Plan.

- ► Gaining access to a particular component often requires the removal of other components first.

- ► Whenever you work on the internal components of a Mac mini, you *must* follow proper ESD procedures.

- ► You must unplug the AC power cord to prevent the Mac mini from turning on during the Take Apart procedure.

- ► When taking apart a Mac mini, you must be very sure of how cables are routed before removing any parts.

- ► Airflow and heat transfer are important considerations with the Mac mini.

16

Reference Files Mac mini Service Source manual (mac_mini_early_late_06.pdf)

Time This lesson takes approximately 1 hour to complete.

Goals Given a Mac mini, locate service procedures, symptom charts, and service issues

Given a problem scenario, return a Mac mini to normal operation using the Apple General Troubleshooting Flowchart and Service Manual

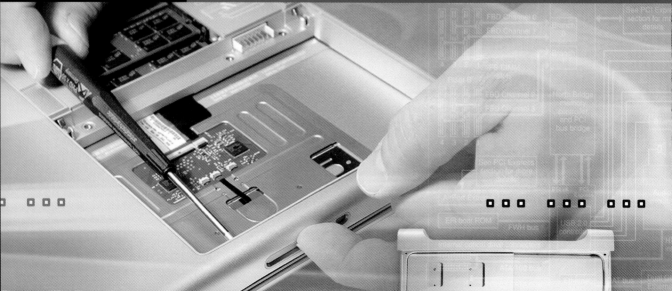

Troubleshooting a Mac mini

In this lesson, you'll find overview information about general trouble-shooting procedures as well as detailed symptom charts, both of which should help you troubleshoot and repair Mac mini computers. Being familiar with some of the basic operations can help you recognize and resolve problems more easily.

It's important to follow the troubleshooting procedures in order; they are presented to address the simplest and least invasive cures first, moving on to more radical solutions only when needed. It's also important to remember that there are slight differences between the models presented here and other models in the same family. When you're working with a particular model, always refer to the most specific resource material available before proceeding.

In Lesson 15, "Taking Apart a Mac mini," we explored the replacement of a faulty logic board. In this lesson consider the troubleshooting steps you would pursue to resolve a Mac mini that won't turn on, has no startup chime, no drive or fan sound, and maybe no power-on LED, as you learn about troubleshooting a Mac mini (Early 2006). Open the Service Manual on this book's companion website (www.peachpit. com/ats.deskport3) and continue with this lesson.

Let's first review some background information that will help in many trouble-shooting situations.

Status LED

The Mac mini has a LED power light located on the front of the computer in the lower-right corner, below the optical drive slot. Depending on the computer's status, the LED displays a steady light, no light, or pulsing light.

If the Mac mini is turned off, the LED is off, too. The LED displays a steady white light during startup, normal operation, and when the display is in sleep mode. If the Mac mini itself is in sleep mode, the LED pulses.

Resetting PRAM and NVRAM

Resetting parameter RAM (PRAM) is a possible cure for several symptoms.

1   Shut down the computer.

2   Turn on the computer.

3   Before the gray screen appears, you must simultaneously press and hold all four of these keys: Command, Option, P, and R.

4   Hold down the keys until the computer restarts and you hear the startup chime for the second time.

5   Release the keys.

    The computer's PRAM and the NVRAM are reset to the default values. On some models, the clock settings may be reset to a default date.

Resetting the SMC

The System Management Controller (SMC) is an integrated circuit (computer chip) typically found on the logic board of Macintosh computers. As its name implies, the SMC is responsible for managing all aspects of the computer's power. If the computer is experiencing any power issue, resetting the SMC may resolve it.

The SMC controls several functions, including the following:

▶   Telling the computer when to turn on, turn off, sleep, wake, idle, and so on

▶   Handling system resets from various commands

▶   Controlling the fans

Resetting the SMC can resolve some computer issues, such as the following:

▶   Not starting up

▶   Not displaying video

▶   Sleep issues

▶   Fan noise issues

Resetting the SMC will not resolve issues in which your computer is unresponsive—in these situations, restarting your computer will generally suffice.

Before you reset the SMC, try restarting the computer instead, which may resolve the issue. If the computer has stopped responding, try these steps, in order, until the computer responds:

1   Force quit (Command-Option-Escape).

2   Restart (Command-Control-Power).

3   Force shut down (press the power button for 10 seconds).

If none of these steps resolves the situation, reset the SMC. Users can reset the SMC with the top housing on without voiding the warranty; Apple Authorized Service Providers (AASPs) also have the option of resetting the SMC with the top housing off.

> **MORE INFO** ▶ Refer to Apple Knowledge Base document 303446, "Intel-based iMac, Intel-based Mac mini: How to reset the System Management Controller."

Resetting the SMC with the Top Housing On

1   Turn off the computer by choosing Shut Down from the Apple menu, or by holding the power button until the computer turns off.

2   Unplug all cables from the computer, including the power cord.

3   Wait 15 seconds.

4   Plug the power cord back in, making sure the power button is not being pressed at the same time. Reconnect the keyboard and mouse to the computer.

5   Press the power button on the back to start up the computer.

> **NOTE** ▶ This procedure does not reset the computer's PRAM.

If these steps do not resolve the situation, reset the SMC with the top housing off as instructed in the following section.

Resetting the SMC with the Top Housing Removed

AASPs can also reset the SMC by directly pressing the SMC reset switch located on the logic board. Follow these steps to access the SMC reset switch on the logic board:

1   Unplug all cables from the computer, including the power cable.

Resetting the SMC   357

2   Remove the top housing.

3   If necessary, remove the internal frame to access the battery.

4   Measure the voltage of the battery in the battery holder.

The battery should measure +2.6 V to +3.0 V. If the battery voltage is good, proceed to step 5. If the battery does not have minimum voltage, replace the battery, wait 10 seconds, and then proceed to step 5.

5   Using a nylon probe tool, press the SMC switch on the logic board once.

Do not press the SMC reset button a second time—it could crash the SMC chip.

NOTE ▶ This procedure does not reset the computer's PRAM.

SMC reset switch (circled in blue)

Symptom Charts

The symptom charts included in this lesson will help you diagnose specific symptoms and follow the guidelines set forth in the Apple General Trouble-shooting Flowchart. Because cures are listed on the charts in the order of most likely solution to least likely, try the cures in the order presented. Verify whether or not the product continues to exhibit the symptom. If the symptom persists, try the next cure. If a cure instructs you to replace a module, and the symptom persists with the new module, reinstall the original module before you proceed to the next cure.

In Lesson 15 we explored the replacement of a faulty logic board. In this lesson, consider the troubleshooting steps you would pursue to resolve a Mac mini that won't turn on, has no startup chime, has no drive or fan sound, and maybe an unlit power-on LED, as you learn about troubleshooting a Mac mini (Early 2006). Open the Service Source Manual on the companion web-site and continue with this lesson.

> **NOTE** ▶ These symptom charts are taken from the service manual that was current at the time of publication and which appears on the compan-ion website. AASPs should download and refer to the latest service manual from AppleCare Service Source before servicing any Apple product.

No Power

The Mac mini won't turn on, no startup chime, no drive or fan sound, power LED may be unlit

In the previous lesson, you replaced the logic board in a computer exhibiting these symptoms. You can imagine following these troubleshooting steps to arrive at that conclusion.

1   Make sure that the power cord is plugged into a working wall outlet and that it's properly connected to the power adapter.

TIP To check if the wall socket is working, plug in a lamp or other electrical device.

2   Make sure that the power adapter is properly connected to the power port on the back of the computer.

3   Disconnect all accessories that are plugged into the computer, such as a printer, hub, or iPod.

4   Reset the SMC.

5   Try plugging a different power cord into the computer. If the computer starts up, replace the old power cord.

6   Try connecting a different power adapter to the computer (if you have a working one available). If the computer starts up, replace the old power adapter.

7   Replace the logic board.

Our scenario would end here, in the replacement of the logic board that was demonstrated in the preceding lesson. Let's continue on to learn about trouble-shooting other symptoms.

No Video

Computer starts up, but no video on display, there is a startup chime, fans and drive spin up, and the power LED is on

1   Make sure that the display is turned on and has power. Make sure that the display's power cord is plugged into a working wall outlet, and that it's properly connected to the power adapter.

2 Check that all video cable connections to the computer video port and to the display are properly connected.

3 Examine the pins on the video cable connector to make sure they are not bent or damaged in any way.

4 Connect a known-good display (if you have an extra one available). If you see no video after doing so, proceed to the next symptom, "No video on the display." If you do not see video, go on to step 5.

5 Reset the computer's NVRAM. (Refer to the "Resetting PRAM and NVRAM" section earlier in this lesson.)

6 Reset the computer's SMC.

7 Reseat the Mac mini's memory.

8 Remove the DIMM and try replacing it with a known-good DIMM to test.

9 Reset the SMC on the logic board.

10 Replace the logic board.

No Video: Other displays work with the Mac mini, but the display shows a black screen or "Out of Range" message

1 Verify that the display used in testing is known-good and is supported by this computer. Refer to Knowledge Base document 300652, "Mac mini: Compatible Apple Displays."

2 If your display is not listed in the document cited above, try using the steps in Knowledge Base document 301345, "Mac mini: Troubleshooting 'Out of Range' alert message."

3 If you still have no video on your display when connected to a Mac mini, try another display of the same type (either same model or same connector and native resolution).

4 Contact Tech Assist through AppleCare Service Source if you require further assistance.

Display Shows Ghosting (Signal Reflection)

1 Verify that the display used in testing is known-good and is supported by this computer.

2 Verify that the cables are correctly installed and firmly seated.

3 Connect a known-good display (if you have an extra one available). If it solves the issue, replace your display.

4 Try a known-good DVI to VGA adapter.

5 Replace the adapter cable.

6 Replace the logic board.

Sharp image   Ghosting

AirPort Extreme Issues

Card Not Recognized

If the Mac mini does not recognize an AirPort Extreme Card, the card may be seated incorrectly or may be inoperable.

1 Reseat the AirPort Extreme Card, making sure it is connected securely into the AirPort slot on the logic board.

Reseat the AirPort Extreme Card as shown.

2 Make sure the AirPort cable is connected to the AirPort card.

3 Reassemble the computer and test. If the AirPort Extreme Card is still not recognized, test with a known-good AirPort Extreme Card. If the known-good card is recognized, replace the AirPort Extreme Card.

4 If a known-good AirPort Extreme Card is still not recognized, replace the logic board and test the computer again.

Poor AirPort Reception: Mac mini is able to connect to the network, but the signal strength is poor

1   Don't put anything on top of your Mac mini, including another Mac mini. Doing so could hamper the signal strength, because the antennas are located in the top of the computer.

2   If the Mac mini is still experiencing poor AirPort reception, refer to Knowledge Base document 58543, "AirPort: Potential sources of interference."

3   Remove the top housing and test the reception. If the reception is good with the top housing removed, check to make sure that the antenna cable and receptors are not damaged or hindered when installing the top housing.

4   Check that the AirPort antenna is securely connected to the AirPort Extreme Card.

5   If a known-good AirPort antenna is still not recognized, replace the AirPort and Bluetooth antennas and test the computer again.

6   Try a known-good AirPort Extreme Card.

7   Replace the AirPort Extreme Card.

8   Replace the logic board.

NOTE ▶ If you replace the AirPort antenna, you must replace the Bluetooth antenna at the same time, and vice versa. The AirPort and Bluetooth antennas *must* be installed by pairing under the same manufacturer (for example, Tyco's Airport antenna with Tyco's Bluetooth antenna). Do not mix different vendors' antennas, or they may interfere with each other.

Can't Connect to the Internet Over AirPort

In this situation, the Mac mini recognizes that an AirPort Extreme Card is installed, but it cannot connect to the Internet over AirPort.

1   Refer to Knowledge Base document 106858, "AirPort troubleshooting guide."

2   If the Knowledge Base document does not resolve the issue, reseat and replace the AirPort antenna.

3   Make sure that the AirPort antenna is seated correctly to the AirPort Extreme Card. Refer to Knowledge Base document 108039, "Properly attaching the antenna on an AirPort Extreme Card."

The boxy part of the connector should be almost flush with the card.

4   Make sure that the AirPort antenna is not damaged or warped on the receiver end of the cable. Make sure that this end is properly seated to the internal frame.

5   Replace the AirPort antenna and test the connection.

6   If the issue persists, replace the AirPort Extreme Card.

Bluetooth issues

The Mac mini does not recognize the Bluetooth board

If the Mac mini does not recognize Bluetooth, the board may not be seated correctly or is inoperable.

1   Reseat the Bluetooth board (located near the AirPort antenna).

Bluetooth card

2 Check that the Bluetooth cable is securely connected to both the Bluetooth board and the interconnect board.

3 Check that the Bluetooth antenna is securely connected to the Bluetooth board.

Bluetooth antenna

4 Reassemble the computer and test. If the Bluetooth board is still not recognized, test with a known-good Bluetooth board. If the known-good board is recognized, replace the Bluetooth board.

5 Replace the logic board.

The Mac mini recognizes the Bluetooth board but cannot pair with wireless devices
If the Mac mini recognizes the Bluetooth board, but you are unable to pair your Apple Wireless Keyboard and Wireless Apple Mouse, try the steps outlined in Knowledge Base document 86496, "Apple Wireless Keyboard and Mouse: Troubleshooting Connection Issues."

1 Make sure that the Bluetooth antenna is connected firmly to the Bluetooth board.

2 With the top housing removed, make sure that the Bluetooth antenna is not damaged or warped on the receiver end of the cable. Make sure that this end is seated properly to the internal frame of the Mac mini.

3   Check to make sure that the antenna cable and receptors are not damaged or hindered when installing the top housing.

4   Replace the Bluetooth antenna and test the computer.

5   If the issue persists, replace the Bluetooth board.

6   Replace the cable connecting the Bluetooth and interconnect boards.

7   Replace the interconnect board.

8   Replace the logic board.

IR Remote

Remote won't communicate with system applications such as iTunes or iPhoto, or with the optical drive.

Make sure of the following when using the Apple Remote:

▶   You are within 30 feet of the front of the computer.

▶   You have an unobstructed line-of-sight to the front of the computer.

▶   You are pointing the lens end of the Apple Remote directly at the front of the computer.

▶   The computer is powered on and awake.

▶   The "Disable remote control infrared receiver" checkbox in the Security pane of System Preferences is not selected.

▶   Make sure the active application works with Apple Remote. Apple Remote uses Front Row, and from Front Row it can access DVD Player, iPhoto, iTunes, and QuickTime Player.

▶   Make sure this particular remote is paired with the computer. Access Security preferences and select "Unpair" if available. Close Security preferences and re-pair the Apple Remote with the computer.

NOTE ▶ For additional information on the Apple Remote, consult Knowledge Base document 302545, "Pairing your Apple Remote with your computer."

The following steps will help troubleshoot the issue.

1   Use a digital camera to test your Apple Remote.

If you have a digital camera or DV camera with an LCD screen, you can use it to see if your Apple Remote is emitting a signal. Infrared beams are invisible to the human eye, but most digital cameras and video cameras use Charged-Coupled Device (CCD) chips or image sensors that are sensitive to infrared light.

To use a camera to test your Apple Remote, follow these steps:

▶   Turn on your digital camera or DV camera and remove any lens cover.

▶   Point your Apple Remote toward the camera lens.

▶   Press and hold the Menu button on the remote while looking at your camera's LCD screen.

▶   If you see a faint blinking light coming from the Apple Remote in the camera's LCD, then the remote is working properly.

▶   If you don't see any blinking light in the camera's LCD, replace the battery in your Apple Remote and then test it again with your computer.

2   Does the IR Remote now communicate with an active application that works with Apple Remote?

Yes: IR Remote is functioning correctly.

No: Replace Apple Remote.

IR (Infrared) Sensor/Receiver

Supported applications do not respond to input from the remote control

1   Check the IR Remote with supported applications to verify that Apple Remote is functioning correctly. Do supported applications now respond to input from the IR Remote? If not, continue to the next step.

MORE INFO ▶ For additional information on the Apple Remote, consult Knowledge Base documents 302504, "About the Apple Remote Control," 303377, "Mac mini (Early 2006): About the IR Sensor," and 302543, "How to replace the Apple Remote battery."

2   Verify that the IR Sensor can be seen in System Profiler. Open System Profiler and click on the USB section. You should see the following listed:

```
IR Receiver:

  Version:           0.58
  Bus Power (mA):    100
  Speed:             Up to 12 Mb/sec
  Manufacturer:      Apple Computer, Inc.
  Product ID:        0x8240
  Vendor ID:         0x05ac  (Apple Computer, Inc.)
```

Do you see the IR Receiver listed under the USB section of System Profiler?

Yes: Go on to step 3.

No: Replace the IR board and retest. Refer to the IR Board procedure in Take Apart.

Do supported applications now respond to input from the IR remote?

Yes: Problem resolved.

No: Replace the IR board and retest. Refer to the IR Board procedure in Take Apart. If the issue persists after replacing these parts, replace the logic board.

3   Access System Preferences and click Security. In the Security pane, check the following:

▶ Make sure the "Disable remote control infrared receiver" checkbox is not selected.

▶ If Unpair is available in Security preferences, another Apple Remote may be paired to the computer (pairing allows only one Apple Remote to control the computer). To delete a pairing between the remote and the Mac mini, click Unpair. (You may have to enter an administrator password to make changes in Security preferences.)

After making sure these features are disabled, does the Apple Remote control the machine now?

Yes: Problem resolved.

No: Replace the IR board and retest. Refer to the IR Board procedure in Take Apart.

Battery

If the computer won't keep date and time, or if the date and time reset when the computer is powered off or unplugged, the problem may be the battery.

1 Make sure the electrical outlet works by plugging in a different device, or plug the computer into a different outlet.

2 Try a known-good power cord.

3 Check the connection of the power cord on both ends. Make sure that the plug is securely plugged into both the electrical outlet and the back of the computer.

4 Disconnect the keyboard, mouse, and all other peripherals such as speakers.

5 Remove the top housing and, if necessary, remove the internal frame.

6 Measure the voltage of the battery in the battery holder.

The battery should measure +2.6 V to +3.0 V. If the battery voltage is good, go on to step 7. If the battery does not have minimum voltage, replace the battery, wait 10 seconds, then go on to the next step.

7 Using a nylon probe tool, press the SMC switch on the logic board once.

Do not press the SMC reset button a second time—it could crash the SMC chip.

8 If the issue continues after resetting the SMC, replace the logic board.

Error Beeps

The computer automatically performs a power-on self test (POST) when it is turned on after being fully shut down (not a restart). This section describes what to do if you hear beeps during startup.

Computer Beeps at Startup

1 Check that the memory DIMM is compliant.

2 Reseat the memory into the slot.

3 Replace the memory.

4 Replace the logic board.

NOTE ▶ The maximum amount of SDRAM supported by the Mac mini (Early/Late 2006) is 2 GB (one 1 GB SO-DIMM in each slot) with the following specifications: PC2-5300, unbuffered, nonparity, 200-pin, 667 MHz DDR2 SDRAM.

Optical Drive

Optical Drive Does Not Accept Discs (Mechanical Failure)

1 Verify the disc is not warped.

2 Try another known-good disc.

3 Reseat the optical drive to the interconnect board.

4 Replace the optical drive.

5 Replace the interconnect board.

6 Replace the logic board.

Disc Icon Does Not Show Up on the Desktop, or a Dialog Appears to Initialize the Disc

1 Verify that you are using the correct type of disc for the type of drive (a CD-ROM or CD-RW drive reads CD discs only; a DVD-ROM or Combo drive reads CD or DVD discs).

2 Try cleaning the disc. If it is dirty or scratched, it may not mount.

3 Try a known-good disc.

4 Reseat the optical drive to the interconnect board.

5 Replace the optical drive.

6 Replace the interconnect board.

7 Replace the logic board.

Optical Drive Does Not Eject the Disc

1 Check the disc. Nonstandard discs should not be used with the Mac mini. Refer to Knowledge Base document 58641, "Using nonstandard discs in optical drives."

2 Verify the disc is not in use by quitting any applications that may be using it.

3 Press and hold the Media Eject key at the upper-right corner of Apple keyboard. If that does not work, hold down the Function (fn) key and the Media Eject key.

4 Drag the disc icon to the Trash or select it and press Command-E.

5 Choose Restart from the Apple menu, then immediately hold down the mouse button to eject the disc.

6 Refer to Take Apart to remove the stuck disc and replace the optical drive.

MORE INFO ▶ For additional information, refer to Knowledge Base document 106752, "Macintosh: How to Eject a Disc When Other Options Do Not Work."

Hard Drive

Hard Drive Fails to Boot to the Desktop

1 Boot from the Mac mini Mac OS X Install DVD and see if the hard drive is available in the installer.

2 Run Apple Hardware Test (AHT), located on the install DVD.

3 Run Disk Utility, and repair any directory and permissions issues.

4 Verify that the hard drive is connected firmly to the interconnect board.

5 Try a known-good hard drive.

6 Back up the original hard drive, erase it, then restore from backup or reinstall Mac OS and applications from original discs.

7 Try a known-good interconnect board.

8 Replace the hard drive.

9 Replace the interconnect board.

10 Replace the logic board.

Internal Hard Drive Does Not Spin

1 Disconnect any connected peripherals.

2 Try a known-good power outlet.

3 Try a known-good power cord.

4 Boot from the Mac mini Mac OS X Install DVD and see if the hard drive is available in the installer.

5 Run AHT, located on the install DVD.

6 Run Disk Utility, and repair any directory and permissions issues.

7 Verify that the hard drive is connected to the interconnect board.

8 Try a known-good hard drive.

9 Back up the original hard drive, erase it, then restore from backup or reinstall Mac OS and applications from original discs.

10 Try a known-good interconnect board.

11 Replace the hard drive.

12 Replace the interconnect board.

13 Replace the logic board.

System Hangs During Normal Startup Process

1   Boot from the Mac mini Mac OS X Install DVD and see if the hard drive is available in the installer.

2   Run Apple Hardware Test (AHT), located on the install DVD.

3   Run Disk Utility, and repair any directory and permissions issues.

4   Verify that the hard drive is connected to the interconnect board.

5   Try a known-good hard drive.

6   Back up the original hard drive, erase it, then restore from backup or reinstall Mac OS and applications from original discs.

7   Try a known-good interconnect board.

8   Replace the hard drive.

9   Replace the interconnect board.

10 Replace the logic board.

Flashing Question Mark Appears on the Screen

Flashing question mark

1   Boot from the Mac mini Mac OS X Install DVD and see if the hard drive is available in the installer.

2   Run AHT, located on the install DVD.

3   Run Disk Utility, and repair any directory and permissions issues.

4   Verify that the hard drive is connected to the interconnect board.

5   Try a known-good hard drive.

6   Try a known-good interconnect board.

7   Replace the hard drive.

8   Replace the interconnect board.

9   Replace the logic board.

Keyboard

No Response from Any Key on the USB Keyboard

1   Check that the mouse and keyboard are compliant with the USB specification.

    The Mac mini has two USB 2.0 ports, which can be used with any USB 1.1 or USB 2.0 keyboard and mouse.

2   Remove any connected peripherals.

3   Boot from the Mac mini Mac OS X Install DVD to verify that it is not a software problem.

4   Disconnect the keyboard connector and inspect connectors.

5 Replace the keyboard.

6 Replace the logic board.

No Response from the Wireless Keyboard

1 Run System Profiler to determine if Bluetooth is present.

2 Try a known-good wireless keyboard.

3 Replace the batteries in the wireless keyboard.

4 Replace the keyboard.

5 Remove the top housing.

6 Check for kinks in the Bluetooth antenna cable. Test the reception before replacing the top housing.

7 If the reception goes away when the top housing is replaced, remove the top housing and reseat the Bluetooth antenna on the internal frame. Test the reception again.

8 Make sure that the Bluetooth antenna is connected firmly to the Bluetooth board.

9 Make sure that the Bluetooth antenna is not damaged or warped on the receiver end of the cable. Make sure that the antenna is seated properly to the internal frame of the Mac mini.

10 Replace the Bluetooth antenna and test the computer.

11 If the issue persists, replace the Bluetooth board.

12 Replace the logic board.

Ports

FireWire or USB Port Is Not Recognizing Devices

1 Choose Shut Down from the Apple menu, then press the power button to restart the computer.

2 Choose Software Update from the Apple menu to verify that the latest software is installed.

3 Run System Profiler to verify that the computer recognizes the bus.

4 For USB, test the port with a compliant keyboard or mouse.

5 For FireWire, test the port by connecting another computer in FireWire Target Disk Mode.

> **MORE INFO** ▶ Refer to Knowledge Base document 58583, "How to Use FireWire target disk mode."

6 Verify that drivers are installed properly for third-party hardware, if needed.

7 Try a different cable.

8 Try a known-good device.

9 If the device is self-powered, make sure that the power supply is connected and the device's LED indicates that it is getting power.

10 Replace the logic board.

Sound

Distorted Sound from Speakers

1   Check the balance setting in the Output pane of Sound preferences.

2   Check to see if the sound is the same from the internal speaker as compared to the external speakers.

3   Check that speakers are inserted correctly, and check cables for damage.

4   Compare the same sound with two different computers to make sure that sound is actually distorted.

5   Remove the top housing and internal frame.

6   Check that the speaker is seated correctly and screwed to the internal frame.

7   Check for speaker cable damage and that the cable is connected securely to the interconnect board.

8   Replace the speaker.

9   Replace the interconnect board.

10 Replace the logic board.

No Sound from Speakers

1   Check the balance setting in the Output pane of Sound preferences.

2   Check to see if the sound is the same from the internal speaker as compared to the external speakers.

3   Verify that no external speakers or headphones are plugged in.

4   Choose Restart from the Apple menu.

5   Reset NVRAM. (Press the power button, then hold down the Option-Command-P-R keys until you hear the startup chime at least one additional time after the initial startup chime.)

6   Remove the top housing and internal frame.

7   Check that the speaker is seated correctly and screwed to the internal frame.

8   Check for speaker cable damage and that the cable is securely connected to the interconnect board.

9   Replace the speaker.

10 Replace the interconnect board.

11 Replace the logic board.

Display

Display Is Dim But Computer Appears to Operate Correctly

1   Check that the display is compatible with the Mac mini. Refer to Knowledge Base document 300652, "Mac mini: compatible Apple displays."

2   Check the brightness level in Display preferences.

3   Make sure that the display is turned on and has power. Make sure that the display's power cord is plugged into a working wall outlet, and that it's properly connected to the power adapter. (To check if the wall socket is working, plug in a known-good lamp or other electrical device.)

4 Check that all video cable connections to the computer video port and to the display are connected properly.

5 Examine the pins on the video cable connector to make sure they are not bent or damaged in any way.

6 Connect a known-good display (if you have an extra one available). If you see video after doing so, replace the old display.

7 If the known-good display shows the same issue, replace the logic board.

Scrambled or Distorted Video

1 Check that the display is compatible with the Mac mini. Refer to Knowledge Base document 300652, "Mac mini: compatible Apple displays."

2 Check connections on the back of the Mac mini.

3 Check that you are using the correct adapter (if necessary).

4 Try a known-good display. If the known-good display solves the issue, replace the old display.

5 If the known-good display shows the same issue, replace the logic board.

Fan

Fan Failure

1 Remove the top housing and the internal frame.

2 Check the fan cable connection to the interconnect board, and check the cable for damage.

3 Check that the hard drive sensor cable is connected to the logic board.

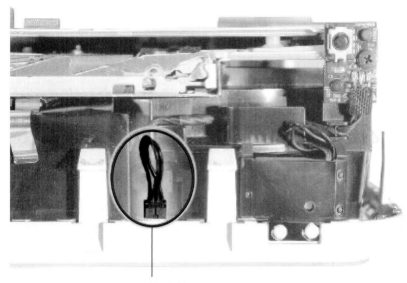

Hard drive sensor cable

4 Replace the fan.

5 Replace the interconnect board.

6 Replace the logic board.

Lesson Review

1. How many status LEDs are present on the Mac mini?

    a. One

    b. Two

    c. Three

2. True or false: The LED pulses when the Mac mini computer's display is in sleep mode.

3. True or false: You can reset the Mac mini computer's SMC with the top housing either on or off.

4. True or false: Resetting the Mac mini computer's SMC also resets PRAM.

5. What is the first thing to check if the Mac mini refuses to turn on?

    a. All accessories are unplugged from the Mac mini.

    b. The power adapter connector on the Mac mini is not bent.

    c. The power cord is plugged into a working wall outlet.

6. When you hear an error beep upon startup, what is the usual cause?

    a. Power issue

    b. Memory issue

    c. Hard drive failure

Answer Key

1. a; 2. False, the LED pulses when the computer is asleep and is steady when only the display is asleep; 3. True; 4. False; 5. c; 6. b

17

Time   This lesson takes approximately 1 hour to complete.

Goal   Describe the Mac Pro and the Mac Pro build-to-order options

About Mac Pro

Mac Pro computers are similar to the preceding Power Mac G5 models in form. However, there are major internal changes, including the use of dual-core Xeon processors from Intel.

Hardware features include the following:

► Two dual-core Intel Xeon processors in all Mac Pro models: This effectively makes them quad-processor computers.

► FB-DIMM DDR2 system memory supporting ECC memory and up to 16 GB of RAM: The system has more room to grow when using high-performance computing applications.

► Four internal HDDs: The Mac Pro supports up to four internal hard disk drives.

► Two optical drives: The Mac Pro has support for two optical drives.

The following chart outlines the major technical specifications of the Mac Pro standard model and the Mac Pro build-to-order options. Use this chart to distinguish between models and to determine the capabilities of each.

Mac Pro (August 2006)

	Mac Pro 2x2.66 GHz Dual Core Standard Configuration	**Build-to-Order Options**
Introduced	August 2006	August 2006
Mac OS (minimum)	Mac OS X 10.4	Mac OS X 10.4
Display		Optional 20/23/30-inch Apple Cinema Display HD
Technical specifications	http://support.apple.com/specs/macpro/Mac_Pro.html	
Processor	2x 2.66 GHz dual-core Intel Xeon	2x 2.0 GHz, 2.66 GHz, or 3.0 GHz dual-core Intel Xeon
Cache	4 MB shared L2 cache per processor	

	Mac Pro 2x2.66 GHz Dual Core Standard Configuration	Build-to-Order Options
Memory	1 GB DDR2 Fully-buffered DIMM ECC	Up to 16 GB
Hard disk	250 GB Serial ATA	Up to 2 TB of internal storage
Hard drive bays	4 3.5-inch hard drive bays (3 open)	
Optical drive	16x SuperDrive	2 16x SuperDrives
Graphics	NVIDIA GeForce 7300 GT w/256MB of GDDR2 SDRAM/ dual-display support ATI Radeon X1900 XT Dual DVI	NVIDIA Quadro FX 4500 (G70), Dual DVI
Expansion	5 USB 2.0 ports 2 FireWire 400 ports 2 FireWire 800 ports 2 10/100/1000 Base-T Ethernet ports	AirPort Extreme Bluetooth 2.0 External Apple USB modem

Lesson Review

1. Name as many of the Mac Pro model's new port layout and features as you can, then use the answer key to fill in any you may have missed.

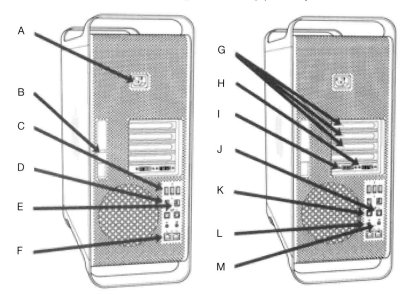

2. What is the Mac Pro computer's maximum internal hard disk space?

    a.   500 GB

    b.   1 TB

    c.   2 TB

3. What display is bundled with the MacPro?

    a.   23-inch Apple Cinema Display HD

    b.   30-inch Apple Cinema Display HD

    c.   No display is bundled with the product. Displays are sold separately.

4. The two dual-core Intel Xeon processors in the Mac Pro effectively make it:

    a.   A quad-processor computer

    b.   Apple's showcase product

    c.   Xserve compatible

Answer Key

1. A. Power socket

   B. Locking latch

   C. USB 2.0 ports (3)

   D. FireWire 400 port

   E. FireWire 800 port

   F. Gigabit Ethernet ports (2)

   G. PCI Express expansion slots (3)

   H. DVI display port 1

   I. DVI display port 2

   J. Optical digital audio-out port

   K. Optical digital audio-in port

   L. Audio line-in port

   M. Audio line-out port

2. c; 3. c; 4. a

18

Lesson **18**

Upgrading a Mac Pro

The Mac Pro is similar to its predecessor, the Power Mac G5, in its external appearance. Both designs incorporate the convenience of easy expansion and accessibility. Components and expansion options are easily reached through the removal of a side access panel.

However, the Mac Pro features many new hardware enhancements that are improvements over the Power Mac G5, including two dual-core Intel processors, higher performance memory, capacity for four internal drives in easy-to-install drive carriers, and space for two optical drives.

This lesson explains how to upgrade the Mac Pro. We'll explore the installation of additional random-access memory (RAM) to increase performance, an additional hard drive to increase storage capacity, and the installation of a Peripheral Component Interconnect (PCI) Express card to expand its capabilities.

Required Tools and Equipment

To complete this lesson, you need the following:

▶ Electrostatic discharge (ESD) wrist strap and mat

▶ Phillips #1 screwdriver

▶ 667 MHz fully buffered dual inline memory modules (FB-DIMMs) (see specifications)

▶ PCI Express card

▶ Serial ATA hard drive

▶ Apple Hardware Test (AHT)

Before You Do Anything

Follow the normal antistatic procedures discussed in Lesson 4, "Safe Working Procedures and General Maintenance." It is vital that you follow these instructions and that you do so in the order presented. Disconnecting some peripherals while in use can damage them or the computer, and stray electrostatic discharges (from something even as innocent as a dry day) can do permanent harm to the computer.

Opening a Mac Pro

Prior to opening the Mac Pro, open the service manual on this book's companion website, www.peachpit.com/ats.deskport3, and familiarize yourself with its precautions and procedures. Always use the latest service manual or user's guide if actually performing an upgrade.

Whenever opening a Mac Pro, follow these simple procedures:

1 Shut down the computer.

> **WARNING** ▶ Always shut down the computer before opening it to avoid damaging its internal components or the components you are installing. Do not open the computer or attempt to install items inside it while it is on.

2   Wait 5 to 10 minutes to allow the computer's internal components to cool down.

   WARNING ▶ After you shut down the system, the internal components can be very hot. You must let the computer cool down before continuing.

3   Touch the metal on the outside of the computer to discharge any static electricity from your body.

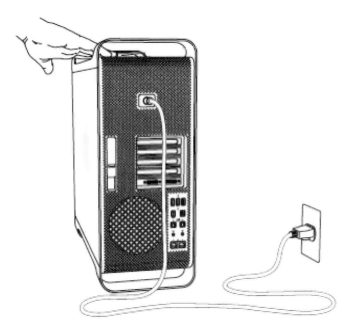

   NOTE ▶ Always discharge static before you touch any parts or install any components inside the computer. To avoid generating static electricity, do not walk around the room until you have finished working and closed the computer. For additional information on ESD, visit http://en.wikipedia.org/wiki/Electrostatic_discharge.

4   Unplug all external cables and peripherals from the computer.

5 Unplug the power cord from the outlet and computer.

WARNING ▶ To avoid damaging the computer's internal components or the components you want to install, always unplug the computer before attempting any upgrade procedure.

6 Put on your ESD wrist strap.

7 Hold the side access panel and lift the latch on the back of the computer.

WARNING ▶ The edges of the access panel and the enclosure can be sharp. Be very careful when handling them.

8 Remove the access panel and place it on a flat surface covered by a soft, clean cloth.

NOTE ▸ Make sure the latch is in the up position before you replace the access panel. If the latch is down, the access panel will not seat correctly in the enclosure.

Installing RAM

The Mac Pro has two memory riser cards with a total of eight memory slots. On each card, the slots are arranged as two banks of two slots each. The computer comes with a minimum of 1 GB of memory, installed as a pair of 512 MB FB-DIMMs in two of the DIMM slots. Additional DIMMs can be installed in the open DIMM slots.

DIMMs must be installed in equal-sized pairs from the same vendor and fit these specifications:

▸ 667 MHz FB-DIMMS

▸ 72-bit–wide 240-pin modules

▸ Maximum 36 devices per DIMM

▸ Error-correcting code (ECC)

NOTE ▸ When purchasing DIMMs for use in Mac computers, make sure that the memory vendor conforms to the Joint Electron Device Engineering Council (JEDEC) specification. Check with the memory vendor to ensure that the DIMMs support the correct timing modes and that the Serial Presence Detect (SPD) feature has been programmed properly, as described in the JEDEC specification.

Install DIMMs in the sequence illustrated by the numbers in the following image. DIMMs in one numbered pair do not need to match DIMMs in a different numbered pair.

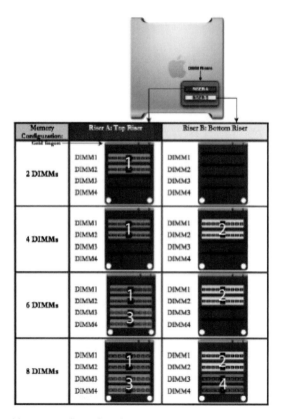

Memory configuration chart

1 Before you begin, lay the open computer on its side with the access side facing up.

2   Holding the memory riser card by the two finger holes, pull it out of the memory cage and place the card on the ESD mat.

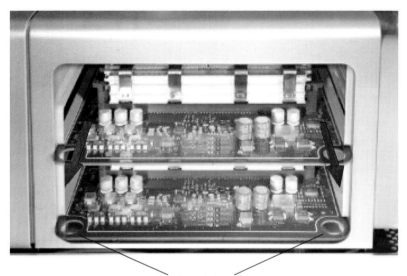

Finger holes

3   If you need to move a memory module or upgrade the module to a larger one, open the ejectors on the DIMM slot by pushing them out to the sides, and remove the DIMM from the riser card.

4   Repeat to remove the second DIMM, if needed. If you are simply adding additional DIMMs, no removal is required and you may proceed to step 5.

NOTE ▶ If you have one pair of DIMMs installed, they are usually in slots 1 and 2 on the top riser card.

5   Following the memory configuration chart, align the first FB-DIMM
    in the correct slot, making sure that the notches line up with the ribs
    inside the slot.

6   Push down on both ends of the FB-DIMM until the tabs are vertical and
    the ejectors snap into place. Repeat to install the second FB-DIMM. Don't
    touch the gold connectors.

NOTE ▶ FB-DIMMs carry heatsinks on both sides. Never attempt to remove the heatsinks. Doing so could damage the memory modules.

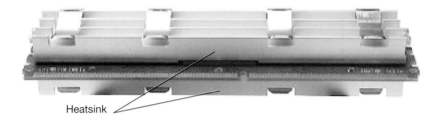

Heatsink

7   Repeat steps 2 through 6 to install additional memory as needed.

8   Replace the access panel, reconnect the power cord and remaining cables, and power on the computer.

9   After logging in, choose About This Mac from the Apple menu to verify that the computer recognizes the newly installed memory.

Installing a Hard Drive

The Mac Pro has room for six internal drives: two optical drives and four hard disk drives. In most configurations, a single hard disk drive occupies the first hard drive bay and an optical drive is located in the top optical drive bay.

You can add up to three additional Serial ATA (SATA) 3 Gbps hard disk drives to the empty hard drive bays. The drives must meet these specifications:

▶   Type: SATA 3 Gbps

▶   Width: 3.9 inches (102 mm)

▶   Depth: 5.7 inches (147 mm)

▶   Height: 1.0 inch

NOTE ▶ When you install ATA or optical drives, use the original Apple cables that came with the Macintosh.

The following installation process is extremely simple. It assumes you have already removed the Mac Pro computer's access panel and grounded yourself following the steps on the previous pages.

1   Make sure the latch on the back panel is up. When the latch is down, the drive and carriers are locked in the drive bays and cannot be removed.

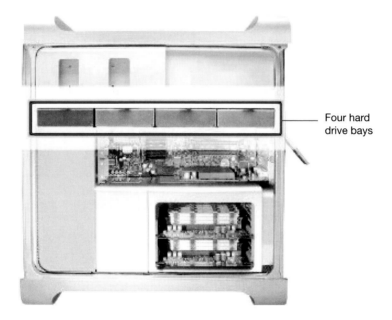

Four hard drive bays

NOTE ▶ If the printed circuit board (PCB) is exposed on the bottom of the hard drive, hold the drive by its sides. To avoid damaging the drive, take care not to touch the PCB during installation.

2   Pull the hard drive carrier out of the drive bay.

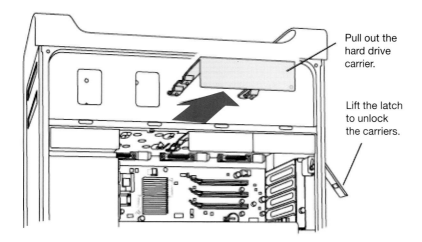

Pull out the
hard drive
carrier.

Lift the latch
to unlock
the carriers.

3   Use the four screws on the carrier to attach the hard disk drive to the carrier.

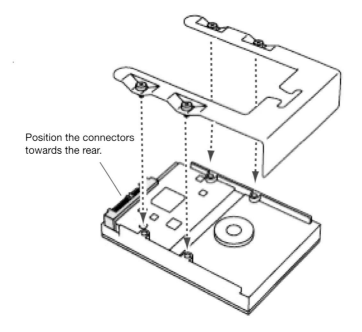

Position the connectors
towards the rear.

4 Lift the latch, and slide the carrier over the guides and into the drive bay, until it is seated in the bay and snaps into place.

5 Replace the side access panel and push the latch down to secure it.

6 Reconnect the power cord and remaining cables, and power on the computer.

7 After logging in, double-click Disk Utility (Applications/Utilities). If you have installed the additional hard drive successfully, Disk Utility will display information about the drive.

8 You may proceed to partition and format the drive, if it is new. If the drive will be a bootable drive, select GUID Partition Table in the partition options.

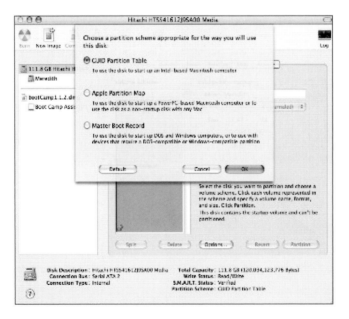

9 Run System Profiler and, in the left column under Hardware, select Serial-ATA. Hard disk drive details including capacity and available space will be available for review.

Adding a PCI Express Card

You can expand the capabilities of the Mac Pro by installing cards in the PCI Express slots. The Mac Pro has one double-wide PCI Express graphics slot and three PCI Express expansion slots.

The Mac Pro comes with a high-performance PCI Express graphics card in slot one. This card contains the graphics processor unit (GPU) and provides the computer's display ports.

> **NOTE** ▶ Graphics cards from previous Power Mac G5 models are not compatible with Mac Pro. In addition, Mac Pro graphics cards are not compatible with Power Mac G5 models.

Each PCI Express slot has a 3.3 V and a 12 V power rail. On the 3.3 V rail, each slot may use a maximum of 10 W. On the 12 V rail, each slot may use a maximum of 65 W, (not including auxiliary power through a booster cable), subject to the total wattage rules listed below.

When populating the four PCI Express slots, follow these total wattage rules:

Slots 1 and 2 (not including aux. power), max. slot power per slot	75 W
Slots 3 and 4 (not including aux. power), max. slot power per slot	40 W
All four slots (not including aux. power), max. total power	200 W
Max. aux. power per connector	75 W
Max. aux. power for both connectors	150 W
Max. total PCI Express power (slot power and aux. connector power)	300 W

> **NOTE** ▶ The combined maximum power consumption for all four PCI Express slots must not exceed 300 watts (slot and aux. power) or 200 watts total (slot power only). Before installing a card, check the manufacturer's specifications to make sure that it can operate in the Mac Pro, and obtain the wattage of the device.

Before we begin, we will assume you have already removed the Mac Pro computer's side access panel, grounded yourself following the steps on the previous pages, and taken any precautions noted.

1   Lay the Mac Pro on its side on a soft, clean cloth to avoid scratching the work surface and the computer itself.

2   Unscrew the two captive screws in the PCI bracket and remove the bracket.

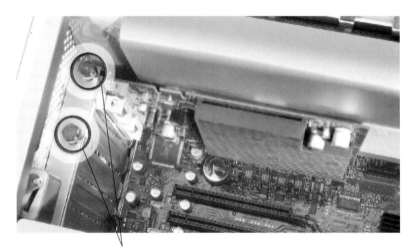

Captive screws

3   Remove the port access cover from the slot in which you plan to install the card. If you remove a card and don't install a replacement, place a port access cover over the empty slot to keep foreign objects out of the enclosure. An uncovered slot affects the airflow that cools the internal components and may cause damage.

TIP It may be easier to install a PCI card if you remove the hard disk drives and carriers, and remove adjacent cards. If you have a full-length card, install the end of the card in the card guide first, and then align the card with the PCI slot to finish installing it.

4   Remove the new PCI Express card from its static-proof bag and hold it by its corners. Don't touch the gold connector or the component on the card. If the card has a booster cable, connect it to the card.

5   Align the card's connector with the expansion slot and press the card into the slot.

6   Press the card gently but firmly until the connector is fully inserted. Press only on the bare areas of the card to avoid damaging the components.

7   Pull the card gently to see if it is properly connected. If it stays in place and its gold connectors are barely visible, the card is connected. If the card has a booster cable, connect it to the logic board.

> **NOTE** ▸ There are two logic board connectors for booster cables. Connect the booster cable for a card in PCI slot 1 to the connector that is closest to the heatsink cover. Connect the booster cable for a card in PCI slot 2 to the connector closest to the media shelf.

8   Replace the PCI bracket and tighten the captive screws to secure the card.

9   Replace the side access panel and push the latch down to secure it.

You will need to configure the PCI Express expansion slot for multiple cards. As indicated earlier, the Mac Pro features four PCI Express slots on the main logic board. PCI Express uses dedicated, unidirectional, point-to-point connections known as *lanes* to communicate with PCI Express devices. In PCI Express, these are known as x16 slots. PCI Express cards will work in slots that are at least as large as the card is. In other words, the x16 slots in the Mac Pro computer also support x1 and x4 cards. However, all four slots cannot simultaneously support four cards that use the same lane configuration.

> **NOTE** ▸ For additional information on PCI-E slots, refer to Apple Knowledge Base document 304122, "Mac Pro: About the PCI-E slots."

To configure the PCI Express expansion slots and lanes:

1   Open the Expansion Slot Utility, located in System/Library/Core Services.

The example below shows a x16 graphics card occupying the first slot, and the other slots are configured to support an x1 card in slot two and x4 cards in slots three and four. The example shows the other options available.

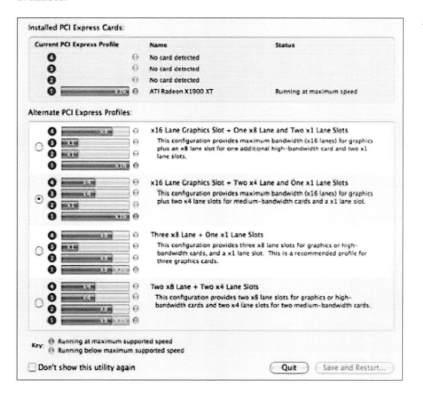

2   When you have picked the appropriate configuration of slots to support your PCI Express cards, click the Save and Restart button to implement the configuration.

3 Open System Profiler and select PCI Cards. The PCI Express card you installed should be visible.

If there is a problem with the installation, you may see a screen similar to the picture below.

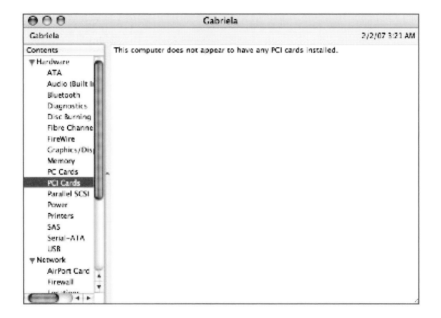

NOTE ▶ The PCI Express card manufacturer may include additional instructions to follow. These instructions may include additional software that needs to be installed for the card to be detected and function properly.

Lesson Review

1. True or false: There is no need to allow the Mac Pro to cool down before opening.

2. True or false: DIMMs must be installed in pairs of equal size from the same vendor.

3. For how many internal hard drives does the Mac Pro have the capacity?

   a. 2

   b. 4

   c. 6

4. True or false: The Mac Pro in its typical configuration has room for three additional SATA drives of the correct size.

5. True or false: Once the access panel on the Mac Pro has been removed, the hard drive carrier is free to be removed.

6. True or false: PCI Express power in the Mac Pro is rated for a total of 300 watts.

7. True or false: Leaving port access covers off on unused PCI Express slots on the Mac Pro is advised, as it adds additional ventilation to the unit.

8. The Mac Pro accepts only which types PCI Express cards?

   a. 1x and 4x

   b. Up to x16

   c. Any one type

Answer Key

1. False, the Mac Pro should cool down for 5 to 10 minutes before opening;
2. True; 3. b; 4. True; 5. False, the access latch must be raised to unlock the carriers; 6. True; 7. False, unused PCI Express slots should be covered to maintain proper ventilation and protect from foreign objects; 8. b

19

Reference Files   Mac Pro Service Source manual (macpro.pdf)

Mac Pro user's guide (Mac_Pro_User_Guide.pdf)

Time   This lesson takes approximately 30 minutes to complete.

Goals   Remove an optical drive and AirPort Extreme Card from a Mac Pro

Replace a battery

Taking Apart a Mac Pro

In the previous lesson, you learned how to install an additional memory module, a hard drive, and a PCI Express card in a Mac Pro.

In this lesson, you'll take apart all the components necessary to remove a faulty optical drive, and AirPort Extreme Card, as well as replace a battery on the Mac Pro.

This text accompanies the Apple Service Source manual, which demonstrates the procedures in full detail. The service manual is located on this book's companion website, www.peachpit.com/ats.deskport3. If you are an AASP, practice the Take Apart and reassembly at your own speed until you feel confident that you can replace any Mac Pro component with skill and efficiency. AASPs should download and refer to the latest service manual from AppleCare Service Source before servicing any Apple product. Non-AASPs should read the service manual and this text to become familiar with the procedures.

NOTE ▶ If anyone other than an AASP opens a Mac Pro for any reason, and any damage to the unit results, the repair of such damage will not be covered under the Apple warranty or the AppleCare Protection Plan.

Required Tools and Equipment

In addition to the standard electrostatic discharge (ESD) wrist strap and mat—which you should always use, following the guidelines discussed in Lesson 4, "Safe Working Procedures and General Maintenance"—you will need the following tools and equipment:

▶ Soft cloth

▶ Apple Hardware Test (AHT) diagnostic disc for the Mac Pro

▶ Magnetized jeweler's Phillips #1 screwdriver

▶ Flat-blade screwdriver

TIP ▶ Remember to eject any media from the drives. To eject the top drive, press the Eject key. To eject the bottom drive, press the Option and Eject keys. If for some reason you do not have a keyboard handy, you may also eject the top drive upon startup by holding down the mouse button.

Taking Apart a Mac Pro

Normally you will find that only one part is required per repair. For this scenario, you will replace three components to enhance your training. Assume the lead technician has already performed the required troubleshooting and determined the optical drive, AirPort Extreme Card, and battery need replacement. Let's begin by performing some preliminary steps.

1 Shut down the computer.

Always shut down the computer before opening it to avoid damaging its internal components or the components you are installing. Do not open the computer or attempt to install items inside it while it is on.

2 Wait 5 to 10 minutes to allow the computer's internal components to cool down.

> **WARNING** ▶ After you shut down the system, the internal components can be very hot. You must let the computer cool down before continuing.

3 Unplug all external cables from the computer except the power cord.

4 Touch the metal PCI access cover on the back of the computer to discharge any static electricity from your body. The discharge will flow from the access cover through the grounded plug on the power cord, to the ground receptacle on the electrical outlet.

> **WARNING** ▶ Always discharge static before you touch any parts or install any components inside the computer. To avoid generating static electricity, do not walk around the room until you have finished working and closed the computer.

5 Unplug the power cord.

WARNING ▶ To avoid damaging the computer's internal components or the components you want to install, always unplug the computer before attempting any Take Apart procedure.

6   Put on your ESD wrist strap.

MORE INFO ▶ The Electrostatic Discharge Association (ESDA) estimates that at low humidity, walking on a carpet can cause a discharge of up to 35,000 volts. ESD can cause major damage to electronic components. For additional information on this topic consult www.esda.org/esdbasics1.htm.

Side Access Panel

The side access panel must be removed so you can access other internal components.

1   After completing the previous exercise, hold the side access panel and lift the latch on the back of the computer.

▶ **Component Identification**

With the side access panel removed, identify the main components that are visible and locate them in the Take Apart section of the service manual:

- ▶ Hard drive carriers
- ▶ Optical drive carrier
- ▶ Power supply
- ▶ Logic board
- ▶ Bluetooth
- ▶ AirPort Extreme Card
- ▶ PCI Express card(s)
- ▶ Battery
- ▶ Memory riser cards

WARNING ▶ Be very careful when handling the edges of the access panel and the enclosure, which can be sharp.

2   Remove the access panel and place it on a flat surface covered by a soft, clean cloth.

Make sure the latch is in the up position before you replace the access panel. If the latch is down, the access panel will not seat correctly in the enclosure.

Now that the side access panel has been removed, you will remove the optical drive the lead technician has determined to be faulty.

Optical Drive

Proceed to the Mac Pro Service Source manual on page 15, and use this text to accompany the step-by-step procedures.

The Mac Pro can accommodate two SuperDrives in the optical drive bay. If the computer has only one optical drive, it is installed in the top position.

1   Perform steps 1 and 2 on page 16, to pull the carrier partially out of the computer.

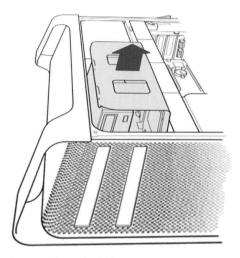

Remove the optical drive carrier in the direction indicated.

2   Perform step 3 on page 17, to disconnect the power and ribbon cables and remove the carrier. Do not stretch or pinch the power or ribbon cables.

 NOTE ▸ Before installing the new drive, set the drive to cable select mode if the manufacturer hasn't already done so.

3   Perform step 4 on page 17, to remove and replace the faulty drive. Use the same four mounting screws that you removed for the replacement drive. Be sure not to cross-thread or overtighten the screws.

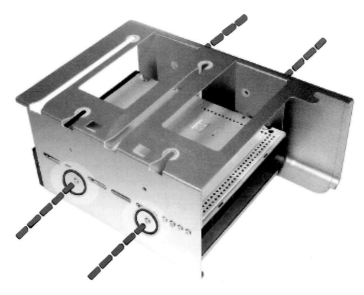

Screw placement locations (in yellow)

4   Perform steps 1 and 2 on page 18 to connect the optical drive.

AirPort Extreme Card

The AirPort Extreme Card provides Wi-Fi connectivity to the Mac Pro. To begin the removal and replacement procedure, open the service manual to page 47.

The Mac Pro computer enclosure includes AirPort antenna wires and a Bluetooth antenna wire. These wires are simple to distinguish because the Bluetooth antenna wire includes a "BT" label (short for Bluetooth). To ensure proper operation, be careful not to connect the Bluetooth antenna wire to the AirPort Extreme Card, or any AirPort antenna wire to the Bluetooth card. You may, however, connect the AirPort antenna wires to either AirPort Extreme Card connector.

For this procedure, we will assume that you have performed all preliminary steps, including shutting off the computer and grounding yourself. Ensure that the computer is on its side with the access door removed.

1   Locate the AirPort Extreme Card.

AirPort Extreme Card (circled in blue)

2   Perform step 1 on page 48 by removing the card mounting screws. Ensure that your screwdriver is magnetized. Do not drop the screws on the logic board.

Mounting screws

3 Perform steps 2 and 3 on page 48 to lift the AirPort Extreme Card and disconnect the wires from it.

4 Perform step 4 on page 49 to remove the card from the enclosure. Place the faulty card in the ESD-safe static bag that was shipped with the replacement card for return to Apple.

To replace the AirPort Extreme Card, perform the following steps:

1   Connect the antenna wires to the card.

Be sure to connect the wires that are marked 1 and 3 to the card; the antenna wire that is marked 2 should be taped out of the way.

2   Insert the card into its logic board connector at an angle, as illustrated.

Insert the AirPort Extreme Card in the direction indicated.

3   Lower the screw end of the card down to the standoffs on the logic board and replace the two mounting screws.

Battery Replacement

Again, we will assume that you have performed all preliminary steps, including shutting the computer off and grounding yourself properly. Ensure that the computer is on its side with the access door removed.

For the battery replacement procedure, you will need to remove any PCI Express cards that block access to the battery.

> **NOTE** ▶ Consult page 24 in the service manual to remove the PCI Express card(s) prior to performing the battery replacement procedure.

Go to page 51 of the service manual to begin the procedure.

1 Locate the battery.

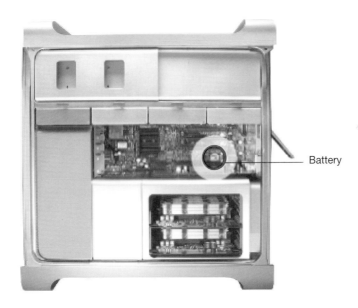

Battery

2   Perform steps 1 and 2 on page 52 to remove the faulty battery from its
holder.

Remove the battery in the direction indicated.

3   Because batteries contain chemicals harmful to the environment, dispose
of the faulty battery in accordance with local environmental laws.

4   To replace the battery, insert the new battery into the holder, making sure
the battery's positive symbol (+) faces up.

WARNING ► Installing the battery incorrectly may cause an explosion. Be
sure the battery's positive and negative sides are correctly oriented in the
holder. Use only the same type of battery or an equivalent recommended
by the manufacturer of the original.

When You Are Finished

1   Reassemble the unit as indicated in the service manual on page 10.

2   Return the faulty parts to Apple in the packaging provided.

3   Start up the computer.

4 Run System Profiler to verify that the replacement AirPort Extreme Card and optical drive appear under the hardware section.

5 Run AHT. By doing so, you will be booting off of the replacement optical drive and can also test the system.

6 Perform a few user tasks that involve the optical drive (such as installing software or burning a disc in iTunes).

7 Test the AirPort Extreme Card using a known-good wireless connection.

8 Verify that everything works correctly by starting up the computer and running AHT.

Lesson Summary

▶ Each Mac Pro model has different Take Apart procedures that are explained in detail in that model's service manual. The information presented in this chapter applies to the Mac Pro only.

▶ Gaining access to a particular component often requires the removal of other components first.

▶ Accessing almost all of the Mac Pro components requires opening the side access panel.

▶ Whenever you work on the internal components of a Mac Pro, it's imperative to follow proper ESD procedures.

▶ You must unplug the AC power cord to prevent the Mac Pro from turning on during the Take Apart procedure.

▶ Always exercise care and do not exert too much pressure when disassembling the Mac Pro; internal components are fragile.

▶ Observing the battery's polarity during battery installation will ensure proper operation of the unit.

20

Reference Files   Mac Pro Service Source manual (macpro.pdf)

Time   This lesson takes approximately 1.5 hours to complete.

Goals   Given a Mac Pro, locate service procedures, symptom charts, and service issues

Given a problem scenario or malfunctioning Mac Pro and the Apple General Troubleshooting Flowchart, return the computer to normal operation

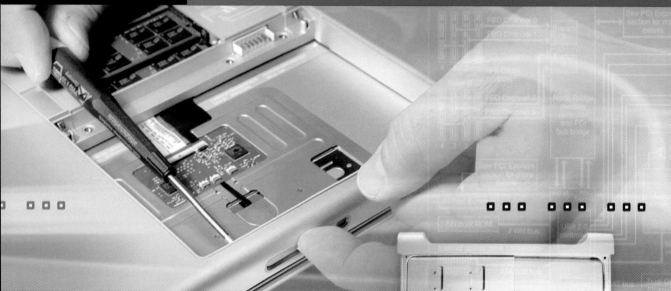

Troubleshooting a Mac Pro

In this lesson, we focus on the resources required to effectively trouble-shoot and repair the Mac Pro, including general technical information, symptom charts, and Apple online resources. Your familiarity with these resources and an understanding of the operation of the Mac Pro will help you troubleshoot and resolve problems more easily.

In situations where you have to troubleshoot or take apart an Apple computer, such as the Mac Pro, the Apple Service Source manual is your best resource.

During the time before a product is released, service writers at Apple are part of the product development process. It is their job to identify and document challenges that impact how a service technician will troubleshoot an issue, arrive at a solution, and replace the part required. After a product is released, the service writers continue to update and maintain all technical resources, and are always working to hone the troubleshooting procedures.

It's important to follow these troubleshooting procedures in order, as they address the most likely and simplest cures first, before moving on to more complex solutions.

TIP ▶ Apple continuously updates the technical resources required to troubleshoot and service their products. Before performing service on any Apple product, be sure you have the most current service manual or user guide for the model you are servicing.

General Information

In this section, we'll discuss some of the main components of a Mac Pro, with the aim of assessing where and why things most commonly go wrong.

Memory

In Lesson 18, "Upgrading a Mac Pro," you learned how to upgrade the memory of the Mac Pro, keeping in mind its memory specifications and how the memory is paired.

Issues related to memory can be fairly simple to troubleshoot, and usually result from not following memory recommendations or from memory that does not meet specifications.

Apple recommends that only approved fully buffered dual inline memory modules (FB-DIMMs) be used. Apple FB-DIMMs come with heat sinks that have been specifically designed and tested for the Mac Pro to offer the best integrated thermal solution. Apple FB-DIMMs have an accurate, integral thermal sensor that aids in tracking thermal requirements and therefore optimizes performance. FB-DIMMs give the best system performance, and fan speeds have been optimized for the quietest system operation. Using inferior FB-DIMMs may result in performance issues.

NOTE ▶ To check the compatibility of the FB-DIMMs, see the Macintosh Products Guide on the Apple website at www.apple.com/guide.

Apple FB-DIMMs

DIMMs from older Mac computers cannot be used in the Mac Pro; attempting to do so may damage the system and void its warranty.

To achieve optimal performance when running certain memory-intensive applications, such as Final Cut Pro, memory DIMM pairs should be installed evenly on both risers.

Intel-based Macintosh models such as the Mac Pro rely on a combination of tones and blinking LEDs to display power-on self test (POST) error codes, which are covered later in this lesson. These codes will assist you in troubleshooting the system and in resolving memory-related issues.

PCI Express Cards

The Mac Pro logic board includes one double-wide PCI Express graphics slot and three PCI Express expansion slots, for a total of four slots. The computer comes with a graphics card installed in slot 1. You can install additional PCI Express graphics and expansion cards in the remaining three PCI Express expansion slots.

NOTE ▶ Combined maximum power consumption for all four PCI Express slots must not exceed 300 watts (W).

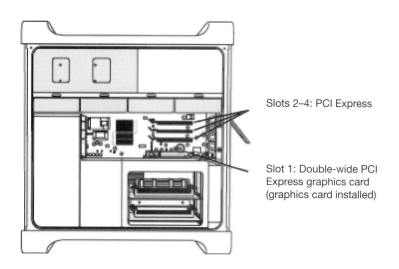

Slots 2–4: PCI Express

Slot 1: Double-wide PCI Express graphics card (graphics card installed)

NOTE ▶ Port 2 of the ATI Radeon X1900 XT graphics card is compatible with the Apple DVI-to-video adapter. For additional information, refer to Apple Knowledge Base document 304910, "Mac Pro: Graphic card video compatibility with Apple DVI-to-video adapter."

Issues with PCI Express Cards often result from improper installation or card incompatibility. Should a card be malfunctioning, verify that the PCI Express Card is compatible with this model, and follow the PCI Express Card replacement instructions in the service manual to reinstall the card.

Internal Cabling Matrix

The Mac Pro logic board is a complex printed circuit board (PCB) with thousands of semiconductor components that form its many circuits. The logic board's cables (wiring) send and receive signals and power to a multitude of internal components, sensors, and associated circuitry.

Most cable connectors are keyed, but locating the connector it plugs into can be difficult with so many connectors present on the logic board. By using the proper resources to troubleshoot cables and connectors, you can identify issues more efficiently.

Each cable connector at the end of a cable has a matching cable connector grid location on the logic board. Cable connectors are conveniently labeled for identification.

The entire internal cable connector and signal matrix is located on pages 133–135 of the service manual. Some examples follow.

Cable Description	Logic Board Connector Location	Logic Board Connector Label	Power / Signals Carried
HDD SATA drive	B-1	SATA	Serial ATA
HDD thermal sensor	A-2	HDD SNS	Thermal sensor signals
Front panel Board panel	K-7	FP MISC	Several power and control signals

To find where the cable connector is located on the logic board, find the logic board connector location, and then find the corresponding grid location on the logic board grid. For example, the HDD SATA drive cable has a connector location of B-1. Follow column B until it intersects with row 1 to locate this connector.

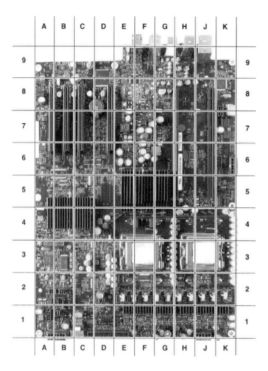

Logic Board Resets

You can resolve many system problems by resetting the logic board.

There are three reset switches on the logic board that you can use to troubleshoot various issues:

▶ SMC reset: If the computer is experiencing a power issue, resetting the system management controller (SMC) may resolve it.

▶ RTC reset: If the computer is experiencing a booting issue, resetting the Real Time Clock (RTC) may resolve it.

▶ System reset: You can use this switch to determine if a computer that won't consistently boot from a cold start has power supply issues.

System Management Controller

The SMC is a chip on the logic board that controls all power functions for your computer. The SMC controls several functions, including:

▶ Telling the computer when to turn on, turn off, sleep, wake, and idle

▶ Handling system resets from various commands

▶ Controlling the fans

Resetting the SMC can resolve some computer issues such as not starting up, not displaying video, sleep issues, and fan noise issues.

Resetting the SMC does not reset the parameter random-access memory (PRAM) or resolve issues in which your computer is unresponsive—in these situations, restarting your computer will generally suffice. If your computer isn't responding, perform these steps one at a time, in this order, until the issue has been resolved:

1 Force quit (Option-Command-Escape).

2 Restart (Control-Command-Power).

3 Force shut down (press the power button for 10 seconds).

If your computer still exhibits these types of issues after you've restarted the computer, try resetting the SMC. To reset the SMC on a Mac Pro:

1 From the Apple menu, choose Shut Down (or if the computer is not responding, hold the power button until it turns off).

2 Unplug all cables from the computer, including the power cord and any display cables.

3 Wait at least 2 minutes.

4   Plug the power cord back in, making sure you are not pressing the power
button at the same time. Then reconnect the keyboard and mouse to the
computer.

5   Press the power button to start up the computer.

An alternate way to reset the SMC on a Mac Pro computer is as follows:

1   From the Apple menu, choose Shut Down (or if the computer is not
responding, hold the power button until it turns off).

2   Open and remove the side access panel.

3   Press the SMC_RST switch that is located slightly below and to the right
of the row of diagnostic LEDs. Use a nonmetallic, nonconductive object,
such as a nylon probe tool.

4   Replace the side access panel.

5   Press the power button to start up the computer.

> **NOTE ▶** Unlike earlier models of Power Mac G5 or Power Mac G4 com-
> puters, the Mac Pro computer does not have a power management unit
> (PMU). The SMC replaces this functionality.

Real Time Clock

The RTC is a chip on the logic board that controls the date and time functions
of the computer. If the computer is experiencing a booting issue, resetting the
RTC may resolve it. Follow these steps to reset the RTC:

1   From the Apple menu, choose Shut Down (or if the computer is not
responding, hold the power button until it turns off).

2   Unplug the AC power cord.

3   Remove the RTC backup battery for at least 20 seconds. You may need to remove a PCI Express Card to gain access to the battery.

System Reset

Mac Pro has a system reset switch on the logic board that you may use to restart the system while it is powered up. You can use this switch to determine if a computer that won't consistently boot from a cold start has power supply issues. Follow these steps to reset the system:

1   Start up the computer.

2   With a nylon probe tool, press the system reset switch located in the upper right-hand corner of the logic board.

If the computer boots after you press the system reset switch, try shutting off the computer and restarting by pressing the front power button. If the computer restarts when you press the system reset switch but not from a cold start, the power supply may need to be replaced.

Power-On Self Test

A POST in the computer's read-only memory (ROM) runs automatically whenever the computer is started up after being fully shut down (the test does not run if the computer is only restarted). If the test detects a problem, the status LED located above the power button on the front of the computer will flash in the following ways:

▶   One Flash: No random-access memory (RAM) is installed or detected, or the quick memory test failed. An LED lights up on the DIMM riser card next to the affected DIMM.

▶   Three Flashes: A RAM bank failed extended memory testing. An LED lights up on the memory riser card next to the affected DIMM.

To troubleshoot, try reseating the memory DIMMs. Check memory installation instructions for proper installation order. Swap the affected DIMM with a known-good DIMM.

Status light

Power button

NOTE ▶ The status LED lights up when the power button is pressed at startup. Do not count this light as one of the diagnostic flashes.

Diagnostic LEDs

The Mac Pro logic board includes a set of LEDs to help service providers troubleshoot the computer. The LEDs are located toward the rear of the logic board, under the memory cage, next to PCI card slot 1. You can view these LEDs by removing the computer's side access panel and looking through the memory cage to the logic board below.

SLEEP LED not installed

DIAG LED button (white button surrounded by a metal square)

Diagnostic LEDs location on the logic board, numbered 1–8 from left to right

LEDs 2, 3, 4, and 5 are normally off and will illuminate automatically if an error occurs. To read LEDs 1, 6, 7, and 8, you must press the DIAG_LED button, which is adjacent to the LEDs. To press the DIAG_LED button, use the nylon probe tool.

NOTE ▶ There is a position on the logic board next to LED 1 for a SLEEP LED that does not have any LED installed. This is normal; the LED was used only in development. To determine if a Mac Pro computer is in sleep mode, watch the power LED on the front of the computer. It will slowly change brightness levels if the computer is sleeping.

Interpreting the LEDs

Use the chart below to interpret the Diagnostic LEDs when troubleshooting.

Location	Name	Color	Status	LED Button to Display	Indicates
LED 1	Trickle power	Yellow	On	Yes	Power supply is providing trickle power
LED 2	CPU B (lower processor) Error	Red	Off	No	CPU B halts on an IERR (instruction error)
LED 3	CPU A (upper processor) Error	Red	Off	No	CPU A halts on an IERR (instruction error)
LED 4	CPU B (lower processor) Overtemp	Red	Off	No	CPU B is over temperature
LED 5	CPU A (lower processor) Overtemp	Red	Off	No	CPU A is over temperature
LED 6	GPU present	Green	On	Yes	EFI has configured the graphics card
LED 7	Power on	Green	On	Yes	All power rails are functioning
LED 8	EFI done	Green	On	Yes	EFI is done loading

LED 1 Trickle Power

LED 1 is normally on when the DIAG_LED button is pressed. If LED 1 is not on, the symptom is that the computer won't power on.

Troubleshooting:

1   Check that the AC cord is connected to a working AC wall outlet.

2   Reseat the AC plug.

3   Check the connections of the power supply cables to the logic board.

4   Check the power supply cable connections at the power supply.

5   Replace the power supply.

LED 2 CPU B (Lower Processor) Error and LED 3 CPU A (Upper Processor) Error

LEDs 2 and 3 are normally off. They turn on if an error occurs or if the BootROM is corrupted. They do not depend on the DIAG_LED button being pressed.

Related symptoms include no video or the computer is not responding. If the BootROM is corrupted, the optical drive tray should eject, prompting for the insertion of a recovery disc to restore the BootROM.

Troubleshooting:

1   With the computer booted up, press the SYS_RESET switch. If this clears the CPU Error LED, check for incompatible device driver software that may have been installed for added hardware.

2   If the Error LED is still on, power down the computer and try pressing the SMC_RESET switch. Restart the computer.

3   Reset the power supply by unplugging the AC cord for 10 seconds.

4   Unplug the AC cord and remove any added DIMMs and PCI Express Cards. If this causes the LED to go off, repopulate the DIMMs and/or PCI Express Cards to find the combination that caused the LED to come on. Overheated memory could be a possible cause for this CPU Error LED to come on. Check fan operation.

5   Unplug the AC cord and remove the RTC battery for 10 seconds. You may need to remove a PCI Express Card to get to the RTC battery. Reinstall the battery and restart the computer. Try swapping CPU A and CPU B locations. If the CPU Error LED follows the CPU, replace that CPU.

6   Try replacing the logic board.

LED 4 CPU B (Lower Processor) Overtemp and LED 5 CPU A (Upper Processor) Overtemp

LEDs 4 and 5 are normally off. They turn on if an error occurs. They do not depend on the DIAG_LED button being pressed.

These LEDs can operate in two different modes; they will either flash or stay on. If either LED is flashing, it may indicate an initial processor over-temperature condition. If either LED is solidly on, it may indicate a chronic processor over-temperature condition. Initial processor over-temperature can cause symptoms such as sluggish computer performance. Chronic processor over-temperature can cause the computer to hang completely.

Troubleshooting:

1   Verify proper heat sink installation.

2   Verify that all thermal sensors are connected properly.

3   Verify that all fans, especially the front intake fan, are operating properly.

LED 6 GPU Present

LED 6 is normally on when the DIAG_LED button is pressed.

If this LED is on, it indicates there is a graphics card installed and recognized by the computer. It does not indicate that the graphics card is fully functional. Some graphics cards require additional power to function, which is available from connectors on the logic board. For these cards, if the auxiliary booster power cable is not connected between the logic board and the graphics card, an error message reminding about this additional power connection will be displayed as Mac OS X starts up.

Troubleshooting:

1   Check that the graphics card is seated correctly in its PCI slot.

2   Check that the card's auxiliary booster power cable is connected properly (if the card requires one).

3   Try the graphics card in a different PCI slot.

4   Try a different graphics card.

5   Replace the logic board.

6   If an error message about graphic card booster power connection is displayed, check that the appropriate booster power cable is firmly connected between the logic board and the graphics card.

LED 7 Power On

LED 7 is normally on when the DIAG_LED button is pressed. If this LED is on, it indicates the power supply is functioning.

Troubleshooting:

1   Check that the power cables to the logic board are attached properly.

2   Check the cable connections at the power supply.

3   Check for any signs of an obvious electrical short, for example, metal screws or PCI card slot cover loose inside the computer touching the logic board.

LED 8 EFI Good

LED 8 is normally on when the DIAG_LED button is pressed. Wait approximately 5 seconds after power-up for the LED to register properly.

If this LED is on, it indicates that the computer has completed the on-board Extensible Firmware Interface (EFI) operations and the operating system is now in control.

Troubleshooting:

1   Check that LED 7, Power On LED, is on.

2   Check that LEDs 2, 3, 4, and 5 are off.

3   Try removing any added hardware.

4   Try removing any added DIMMs.

Memory Diagnostic LEDs

Both of the memory riser cards include diagnostic LEDs for each DIMM. Each of the LEDs lights if it detects an issue with the corresponding installed DIMM. These LEDs also flash briefly when you start up the computer or shut it down, and when it goes in and out of sleep mode. This is a normal behavior.

Troubleshooting:

1   Shut down and restart the computer.

2   Try reseating the DIMMs.

3   Check the memory installation instructions for proper installation order.

4   Swap the affected DIMM with a known-good DIMM.

5   Try moving the DIMM to another slot (within the same bank of two) to see if the failure LED follows the DIMM. If so, replace the DIMM with a known-good DIMM.

Video Diagnostic LEDs

Though not part of the default configuration, the Radeon X1900 XT video card also has diagnostic LEDs. These LEDs also flash briefly when you start up the computer or shut it down, and when it goes in and out of sleep mode. This is a normal behavior.

T_Fault LED

Normally off, the T_Fault LED lights up if the graphics chip gets too hot.

Troubleshooting:

1   Check that the rear fan is working.

2   Try reseating the card in the PCI slot.

3   Make sure the card's auxiliary booster power cable is connected (if there is one).

4   Reboot the computer.

5   Try a different video card.

6   Replace the video card.

Ext_Power LED

Normally off, the Ext_Power LED lights up if the auxiliary power isn't being supplied.

Troubleshooting:

1   Make sure the card's auxiliary booster power cable is connected (if there is one).

2   Check connections from the power supply to the logic board.

3   Try a different auxiliary power cable.

4   Try a different video card.

5   Replace the video card.

Power Supply Verification

To power on, the computer's logic board requires "trickle" power. If the system fails to power on, first reset the SMC as described in this lesson. If the computer still doesn't power on, follow the procedure outlined below to determine whether the issue is related to the power supply:

1   Verify that trickle power is present. Diagnostic LED 1 indicates the presence of trickle power required by the logic board to begin the startup process. LED 1 should be yellow when the DIAG_ LED button is pressed.

2   Verify that the power supply is providing power. Diagnostic LED 7 indicates that the main power is OK and within regulation. Plug in the AC power cord and press the power button on the front panel. LED 7 should be green when the DIAG_ LED button is pressed.

Symptom Charts

The symptom charts included in this lesson will help you diagnose specific symptoms by following the guidelines set forth in the Apple General Trouble-shooting Flowchart. Because cures are listed on the charts in the order of most likely solution to least likely, try the cures in the order presented. Verify whether or not the product continues to exhibit the symptom. If the symptom persists, try the next cure. If a cure instructs you to replace a module and the symptom persists with the new module, reinstall the original module before you proceed to the next cure.

For troubleshooting purposes, Mac Pro computers may be started up and diagnosed with a single processor installed in either the upper (CPU A) or lower (CPU B) position.

NOTE ▶ These symptom charts are taken from the service manual that was current at the time of publication and that appears on this book's companion website, www.peachpit.com/ats.deskport3. Apple Authorized Service Providers (AASPs) should download and refer to the latest service manual from Apple Service Source before servicing any Apple product.

Startup Failures

When testing a computer for the following symptoms, remove the side access panel so you can better observe or listen for fan movement.

Power-on LED Does Not Illuminate When Power Button Is Pressed, Fans Do Not Spin, and There Is No Boot Tone or Video

1 Verify that the power outlet is good.

2 Check that diagnostic LED 1 is on when the power cord is connected.

3 Replace the power cord.

4   Check that diagnostic LED 1 is on when the power cord is connected.

5   Reset the logic board. Refer to "Logic Board Resets," earlier in this lesson.

6   Verify that the power supply cables are seated properly.

7   Verify that the processors are seated properly. Check diagnostic LED 2 and/or LED 3.

8   Verify that the processors' mounting clamps are tightened properly.

9   Test whether the front panel board or power button is at fault. Remove the installed front panel board and test with a known-good front panel board.

10 Replace the front panel board.

11 Replace the power button.

12 Replace the power supply.

13 Replace the logic board.

Power-on LED Illuminates When Pressed, but Goes Out When Button Is Released, There Is No Boot Tone or Video, but You Can Hear a Small Click

1   Check diagnostic LED 1 for trickle voltage from the power supply. Refer to "Power Supply Verification," earlier in this lesson. If verification fails, replace the power supply.

2   Verify that the processors are seated properly. Check diagnostic LED 2 and/or LED 3.

3   Verify that the processor mounting clamps are tightened properly.

4   Verify that the power supply cables are seated properly.

5   Replace the power supply.

Power-on Led Illuminates When Power Button Is Pressed but Fans Do Not Spin (or Spin Only Momentarily) and There Is No Boot Tone or Video

1   Reseat the video card. (Make sure the video card is fully inserted in the connector and the end of the card is secured by the connector latch.) For video cards that require power cables, check that they are connected.

2   Reset the logic board. Refer to "Logic Board Resets," earlier in this lesson.

3   Verify that the power supply cables are seated properly.

4   Check diagnostic LED 2 and/or LED 3 for processor connection.

5   Reseat the processors and check for bent pins.

6   Check diagnostic LED 1 for trickle voltage from the power supply. Refer to "Power Supply Verification," earlier in this lesson. If verification fails, replace the power supply.

7   Replace the logic board.

8   Replace the processor.

Power-on Led Illuminates When Power Button Is Pressed and Fans Spin Continuously but There Is No Boot Tone or Video

1   Reseat the video card. (Make sure the video card is fully inserted in the connector and the end of the card is secured by the connector latch.) For video cards that require power cables, check that they are connected.

2   Verify that the speaker cable is fully seated.

3   Reset the logic board. Refer to "Logic Board Resets," earlier in this lesson.

4   Verify that the power supply cables are seated properly.

5   Check diagnostic LED 2 and/or LED 3 for processor connection. If only one of the CPU Error LEDs (LED 2 or 3) comes on, try swapping the processors. If the Error LED follows the processor to the other processor location, replace that processor.

6   Replace the logic board.

Power-on LED Illuminates When Power Button Is Pressed, Fans Spin, and Boot Tone Chimes, but There Is No Video

1   Verify that the display is connected properly and powered on.

2   Check the video card connector and display cable for any bent pins.

3   Reseat the video card. (Make sure the video card is fully inserted in the connector and the end of the card is secured by the connector latch.) For video cards that require power cables, check that they are connected.

4   Reset PRAM (restart the computer while holding down the Command-Option-P-R keys until the second boot tone chimes).

5   Reset the logic board. Refer to "Logic Board Resets," earlier in this lesson.

6   Verify that the power supply cables are seated properly.

7   Replace the video card.

8   Replace the logic board.

Power-on LED Does Not Illuminate When Power Button Is Pressed, but Fans Spin, Boot Tone Chimes, and There Is Video

1   Verify that the power supply cables are seated properly.

2   Reseat the front panel board.

3 Replace the front panel board.

4 Replace the logic board.

5 Replace the power supply.

Power-on LED Illuminates, Fans Spin Up, No Boot Tone, and the System Shuts Down Within a Few Minutes

1 Open the side access panel and observe all diagnostic LEDs. Refer to "Diagnostic LEDs," earlier in this lesson, for more information on how to locate and interpret these LEDs. Troubleshoot further if any LEDs indicate any failure.

2 Verify that the power supply cables are seated properly.

3 Reseat the processors and check for bent pins.

4 Replace the processors.

5 Replace the logic board.

6 Replace the power supply.

Fans

Individual Fan Failure

1 Verify that the fan is connected properly.

2 Verify that all other fans are working properly. If all fans seem to have failed, the problem is most likely not the fans. Reset the logic board to see if this resolves this problem.

3 Replace the fan.

4 Replace the logic board.

Fans Run at High Speed (Computer May Shut Down or May Be Unresponsive and Not Shut Down As a Result)

1   Check for proper ventilation around the exterior of the computer.

2   Remove the computer's side access panel and observe the diagnostic LEDs, specifically LEDs 4 and 5 (the CPU A and B Overtemp LEDs). Refer to "Diagnostic LEDs," earlier in this lesson, for more information on how to locate and interpret these LEDs. If either LED is flashing, it may indicate an initial processor over-temperature condition. If either LED is solidly on, it may indicate a chronic processor over-temperature condition.

3   Verify proper processor heat sink installation. (See the Take Apart section of the service manual for more information on heat sink installation.)

4   Verify that all thermal sensors, especially the ambient temperature sensor board, and their cables are connected properly.

5   Verify that all fans, especially the front intake fan, are operating properly and are unobstructed.

6   Verify that the proper type of memory is installed. (See "Memory" in the Take Apart chapter of the service manual for more information.)

7   Replace the power supply.

Computer Performance Seems Sluggish or Slow, or Computer Is Completely Unresponsive

1   Start up the computer from a known-good volume, such as its Install disc or an external hard drive, to isolate the issue to software or hardware. If the computer seems to perform adequately when booted in this way, troubleshoot as a software issue. If the computer continues to perform sluggishly when booted this way, continue following the steps below.

2   Run Apple Service Diagnostic (ASD) to verify that hardware is functional. Address any diagnostic failures as necessary.

3   Check for proper ventilation around the exterior of the computer.

4   Remove the computer's side access panel and observe the diagnostic LEDs, specifically LEDs 4 and LED 5 (the CPU A and B Overtemp LEDs). Refer to "Diagnostic LEDs," earlier in this lesson, for more information on how to locate and interpret these LEDs. If either of these LEDs is flashing, this may indicate an initial processor over-temperature condition. If either of these LEDs is solidly on, this may indicate a chronic processor over-temperature condition. Initial processor over-temperature can cause symptoms such as sluggish computer performance. A chronic processor over-temperature condition can cause the computer to be completely unresponsive.

5   Verify proper processor heat sink installation. (Refer to "Processor Heatsinks" in the Take Apart chapter of the service manual for more information.)

6   Verify that all thermal sensors, especially the ambient temperature sensor board, and their cables are connected properly.

7   Verify that all fans, especially the front intake fan, are operating properly and are unobstructed.

Other Failures

Optical Drive

1   Try different optical media.

2   If two drives are installed, check the Master/Slave or Cable Select jumpers on both optical drives (this will depend on drive vendor). Both drives should be set to Cable Select mode for proper operation.

3 If two drives are installed, test one optical drive at a time by disconnecting one of the drives to see if the other one works.

4 Replace the optical drive cable.

5 Replace the optical drive.

6 Replace the logic board.

Front Panel FireWire Port

1 Reseat the front panel board cable.

2 Replace the front panel board cable.

3 Reseat the front panel board.

4 Replace the front panel board.

5 Replace the logic board.

Rear FireWire Port

Replace the logic board.

Front Panel USB 2.0 Port

1 Reseat the front panel board cables.

2 Replace the front panel board cables.

3 Reseat the front panel board.

4 Replace the front panel board.

5 Replace the logic board.

Rear USB 2.0

Replace the logic board.

Internal Speaker

1   Check the speaker cable connection.

2   Replace the speaker.

3   Replace the logic board.

AirPort Extreme Card

1   Start up the computer from a known-good volume (such as an external hard drive) with AirPort driver software installed, to isolate the issue to software or hardware. If the computer seems to perform adequately when booted in this way, troubleshoot as a software issue. If the computer continues to exhibit the issue, follow the steps below.

2   Reseat the antenna cables connected to the card.

3   Replace the card.

4   Replace the logic board.

Bluetooth Card

1   Start up the computer from a known-good volume (such as an external hard drive) with Bluetooth driver software installed, to isolate the issue to software or hardware. If the computer seems to perform adequately when booted in this way, troubleshoot as a software issue. If the computer continues to exhibit the issue, follow the steps below.

2   Reseat the antenna cable connected to the card.

3 Replace the card.

4 Replace the logic board.

Audio IO (Front Headphones)

1 Start up the computer from a known-good volume (such as its Install disc or an external hard drive), to isolate the issue to software or hardware. If the computer seems to perform adequately when booted in this way, troubleshoot as a software issue. If the computer continues to exhibit the issue, follow the steps below.

2 Reseat the front panel board.

3 Replace the front panel board.

4 Replace the logic board.

Audio IO (Rear Audio Line In; Rear Audio Line Out)

1 Start up the computer from a known-good volume (such as its Install disc or an external hard drive), to isolate the issue to software or hardware. If the computer seems to perform adequately when booted in this way, troubleshoot as a software issue. If the computer continues to exhibit the issue, follow the steps below.

2 Check the Sound settings in System Preferences.

3 Replace the logic board.

Lesson Review

1. True or false: All FB-DIMMs may be used in the Mac Pro.

2. What is the combined maximum power consumption for all four PCI Express slots?

   a. 100 W

   b. 200 W

   c. 300 W

3. On the Mac Pro, what type of reset may solve a booting issue?

   a. SMC reset

   b. RTC reset

   c. System reset

4. On the Mac Pro, what type of reset may solve a power issue?

   a. SMC reset

   b. RTC reset

   c. System reset

5. True or false: The SMC reset also resets the PRAM.

6. During POST a RAM bank failed extended memory testing. How many flashes will the status LED display?

   a. One

   b. Three

   c. None

7. True or false: The diagnostic LEDs are located toward the front of the logic board.

Answer Key

1. False, Apple approves only certain FB-DIMMs for the Mac Pro; 2. c; 3. b; 4. a; 5. False, resetting the SMC does not reset the PRAM; 6. b; 7. False, the diagnostic LEDs are toward the rear of the logic board, under the memory cage.

Try Quick Fixes

Verify BIOS

Systematic Fault
Isolation

Run Diagnostics

Verify Repair

Inform User

Portables

21

Time This lesson takes approximately 1 hour to complete.

Goals Describe the MacBook model

Explain the differences between the MacBook (13-inch) base
configurations

About MacBook Models

Intel processors first came to Macintosh portables in the MacBook Pro. The MacBook series was introduced in May of 2006 and brought Intel-based processors to Apple's consumer portable line. The MacBook (13-inch) completes Apple's move to the Intel architecture for portables, and though technically enhanced, it keeps the same general look and feel of previous iBook G4 models. The MacBook is offered in three configurations: two white models known as Good and Better, and a Black model known as Best.

The following chart outlines the major technical differences among the MacBook models. Use these charts to distinguish between various models and to determine the capabilities of each.

NOTE ▶ For detailed MacBook support, go to http://support.apple.com/specs/macbook/macbook.html.

MacBook (13-inch)

	1.83 GHz MacBook (Good/White)	2 GHz MacBook (Better/White)	2 GHz MacBook (Best/Black)
Introduced	May 2006	May 2006	May 2006
Mac OS (minimum)	Mac OS X 10.4	Mac OS X 10.4	Mac OS X 10.4
Technical specifications	http://support.apple.com/specs/macbook/macbook.html		
Processor	1.83 GHz Intel Core Duo	2 GHz Intel Core Duo	2 GHz Intel Core Duo
Cache	2 MB L2	2 MB L2	2 MB L2
Memory	512 MB PC2-5300S SO-DIMMs	512 MB PC2-5300S SO-DIMMs	512 MB PC2-5300S SO-DIMMs

	1.83 GHz MacBook (Good/White)	2 GHz MacBook (Better/White)	2 GHz MacBook (Best/Black)
Hard disk	60 GB Serial ATA	60 GB Serial ATA	80 GB Serial ATA 120 GB Serial ATA
Optical drive	Combo	SuperDrive	SuperDrive
Graphics	Intel GMA 950 graphics processor	Intel GMA 950 graphics processor	Intel GMA 950 graphics processor
Expansion	2 USB 2.0 1 FireWire 400 Mini-DVI port with support for DVI, VGA, S-video, and composite video output 10/100/1000Base-T Ethernet AirPort Extreme Bluetooth 2.0	2 USB 2.0 1 FireWire 400 Mini-DVI port with support for DVI, VGA, S-video, and composite video output 10/100/1000Base-T Ethernet AirPort Extreme Bluetooth 2.0	2 USB 2.0 1 FireWire 400 Mini-DVI port with support for DVI, VGA, S-video, and composite video output 10/100/1000 Base-T Ethernet AirPort Extreme Bluetooth 2.0
Video connectors	ADC DVI VGA	ADC DVI VGA	ADC DVI VGA
Video camera	iSight	iSight	iSight

Lesson Review

1. Name as many of the labeled MacBook features as you can. Use the Answer Key to fill in any you may have missed.

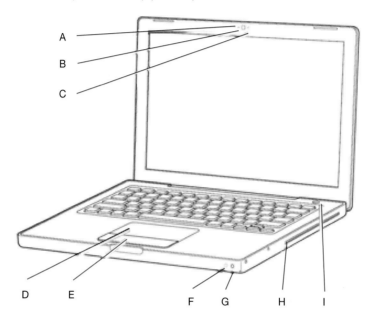

2. True or false: The MacBook (13-inch) (Best) model is available in both black or white.

3. True or false: Only the 2 GHz MacBook (Best/Black) model has built-in iSight.

4. Name as many of the MacBook ports as you can. Use the Answer Key to fill in any you may have missed.

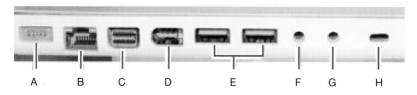

Answer Key

1. A. Microphone; B. iSight camera; C. Camera indicator light; D. Trackpad;
E. Trackpad button; F. Sleep indicator light; G. Infrared sensor for Apple
Remote; H. Optical drive slot; I. Power button; 2. False (black only); 3. False
(all MacBook models have built-in iSight); 4. A. MagSafe power adapter port;
B. Gigabit Ethernet port (10/100/1000Base-T); C. Mini-DVI port; D. FireWire
400 port; E. USB 2.0 ports; F. Combined optical digital/audio line-in port;
G. Headphone out/optical digital audio out port; H. Security slot

22

Reference Files	MacBook Users Guide (MacBook_Late2006_UsersGuide)
Time	This lesson takes approximately 1 hour to complete.
Goals	Install memory in a MacBook
	Replace a hard drive in a MacBook

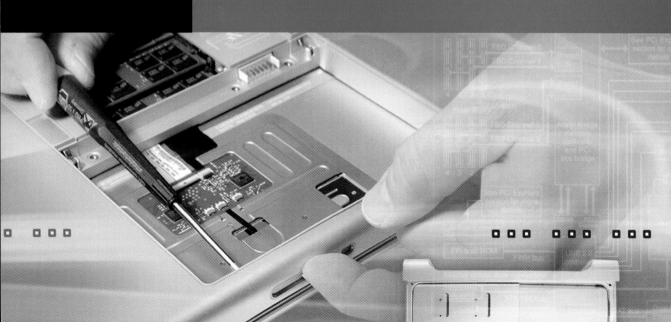

Upgrading a MacBook

The Intel-based MacBook sports many design improvements over its very distant iBook predecessor. As impressive as the MacBook is, technicians will concur that the single most impressive design improvements are in its ease of upgrading and repair.

This lesson explains how to upgrade a MacBook with additional RAM to increase overall system performance. You will also learn how to replace the hard drive.

> **MORE INFO ▶** Apple maintains an extensive online collection of instructions and videos for Do-It-Yourself (DIY) parts. Users can install these replacement parts and upgrades, as they require only a moderate amount of technical ability and common tools. This lesson covers two of the more common procedures; for a complete list of DIY parts, visit www.apple.com/support and look for the Do-It-Yourself link.

Required Tools and Equipment

To complete this lesson, you will need the following:

- ▶ Electrostatic discharge (ESD) wrist strap and mat
- ▶ Clean, soft, lint-free cloth
- ▶ Coin
- ▶ Phillips #0 screwdriver (preferably with a long handle)
- ▶ Stiff, plastic, nonmagnetic card (such as a library card)
- ▶ PC-5300 DDR2 667 MHz memory modules (installed in pairs)

Before You Do Anything

Follow the ESD Safety Guidelines and antistatic procedures discussed in Lesson 4, "Safe Working Procedures and General Maintenance." It is imperative that you follow these guidelines and any instructions given—failure to do so could result in injury, damage the computer, or void its warranty. If you are not an AASP, review the materials for this lesson carefully, but do not perform the procedures. If you are an AASP, practice the upgrade procedures until you are confident in your skills.

Ensure that the memory module you will be installing meets the following criteria:

- ▶ 1.25 inch or smaller
- ▶ 256 MB, 512 MB, or 1 GB
- ▶ 200-pin
- ▶ PC-5300 DDR2 667 MHz type RAM

> **NOTE** ▶ Memory from older portable computers is not compatible with your MacBook.

Before replacing your hard drive, you will need to back up your data. Perform any backup procedures before continuing further in this lesson.

Opening a MacBook

Regardless of the upgrade or repair to be performed, one of the first steps in upgrading a MacBook is to let the unit cool down. Cooling down the internal components properly will help to avoid damage to the unit and injury to you. We will assume you have followed ESD precautions, are wearing an ESD wrist strap, and have properly grounded yourself.

1   Place the computer on a soft clean cloth.

2   Shut down the computer and wait 30 minutes before continuing.

3   Unplug all external cables and peripherals from the computer.

4   Unplug the power cord and adapter last.

> **NOTE ▶** The power supply in your computer is a high-voltage component and should not be opened for any reason, even when the computer is off. If the power supply needs service, contact your Apple reseller or Apple Authorized Service Provider.

5   Turn over the computer.

6   Use a coin to release the battery latch. Turn the coin a quarter turn clockwise to unlock the battery.

Turn the coin clockwise.

7 Lift out the battery from the battery bay.

Removing the battery will prevent you from turning on the computer accidentally, and it will remove power from the system.

NOTE ▶ Removing the battery before shutting down your computer may result in data loss.

8 Touch a metal surface on the inside of the computer to discharge any static electricity.

NOTE ▶ To avoid electrostatic discharge damage, always ground yourself by touching the computer's framework before you touch any parts or install any components inside the computer. To avoid static electricity building back up in your body, do not walk around the room until you have completed the installation and closed the computer. Don't let others come into contact with you, since they may have built up a static charge.

Installing RAM

MacBook comes with a minimum of 512 MB of 667 MHz double data rate 2 (DDR2) synchronous dynamic random-access memory (SDRAM) installed. It has two slots that can accept SDRAM small outline dual inline memory modules (SO-DIMMs).

The slots are side-by-side on the logic board behind the RAM door. Best performance is obtained with memory installed in pairs with an equal-sized memory card in each slot. The maximum amount of memory for this computer is 2 GB, with 1 GB DIMM installed in each slot.

Removing the Installed DIMMs

As you perform this procedure, note the location of the battery and RAM door; they will need to be removed when you upgrade the hard drive.

1   Loosen—but do not try to remove—the three captive screws along the RAM door.

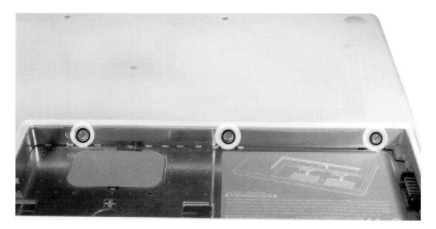

Captive screws (circled in blue)

2 Holding the long end of the L-shaped RAM door, pivot it out from the battery bay. If necessary, use a nonmagnetic, plastic card (such as a library card) to tilt the RAM door up and out of the battery bay. Be careful not to bend the RAM door.

Levers on the memory slots will spring out when you remove the RAM door.

RAM door

NOTE ▶ Remember to replace the RAM door after you have finished working inside your computer. The computer will not function properly if the RAM door is not replaced.

3   To eject the memory cards from the slots, move the levers all the way to the left.

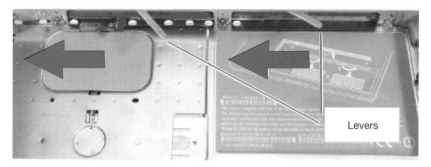

Levers

Move the levers in the direction of the arrows.

NOTE ▶ Like cables and connectors, tabs and latches are very thin and fragile. If you break a latch or tab, you may have to replace the entire part, which can be very costly.

4   Holding the memory cards by the corners, slide them out from the battery bay without touching the gold connectors. Handle the card only by its edges.

Replacing the DIMMs

When installing memory modules into their slots, you may be required to exert some pressure on them during insertion.

1   Align the memory card so that the gold connectors face the slot and the notch is on the left. (The chip side of the board faces down.)

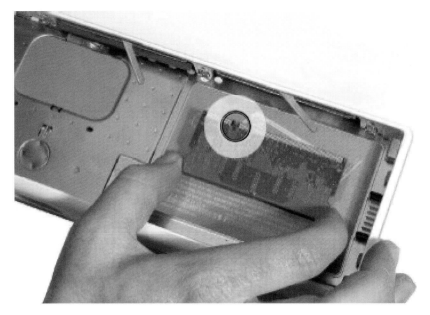

Notch (circled in blue)

2   Use two fingers to push firmly on the edge of the memory cards.

If there is a tight fit, installing the cards may take some force to ensure that they are fully inserted.

When the cards are fully inserted, the edges of the cards are hidden, as shown by the recessed card on the left in the following image.

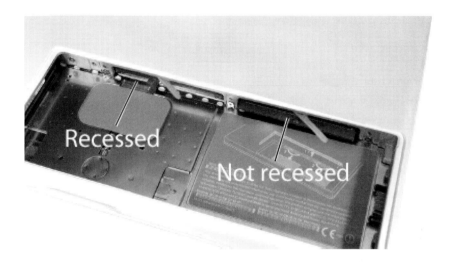

3 If the levers do not return to the closed position automatically, close them manually.

NOTE ▶ Should you wish to upgrade only the memory at this time, proceed to page 38 in the MacBook user's guide to complete the procedure and test the memory.

Upgrading the Hard Drive

The computer is off, and you have just completed installing RAM, so the RAM door is removed. If you'd like to upgrade the hard drive at the same time, you're ready to begin. Be sure to practice proper ESD procedures and wear your ESD wrist strap at all times.

NOTE ▶ If you are upgrading only the hard drive, go to the following MacBook DIY page (www.apple.com/support/macbook/diy/order.html) and locate the Hard Drive Replacement Instructions. Perform all steps on pages 1 through 4 before proceeding.

Removing the Hard Drive

1 Unroll the hard drive pull-tab.

2 Pull the tab straight out to slide the drive out from the recessed rubber rails in the battery bay.

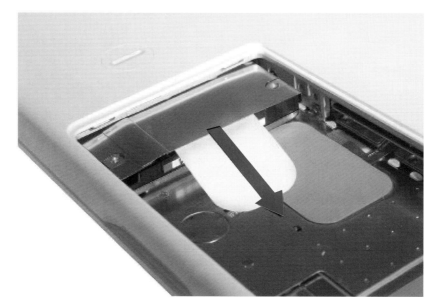

Pull the tab in the direction indicated.

3 Hold the drive only by the sides when removing and replacing it. Place the drive in an antistatic bag.

Replacing the Hard Drive

1   Slide in the replacement hard drive, and tuck the pull-tab underneath the drive.

2   Install the replacement RAM door by first aligning the short end at the notch near the hard drive opening.

RAM door notch (circled in blue)

3   Use a plastic card, if necessary, to tuck in the EMI gaskets (which prevent electromagnetic interference) located on the RAM door so they do not protrude from the edge of the battery bay. Make sure the three screws align with the holes in the bottom case before tightening them.

Closing a MacBook

1   Replace the battery by tilting the foot end of the battery into the battery bay first. Then press and hold down the other end of the battery as you turn the coin to lock it into place.

2   Connect the power cord.

   WARNING ▶ Never turn on the computer unless all of its internal and external parts are in place, and the computer is closed. Operating the computer when it is open or missing parts can damage it or cause injury.

3   Restart your computer and restore the operating system that came with your computer.

4   Restore the data from your backup to the new drive.

   NOTE ▶ Should you wish to reinstall the software that came with your computer, proceed to the following MacBook DIY page (www.apple.com/support/macbook/diy/order.html), and locate the Hard Drive Replacement Instructions. Perform the applicable software reinstallation steps on page 7 before proceeding.

5   Make sure your computer recognizes the new memory by opening System Profiler, clicking More Info, and clicking Memory. You may need to reset the date and time in Date & Time preferences.

Lesson Review

1. True or false: Memory from older portable computers is not compatible with your MacBook.

2. True or false: The maximum amount of memory for this computer is 2 GB per slot (4 GB total).

3. True or false: When installing memory modules into their slots, you may be required to exert some pressure on them during insertion.

4. When the cards are fully inserted, the edges of the cards are…

    a. Not recessed

    b. Recessed

    c. Gold

5. It is important to tuck in the EMI gaskets when reinstalling the RAM door because…

    a. EMI gaskets are expensive.

    b. They prevent electromagnetic interference.

    c. The memory will not function properly without them in place.

6. True or false: It is acceptable to turn on power to the MacBook while some of its internal and external parts are not in place.

Answer Key

1. True; 2. False, the maximum amount of memory is 1 GB per slot (2 GB total); 3. True; 4. b; 5. b; 6. False, to avoid damage and injury, all parts should be in place and access doors closed before the computer is turned on.

23

Reference Files   MacBook (13-inch) service manual (macbook_13in.pdf)

Time   This lesson takes approximately 1 hour to complete.

Goals   Remove a faulty logic board from a MacBook

Taking Apart a MacBook

In the previous lesson, you learned how simple it is to upgrade the MacBook (13-inch), by installing memory and a hard drive. This lesson focuses on a more complete disassembly of the unit leading to the replacement of a faulty logic board.

This lesson is meant to accompany the Apple Service Source manual, provided as a resource on this book's companion website, www.peachpit. com/ats.deskport3, which demonstrates the procedures in full detail including reassembly. If you are an Apple Authorized Service Provider (AASP), practice the Take Apart and reassembly at your own speed until you feel confident that you can replace any MacBook component to factory specifications. AASPs should download and refer to the latest service manual before servicing any Apple product. Non-AASPs should read the service manual and this text to become familiar with the procedures.

NOTE ▶ If anyone other than an AASP opens a MacBook for any reason, and any damage to the unit results, the repair of such damage will not be covered under the Apple warranty or the AppleCare Protection Plan.

Required Tools and Equipment

In addition to the standard electrostatic discharge (ESD) wrist strap and mat—which you should always use, following the guidelines discussed in Lesson 4, "Safe Working Procedures and General Maintenance"—you will need the following tools and equipment:

▶ Magnetic Phillips #0 and #00 screwdrivers

▶ Nylon probe tool (also called a black stick) or other nonconductive nylon or plastic flat-blade tool

▶ Stack of books, weighted boxes, or other means of support for display while removing and replacing left clutch block

▶ Alcohol wipes

▶ Thermal grease syringe

▶ Felt-tip pen

▶ Coin

▶ Clean, soft, lint-free cloth

▶ Access card

Taking Apart a MacBook

At each stage of the Take Apart procedure, we proceed from component to component, from the outside in. The lead technician has assigned to you the task of replacing a faulty logic board in this unit, after performing the required troubleshooting. Proceed to page 112 of the service manual to review the preliminary steps that you must perform prior to removing the logic board. After reviewing these preliminary procedures, go to page 13 in the service manual to familiarize yourself with the battery removal procedure. Always complete steps in the order they are provided.

Battery

A lithium-ion (Li-ion) battery provides power for the MacBook when it is not being powered by its power adapter. Whenever you are opening a MacBook or any portable computer, the first step is to remove all power from the unit, including the power adapter and the battery.

> **WARNING** ▶ Always shut down the computer before opening it to avoid damaging the internal components or causing injury. After you shut down the computer, the internal components can be very hot. Let the computer cool down for 30 minutes before continuing.

1   Complete steps 1 through 6 on page 14 of the service manual to prepare to remove the battery.

2   Complete step 7 to release the battery latch. Use only a coin to unlock the battery to prevent scratching the unit.

3   Perform step 8 and lift the battery from the battery bay. Set aside the battery on a soft cloth.

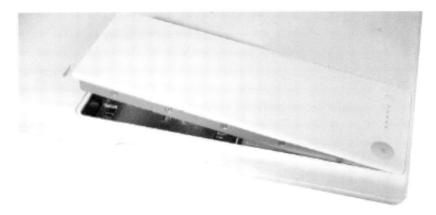

Battery removal

RAM Door (L-Bracket)

Proceed to page 16 in the service manual to become familiar with the random-access memory (RAM) door removal procedure.

1   Perform steps 1 and 2 on page 17 to begin the procedure. The three captive screws will loosen but will not come out.

Captive screws (circled in blue)

2   Perform step 3 on page 18 to remove the L-shaped RAM door. Be careful not to bend it. Set aside the RAM door for later reassembly.

RAM door

Memory

Turn to page 21 of the service manual and review the memory module removal procedure. The memory upgrade you performed in the previous lesson will have made this procedure more familiar to you.

1   Complete steps 1 through 3 on page 21. Pay particular attention to any special cautions or notes. Avoid damaging the dual inline memory module (DIMM) levers by moving them only in a sideways direction, as shown below.

2   Perform step 4 on page 22 to slide out the memory cards from the battery bay.

Top Case (with Keyboard)

Proceed to page 28 in the service manual to become familiar with the top case removal procedures. You will need an access card for this procedure.

You will remove many screws during this procedure, and it is important to keep track of where they came from. It is possible to place a longer screw in the incorrect hole. One suggestion for noting screw locations is to use a large paper packing slip and draw the shape of the computer on the adhesive layer. When you remove the screws, you can place them in the drawing where they belong. Another technique is to use a plastic ice cube tray, and store the screws by component, in the order they were removed. In either case, the goal is to place the correct screw in the hole to which it corresponds.

NOTE ▶ To prevent scratching the computer housing, use a soft cloth as a protective layer.

1   Perform the first two steps in the procedure on page 29 of the service manual, carefully noting the location and length (5.5 mm and 3 mm) of the screws removed.

2   Perform step 3 on page 29 to remove the screws at the back of the computer, again taking note of the different locations and lengths (8 mm and 12 mm).

3   Perform step 4 on page 30 to remove the screws on the bottom case. Take note of the center 11-mm screw: if replaced with a longer screw, it may damage the logic board. Later you will need to install these screws in a particular order, as noted in the service manual.

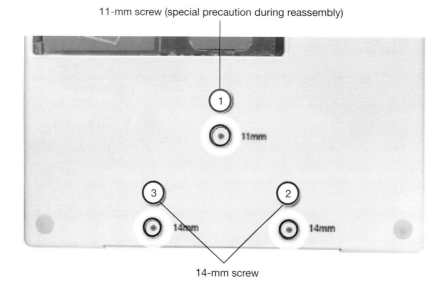

11-mm screw (special precaution during reassembly)

14-mm screw

4   Perform steps 5 and 6 on page 31 to remove the 3-mm front-edge screws. Remove the screws in the order shown.

> **TIP** ▶ You may remember this clever Apple mnemonic when performing this procedure: "2, 4, 7, 9...loosens the top case every time."

5   Perform step 7 on page 31 to remove the 6-mm screws on both outer sides of the battery bay. Do not remove the inner screws near the battery connector.

6   Perform step 8 on page 32 to remove the three screws near the battery bay, near the RAM slots. Due to the recessed location of the screws, you must keep the screwdriver in line with the screw heads as much as possible. Upon reassembly, incorrect installation of these screws could result in the computer wobbling while in use.

7   Review and perform steps 9 and 10 on page 32.

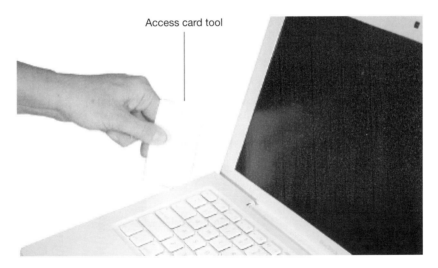

Access card tool

NOTE ▶ Inserting a tool too far or performing this step too quickly could result in breaking some of the snaps that secure the top case. Be especially careful with the left front corner of the top case. Starting at the left corner and working in a counter-clockwise direction, use an access card tool to open the gap along the front of the top case, around the perimeter, and to the right side above the optical drive slot.

8   Perform step 11 on page 33 to release the remaining top case snaps.

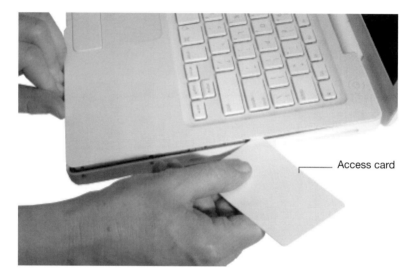

Access card

9   Perform steps 12 and 13 on pages 34 and 35 to disconnect the trackpad cable. Note that both MacBook models are depicted in the service manual.

10 Perform step 14 on page 36 to lift away the top case from the computer, and place it on a soft cloth to protect its surface.

Having removed the top case, the computer is very vulnerable to damage, either from ESD or by leaving a screw dropped inside during reassembly. Take proper precautions during the next steps. Proceed to the next preliminary step.

AirPort Extreme Card

Proceed to page 45 of the service manual and become familiar with the procedure necessary to remove the AirPort Extreme Card.

1 Perform steps 1 and 2 on page 46 to remove the screws that hold the AirPort Extreme Card in place.

2 Perform step 3 on page 46 to remove the AirPort Card.

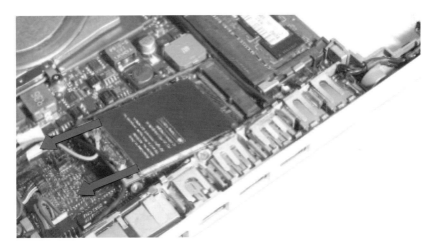

Remove the AirPort Card in the direction shown by the arrows.

3 Perform steps 4 and 5 on page 47 to move aside the speaker cables and disconnect the two antenna cables attached to the AirPort Extreme Card. Place the AirPort Card in an ESD-safe static bag to prevent damage to its sensitive components.

MagSafe DC-In Board

Proceed to page 50 to remove this component.

1   Perform steps 1 and 2 on page 51 to remove the cables and screws from the connector.

2   Perform step 3 on page 52, carefully tilting the MagSafe DC-In Board upwards from the port with a nylon probe tool.

Folded side of the electromagnetic interference (EMI)
shield sandwiched between the EMI flanges

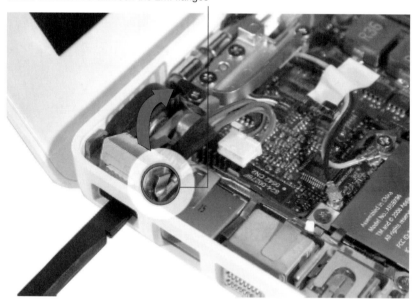

During removal, tilt the connector in the direction indicated by the arrow.

Left Speaker

Proceed to page 54 of the service manual to review the left speaker removal procedure. You completed step 2 of this procedure when you removed the 8.5-mm ground screw during removal of the AirPort Extreme Card. You will not need to perform step 7, as the DC-In was removed during the MagSafe DC-In removal procedure.

> **TIP** ▶ Note the routing of the speaker cable so that you can place it in the same position during reassembly.

1   Perform steps 1 and 3 on page 55 of the service manual.

2   Perform step 4 on page 56 to remove the 6-mm speaker screw.

3   Perform steps 5 and 6 on page 56 to pivot the speaker upward for removal.

4   Place the left speaker in a separate location from the removed screws and other components to avoid contact with the speaker's magnets.

I/O Frame (with Upper EMI Shield)

1   Familiarize yourself with the I/O frame disassembly procedure on page 108 of the service manual, noting the locations and sizes of the screws you will be removing during the procedure.

2   Complete the first step on page 109 of the service manual to remove the screws from the I/O frame.

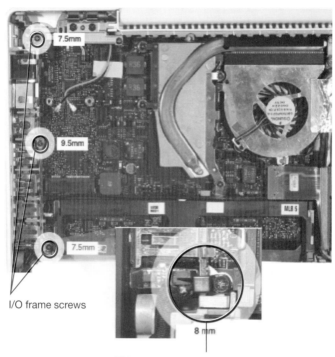

I/O frame screws

This screw may hold a battery cable clip and thus be an 8-mm screw.

3   Perform steps 2 and 3 on pages 110 to remove the EMI shield and I/O frame. Set aside these components for later replacement.

Fan

Review the fan removal procedures on page 70 of the service manual. Pay particular attention to screw placement and size, as well as tape location.

1   Perform steps 1 and 2 on page 71 to remove the fan screws. The 3-mm screw is normally hidden underneath the cable bundles.

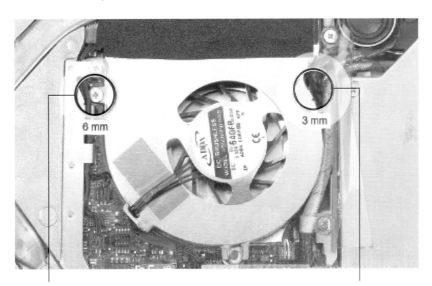

6-mm fan screw   3-mm fan screw under cable bundles

2   Perform steps 3 and 4 on page 72 to tilt up and disconnect the fan cable and remove the fan.

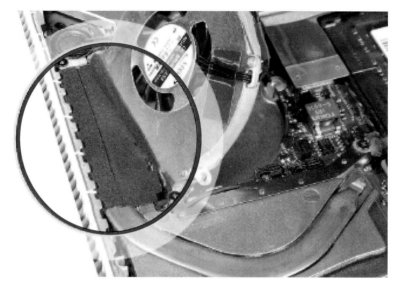

The adhesive foam, circled here, that overlaps the fan and heatsink must be replaced before reassembling the computer, as it tears easily.

Heatsink

Proceed to page 73 in the service manual to become familiar with the heatsink removal procedure, taking care to note screw placement, thermal grease precautions, and heatsink differences.

1   Perform the first step on page 74 of the service manual to remove the four 8-mm screws. Notice the flexible ground tab sandwiched between the lower-right screw and heatsink.

Lower-right screw anchoring the ground tab (circled in blue)

2   Perform steps 2 and 3 on page 75 to loosen the heatsink and disconnect the thermistor connectors from the logic board. Note the routing of the thermistor cables and the placement of the thermal sponge to aid reassembly of the unit.

> NOTE ▶ Proper heat dissipation is crucial to the operation of any computer, but even more so in portable computers that have miniaturized components, including a smaller case and fan. To prevent serious damage to the unit, take the utmost care in following the precautions regarding thermal foam and thermal grease prior to reassembly.

3   Proceed to page 77 in the service manual to review "Checking the Thermal Grease," which will be required during reassembly.

4   Proceed to page 83 to review "Comparing Heatsinks," taking note of the two types of heatsinks. You will use this information during reassembly.

Logic Board

Having performed all ten preliminary steps, you can review the logic board removal procedures on page 112 of the service manual.

1   Perform the first step on page 113 to disconnect the optical drive flex cable from the logic board.

Remove the optical flex drive cable in the direction of the arrow.

2   Perform steps 2 and 3 on page 114 to disconnect the low-voltage differential signaling (LVDS) cable, Bluetooth antenna cable, and hard drive cable connector from the logic board.

3   Perform step 4 on page 115 to remove the 3-mm screw next to the lower end of the midframe.

4   Perform step 5 on page 115 to remove the 3-mm screw between the memory card carriers, as well as four cables. Use a black stick to raise and disconnect the sleep switch.

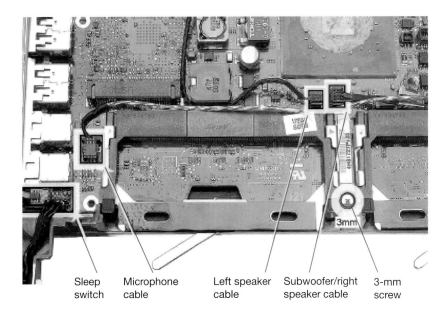

| Sleep | Microphone | Left speaker | Subwoofer/right | 3-mm |
| switch | cable | cable | speaker cable | screw |

5   Perform step 6 and 7 on page 116 of the manual to support the display, disconnect the inverter cable and four screws, and remove the left clutch block and cap.

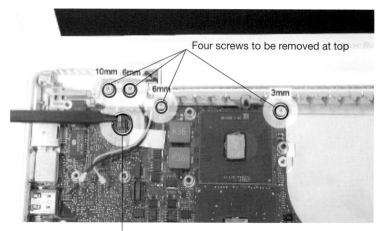

Four screws to be removed at top

10mm 6mm

6mm

3mm

Inverter cable

6   Perform step 8 on page 117 to remove the faulty logic board. If the logic board is not easily removed with a small rocking motion, use a black stick or other nonconductive tool between the side of the bottom housing and ports to gently assist the logic board removal.

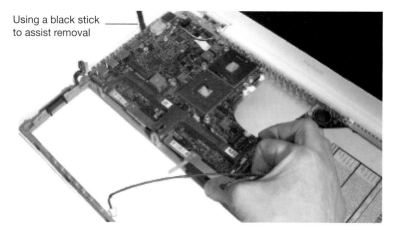

Using a black stick to assist removal

Notice the angle of the logic board as it is being removed.

7   Place the faulty logic board in the ESD-safe static bag that was shipped with the replacement logic board for return to Apple.

When You Are Finished

The Take Apart procedures in this lesson have shown you the step you'll need to take before replacing the logic board. This replacement procedure will require careful attention to detail, since the component can be easily damaged if not replaced correctly.

1 Replace the logic board and preliminary steps components, carefully following the instructions and all precautions in the service manual, beginning on page 118.

2 Verify that the system is working correctly by starting it up, running Apple Hardware Test (AHT), and performing a few user tasks, such as copying files and launching Apple-supplied applications.

Lesson Summary

▶ Whenever you work on the internal components of any computer, it is imperative that you follow proper ESD procedures and follow steps in the service manual in the order provided.

▶ Each product has a different Take Apart procedure, which is explained in detail in its particular service manual. The information presented in this lesson applies to the MacBook (13-inch).

▶ Gaining access to a particular component often requires the removal of several other components first. Each component must be properly protected from damage as it is removed.

▶ You must unplug the power adapter and remove the battery to prevent the MacBook from turning on during the Take Apart procedure.

▶ Some parts, such as thermal foam, must be replaced—not reused—when you reassemble the computer.

▶ Take precautions with fragile internal components to protect them from ESD damage and surface damage. Watch for screws and other small objects that can fall into the computer, shorting the components upon startup.

24

Reference Files	MacBook (13-inch) service manual (macbook_13in.pdf)
Time	This lesson takes approximately 1 hour to complete.
Goals	Given a MacBook, use all technical resources to locate service procedures, symptom charts, and service issues
	Given a problem scenario or malfunctioning MacBook, use the Apple General Troubleshooting Flowchart and the corresponding Apple Service Source manual for this unit, and return the computer to normal operation

Troubleshooting a MacBook

In this lesson, we focus on the Try Quick Fixes and Research Troubleshooting steps of the Apple General Troubleshooting Flowchart, by using symptom charts to effectively troubleshoot and repair MacBook computers. Your familiarity with Apple technical resources coupled with a good understanding of the operation of the MacBook will help you restore a MacBook to normal operation.

> **NOTE ▶** For more detailed information, refer to the Service Source manual for this unit, which can be found on this book's companion website, www.peachpit.com/ats.deskport3.

Before we begin, proceed to the General Information section of the Service Source manual for MacBook (13-inch). On page 314, review both of the kinds of problems that you might see when troubleshooting this unit, and review the Apple General Troubleshooting Flowchart steps.

In the previous lesson, the lead technician assigned you to replace a logic board. In that scenario, the MacBook in question played no sound from its speakers. As you read this lesson, keep this scenario in mind to better understand what procedures the lead technician performed before assigning you to perform this specific part replacement.

NOTE ▸ At the time of publication, there is one service manual that covers both the preproduction and productions models of the MacBook (13-inch). In some of the diagrams, you may notice preproduction model photographs have been used. The operation and troubleshooting of the units is the same, but certain aspects of their construction may be slightly different.

Symptom Charts

The symptom charts included in this lesson will help you diagnose specific symptoms by following the guidelines set forth in the Apple General Trouble-shooting Flowchart. Ensure that you have gathered information, verified the problem, and tried quick fixes as part of your troubleshooting before proceeding. Because cures are listed on the charts in the order of most likely solution to least likely, try the cures in the order presented. Verify whether or not the product continues to exhibit the symptom. If the symptom persists, try the next cure. If a cure instructs you to replace a module, and the symptom persists with the new module, reinstall the original module before you proceed to the next cure.

NOTE ▸ Apple continuously updates the technical resources required to troubleshoot and service their products. It is always recommended that before performing service on any Apple product, that Apple Authorized Service Providers (AASPs) obtain the most current service manual or user guide, appropriate to the model being serviced.

AirPort Extreme Card

AirPort Extreme Card Not Recognized

1   Use Software Update in Mac OS X System Preferences, or see the Apple Software Updates webpage to make sure the latest version of AirPort software is installed.

2 In System Preferences, check the Network pane to verify that the AirPort port is selected.

3 Reseat the AirPort Extreme Card and make sure the AirPort antenna cables are fully connected.

4 Remove and reinstall the AirPort software.

5 Replace with a known-good AirPort Extreme Card.

6 Replace the logic board.

Poor AirPort Reception

1 Refer to Knowledge Base document 88258, "Optimizing AirPort reception in portable computers," which also provides links to useful articles regarding potential sources of interference and how to optimize performance in the AirPort Base Station.

2 Reseat the AirPort Extreme and Bluetooth antenna cables on cards.

3 Check the AirPort Extreme and Bluetooth antenna cables for damage.

4 Replace with known-good AirPort Extreme Card or Bluetooth card.

5 Replace the AirPort Extreme or Bluetooth antenna cables.

NOTE ▶ Remember that devices that operate in the 2.4 GHz band may interfere with wireless connectivity.

Cooling

Unit Unusually Hot

Although this computer runs hotter than previous models, the normal operating temperature is well within safety standards. Your customers may be concerned about the heat generated by the unit. To prevent an unneeded repair, you can compare a customer's computer to a known-good display unit, if available.

> **NOTE ▸** The bottom surface and some areas between the keyboard and liquid crystal display (LCD) hinge of an Apple notebook computer can become hot after extended periods of use. This is normal operating behavior.

1 Verify that the customer uses the computer while it is placed on a flat, hard surface.

2 Verify that the computer is hotter than expected for normal operation. If possible, compare how hot the computer case feels with how hot the case of a running display model feels.

3 Is the computer running hotter than normal?

Yes: Proceed to the next step.

No: The unit is operating normally. Proceed to the Inform Customer step on the flowchart. When speaking with the customer, direct them to Knowledge Base document 30612, "Apple Notebooks: Operating Temperature."

4 Check the processor speed.

5 Is the processor speed running at the setting the customer set?

Yes: Continue with the next step.

No: The computer could be overheating. The operating system will automatically reduce the processor speed if the computer starts to get too hot. Continue with the next step.

6 Check for a failed fan.

7   Can you hear the fan running?

Yes: Continue with the next step.

No: This computer has only one fan. If the unit feels too hot and you do not hear a fan running or cannot feel the air venting over the top of the keyboard, the fan may have failed. Proceed to the Take Apart procedure for replacing the fan.

8   Check for misplaced thermal grease. Each processor chip should have .01 to .12 cc (one-third of a single syringe) of grease on it. It should look completely covered. See the Heatsink section of the service manual on page 73 for complete details.

9   Is the thermal grease applied in the right places and in the right amount, according to the service manual?

Yes: You have eliminated all the immediately known potential causes of an unusually hot unit. Proceed to the Systematic Fault Isolation step of the flowchart.

No: Apply the thermal grease correctly, according to the instructions in the service manual, and then proceed to the Verify Repair step of the flowchart.

Fan fails

1   Check the fan cable connection and check cable for damage.

2   Check the fan for loose parts stuck in fan blades.

NOTE ▶ If you have recently replaced the fan, reinspect the fan unit to ensure that no debris is impeding the fan's normal operation.

3   Replace the fan.

4   Replace the logic board.

Memory

Memory Not Recognized; Beeping Tones

You may need to use increased firm pressure when installing memory. If you or the customer does not fully seat the memory, the computer will not start up or System Profiler may not recognize the memory.

> **NOTE ▶** For further information, refer to Knowledge Base document 303721, "MacBook: How to install memory."

Computer Will Not Start; LED Blinks or Remains On

1 You may need to use increased firm pressure when reseating the memory. Try ejecting the memory and reseating it.

2 Try a known-good memory module.

> **NOTE ▶** If you or the customer do not fully seat the memory, the computer will not start up. See Knowledge Base documents 303083, "Intel-based Mac Power On Self Test RAM error codes," and 303721, "MacBook: How to install memory."

Battery

Battery Will Not Charge

1 Remove any connected peripherals.

2 Try a known-good power outlet.

3 Try a known-good power adapter and power cord.

NOTE ▶ Verify that the power adapter connector glows amber or green. If the power adapter light is green, turn over the computer and press the battery button. If the power adapter is operating correctly, the battery lights should glow green and stay on. Also note that when a lithium polymer battery reaches its end of life, the battery simply ceases to function; there is no downward ramp in performance. This means that any battery issue should prompt questions as to how long the battery has been used. To check the voltage and amperage of the battery, as well as the number of charge cycles the battery has undergone, open System Profiler to the Hardware section, and select Power.

4   Try a known-good battery.

5   Reset the Power Manager by pressing Control-Option-Shift-power.

WARNING ▶ Make sure you do not hold down the Fn (function) key when resetting the Power Manager. Resetting the Power Manager means you will also need to reset the date and time in Date & Time preferences.

6   Try a known-good DC-in board and cable assembly.

7   Replace the battery connector with a sleep switch.

8   Replace the logic board.

NOTE ▶ For information on how to better diagnose short battery life, visit www.apple.com/batteries. Battery calibration is highly recommended to ensure the best possible battery life for the lithium polymer batteries used in the MacBook. Repeat the calibration process occasionally to keep a MacBook battery fully functioning. If the customer uses the MacBook infrequently, it's best to recalibrate the battery at least once a month. Refer to Knowledge Base document 86284, "Calibrating your computer's battery for best performance."

Drives

Optical Drive Does Not Work

There are four clips at the optical drive bezel that can come loose during disassembly or reassembly. If any come loose, they could cause the optical drive to stop functioning.

If, after trying other less-invasive quick fixes, the optical drive still does not function, remove the top case and check that the four clips at the optical drive bezel (shown below) are in place. Refer to the top case Take Apart procedures in the service manual for additional information.

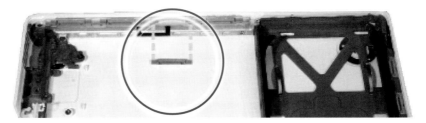

Bezel clips (circled above)

Optical Drive Does Not Accept CD or DVD Disc (Mechanical Failure)

1   Verify that the disc is not warped.

2   Verify that the drive slot has no foreign object in the channel.

3   Verify that the disc is properly seated in the carrier.

4   Replace the optical drive.

NOTE ▶ See Knowledge Base document 88288 "Apple Portables: Tips for inserting discs into the disc drive."

Disc Icon Does Not Show Up on Desktop, or a Dialog Box Appears to Initialize Disc

1 Verify that the correct type of disc is being used.

2 Try cleaning the disc. It may not mount if it is dirty or scratched.

3 Verify that the media is positioned correctly (data side down).

4 Try a different disc.

5 Listen to verify that the disc spins.

6 Reseat the optical drive cable.

7 Verify the logic board connection by trying a known-good optical drive and disc.

8 Replace the optical drive cable.

9 Replace the optical drive.

Disc Will Not Eject

The MacBook optical drive has narrow tolerances for the recommended optical media. If the drive does not accept a disc, it might be the wrong kind of disc. Advise the customer to use discs no thicker than 1.5 mm.

> **NOTE ▶** For further information, refer to Knowledge Base document 88275, "MacBook Pro, MacBook, PowerBook G4, iBook G4: Troubleshooting the slot load disc drive."

1 Verify that the disc is not in use by quitting any applications that may be using it.

2 Press and hold the Media Eject key at the top-right corner of the keyboard. If that does not work, hold down the Fn and Media Eject keys.

3 Drag the disc icon to the Trash or select it and press Command-E.

4 Choose Restart from the Apple menu while holding down the trackpad button.

> **TIP ▶** Foreign objects—coins, staples, paper clips, and other small objects—can be inadvertently inserted into the drive. The limited warranty may not cover the repair under warranty if the cause is foreign object damage.

5 Replace the optical drive.

Target Disk Mode

If you attempt to mount an Intel-based MacBook in Target Disk mode on a Macintosh running Mac OS X 10.3.9 or earlier, you'll see this alert message: "You have inserted a disk containing no volumes that Mac OS X can read." The system you are mounting to must be running Mac OS X 10.4 or later for target disk mode to work.

Power

Power Issues, Power Adapter Dead, No Power

1 Check for damaged pins or magnetic debris on the MagSafe power adapter. If the pins are okay, reseat the power adapter connector and make sure it is fully inserted.

Magnetic debris

NOTE ▶ Refer to Knowledge Base documents 303566, "MacBook Pro: Troubleshooting MagSafe power adapters with stuck pins," and 302461, "Troubleshooting iBook, PowerBook G4, and MacBook Pro power adapters."

2 Remove any connected peripherals.

3 Try a known-good power outlet.

4 Remove the battery and AC power.

5 Press the Caps Lock key to see if the light on the key comes on. If it does, hold the power button down for 6 seconds to shut down the computer and restart.

6 Reset parameter random-access memory (PRAM) by pressing the power button, then holding down the Option-Command-P-R keys until you hear the startup chime at least one additional time after the initial startup chime.

7 Reset the Power Manager.

NOTE ▶ Refer to Knowledge Base document 303319, "Resetting MacBook and MacBook Pro System Management Controller (SMC)."

WARNING ▶ Make sure you do not hold down the Fn key when resetting the Power Manager. Resetting the Power Manager means you will also need to reset the date and time in Date & Time preferences.

8 Test each RAM slot individually with known-good RAM. The computer should still start with only one known-good dual inline memory module (DIMM).

9 Remove the AirPort Extreme Card.

10 If the computer starts on battery power only, try replacing the MagSafe board with a known-good MagSafe DC-in board.

11 Verify cable connections and check cables for damage.

12 Verify that the power button is connected properly to the logic board. If the power button is not functioning correctly or damaged, replace the top case.

13 Replace the logic board.

Computer Shuts Down Intermittently

Apple has released SMC version 1.1 for the MacBook, which improves the computer's internal monitoring system and addresses issues with unexpected shutdowns. This update is recommended for all MacBook systems, including those that received warranty repair. Effective immediately, when repairing MacBook computers with an intermittent shutdown failure, follow these procedures:

1 Make sure the operating system has been updated to Mac OS X 10.4.8 or later and that SMC version 1.1 (or later) has been installed.

NOTE ▶ To verify which SMC firmware version is installed, open System Profiler and select the Hardware section. The Hardware Overview contains useful information that about the computer being repaired. Should you need to update the SMC firmware, consult Knowledge Base document 303880, "Mac OS X: Firmware Updates for Inel-based Macs."

2 Remove all third-party internal and external devices from the computer and test again. If the issue still occurs, go to the next step.

3 Reseat the computer's system memory and test again. If the issue still occurs, go to the next step.

4 Make sure you are testing from a known-good power adapter and a known-good battery that is fully charged.

5 If the intermittent shutdown symptom persists, refer to the final step on pages 324–325 of the service manual.

NOTE ▶ For more details on the MacBook intermittent shutdown issue, refer to Knowledge Base document 304308, "MacBook: Shuts down intermittently."

Input Devices

Trackpad Works Intermittently

The trackpad operation can be affected by hand lotion, humidity, dangling jewelry, and the use of more than one finger on the trackpad.

1   Check for environmental factors such as humidity, hand lotion, or jewelry.

2   Clean the trackpad with a clean, dry lint-free cloth.

> **NOTE ▶** For more information, refer to Knowledge Base document 17228, "Portables: Jumpy or Erratic Trackpad Operation."

Keycap Damaged or Sticking

If a keycap is damaged, you may be able to replace just a keycap rather than the entire top case. Refer to the Additional Procedures section beginning on page 282 of the service manual, to identify the keyboard on the top case and verify whether or not to replace a keycap.

USB Port Is Not Recognizing Known Devices

1   Completely shut down the computer and then press the power button to start it.

2   Use Software Update in Mac OS X System Preferences to verify that the latest software is installed.

3   Use System Profiler to verify that the computer is recognizing the bus.

4   Test the USB port with an Apple keyboard or mouse.

5   Verify that the USB port provides power to the USB device.

6   Verify that the drivers are installed properly for third party, if needed.

7 Try another port, if available.

8 Try a different cable.

9 Try a known-good device.

10 Check that the device's LED indicates that it is getting power.

11 Replace the logic board.

Display

Display Issue: When Displaying a Single Color Over the Screen Area, the LCD Panel Shows One or More Pixels That Are Not Properly Lit

When speaking with customers, please use the following explanation for this issue:

> Active-matrix LCD technology uses rows and columns of addressable locations (pixels) that render text and images on screen. Each pixel location has three separate subpixels (red, green, and blue) that allow the image to be rendered in full color. Each subpixel has a corresponding transistor responsible for turning the subpixel on or off. There are typically millions of these subpixels on an LCD display. For example, the LCD panel used in the Apple Cinema HD display is made up of 2.3 million pixels and 6.9 million red, green, and blue subpixels. Occasionally, a transistor does not work perfectly, which may result in the affected subpixel being turned on (bright) or turned off (dark). With the millions of subpixels on a display, it is quite possible to have a low number of faulty transistors on an LCD. Therefore, a certain number of subpixel anomalies are considered acceptable. Rejecting all but perfect LCD panels would significantly increase the retail price for products using LCD displays. These factors apply to all manufacturers using LCD technology—not just Apple products.

To determine whether or not the display has an acceptable number of pixel anomalies, follow these steps:

1   Set the display image to one of the following colors: all-white display, all-red display, all-green display, or all-blue display.

> **NOTE** ▶ AASPs may refer to Knowledge Base document 112125, "Service Diagnostics Matrix," which has the LCD Tester Diagnostic Utility that generates these patterns on the screen.

2   Using a jeweler's loupe, pocket microscope, or other magnifying device, identify and count each pixel anomaly:

   ▶   Bright subpixel anomaly = subpixel that is always on

   ▶   Dark subpixel anomaly = subpixel that is always off

3   The criteria for the number of acceptable pixel anomalies for this computer are available in this unit's service manual on page 325.

> **NOTE** ▶ When customers express concern about pixel anomalies on their product, AASPs should call Apple technical support for assistance. Do not disclose pixel anomaly procedures or tolerances to the customer.

No Display, or Dim Display, but Computer Appears to Operate Correctly (If Dim, Display Shows Startup Icon and/or Desktop)

1   Remove any connected peripherals.

2   Try a known-good power outlet, power adapter, and power cord.

3   Press F2 (with the Fn key pressed and not pressed) to increase the screen brightness setting.

4   Reboot the computer: Either hold down the Control and Command keys and press the power button; or press and hold the power button for 5 to

10 seconds to shut down the computer, and then press the power button to restart.

5 Reset the Power Manager by pressing Control-Option-Shift-power. Make sure you do not hold down the Fn key when resetting the Power Manager. Resetting the Power Manager means you will also need to reset the date and time in the Date & Time preferences.

6 Reset PRAM by pressing the power button, then holding down the Option-Command-P-R keys until you hear the startup chime at least one additional time after the initial startup chime.

7 Connect an external display and check it for video.

8 If video is fine on the external display, troubleshoot the LCD panel and verify the cable connections to the inverter and the LCD.

9 If the video symptom is the same on the external display, replace the logic board.

10 Verify that the LCD panel cable and LVDS cable connections are seated properly and that the cables are not damaged.

11 Replace the LCD panel.

12 Verify the cable connections and check the cables around the hinges for damage.

13 Replace the logic board.

Sound

Distorted Sound from Speaker(s)

1 Verify that the sound is correct with external speakers/headphones. If sound is correct, replace the top case.

2   Verify that the speaker cables are inserted correctly and check the cables for damage.

3   Open Sound preferences, select Output, and check the balance.

4   Compare the same sound with two different units to make sure that the sound is actually distorted.

5   Open Sound preferences, select Output, and set the slider bar to either the left or right speaker. Play a sound to tell which speaker is not responding and may need replacement. Based on the results, replace either the left or right speaker.

6   Replace the logic board.

No Sound from Speaker(s)

1   Reset PRAM by pressing the power button, then holding down the Option-Command-P-R keys until you hear the startup chime at least one additional time after the initial startup chime.

2   Verify that the speaker cables are connected properly to the logic board, and check cables for damage.

3   Use Software Update to verify that the latest audio update has been installed.

4   Press the F3 key (with the Fn key pressed and not pressed) to verify that mute mode is not enabled.

5   Press the F4 or F5 key (with the Fn key pressed and not pressed) to check the volume setting.

6   Verify that no external speakers or headphones are plugged in.

7   Restart the computer.

8 Open Sound preferences, select Output, and set the slider bar to either the left or right speaker. Play a sound to tell which speaker is not responding and may need replacement. Based on the results, replace either the left or right speaker.

9 Replace the logic board. This is the procedure you performed in the previous lesson. The lead technician had performed this series of troubleshooting steps, prior to assigning the replacement of the logic board to you.

Microsoft

Microsoft Office Applications Will Not Open

Under certain circumstances, if a user installs Final Cut Studio 5.1, Microsoft Office applications may no longer launch.

1 Verify that both Final Cut Studio 5.1 and Microsoft Office are installed, if you have not already done so.

2 Update prebinding. Refer to Knowledge Base document 303677, "Intel-based Mac: Microsoft Office doesn't launch," for instructions.

Windows XP Will Not Install Correctly

Boot Camp Beta lets you install Windows XP on an Intel-based Macintosh. However, Windows XP may not install correctly on this computer when an Apple Mighty Mouse is plugged in. Use the computer's built-in trackpad until after Windows XP is installed and Windows recognizes the mouse.

> **NOTE** ▶ For further information, refer to Knowledge Base document 303575, "Boot Camp Beta: MacBook and MacBook Pro frequently asked questions (FAQ)."

Lesson Review

1. You are troubleshooting a MacBook (13-inch) that is not receiving a response from the trackpad. What does Apple suggest as the first procedure?

   a. Check for environmental factors.

   b. Reset PRAM.

   c. Restart the computer.

   d. Replace the keyboard.

2. True or false: For the MacBook (13-inch), you can test the USB port with an Apple or non-Apple mouse.

3. If the MacBook shuts down intermittently, what does Apple suggest as the first procedure?

   a. Update the computer to Mac OS X 10.4.8.

   b. Install SMC version 1.1 or later.

   c. Both a and b.

   d. None of the above.

4. True or false: The MacBook battery does not require calibration.

5. True or false: The MacBook optical drive will not accept all sizes of optical media.

6. True or false: If you have a MacBook battery that will not charge, you should reset the Power Manager before taking any other troubleshooting steps.

7. The display on a MacBook is dim, but the computer appears to be operating correctly otherwise. Which one of the following troubleshooting steps is not recommended by Apple?

   a. Remove any connected peripherals.

   b. Reboot the computer.

   c. Replace memory.

   d. Verify that the LCD panel cable and LVDS cable are seated properly.

Answer Key

1. a; 2. False, test with an Apple mouse or keyboard only; 3. c; 4. False, the MacBook battery requires occasional calibration, more often if the computer is used infrequently; 5. True; 6. False, resetting the Power Manager is the last troubleshooting step; 7. c

25

This lesson takes approximately 1 hour to complete.

Describe the MacBook Pro models

Explain the differences between the MacBook Pro models

Lesson **25**

About MacBook Pro Models

The MacBook Pro was introduced in January 2006 and is the first Mac notebook powered by the Intel Core Duo processor. The MacBook Pro's Dual Core processors have one single processor chip containing two processor cores. This means that the user can perform multiple tasks simultaneously, such as downloading music and gaming, without compromising speed.

Targeted at the mobile, professional customer, the MacBook Pro has a number of features that appeal specifically to that audience, including Front Row and Apple Remote, which facilitates the remote presentation of photos, videos, and slideshows; iSight camera for video conferencing; a MagSafe Power adapter; illuminated keyboard with ambient light sensor; and scrolling trackpad. Further boosting the performance of the MacBook Pro is a new high-bandwidth architecture using PCI Express and the leading-edge graphics processor from ATI, the Radeon X1600.

The following charts outline the major technical differences among the MacBook Pro models. Use this chart to distinguish between various models and to determine the capabilities of each.

NOTE ▶ For detailed MacBook Pro support go to:

▶ http://support.apple.com/specs/macbookpro/MacBook_Pro.html

▶ http://support.apple.com/specs/macbookpro/MacBook_Pro_
17-inch.html

▶ http://support.apple.com/specs/macbookpro/MacBook_Pro_
15-inch_Glossy.html

▶ http://www.apple.com/macbookpro/specs.html

MacBook Pro

	MacBook Pro (15-inch 1.83 GHz)	MacBook Pro (15-inch 2.0 GHz)
Introduced	January 2006	January 2006
Mac OS (minimum)	Mac OS X 10.4.5	Mac OS X 10.4.5
Display	1.54-inch TFT LCD	1.54-inch TFT LCD
Technical specifications	http://support.apple.com/specs/macbookpro/ MacBook_Pro.html	
Processor	1.83 GHz Intel Core Duo	2.0 GHz Intel Core Duo
Cache	2 MB L2	2 MB L2
Memory	512 MB PC2-5300 SO-DIMM two slots support up to 2 GB	1 GB PC2-5300 SO-DIMM two slots support up to 2 GB
Hard disk	80 GB Serial ATA	100 GB Serial ATA
Optical drive	SuperDrive	SuperDrive

	MacBook Pro (15-inch 1.83 GHz)	MacBook Pro (15-inch 2.0 GHz)
Graphics	ATI Mobility Radeon X1600 graphics processor, 128 MB GDDR3 VRAM, dual-link DVI support	ATI Mobility Radeon X1600 graphics processor, 256 MB GDDR3 VRAM, dual-link DVI support
Expansion	ExpressCard/34 slot 1 FireWire 400 2 USB 2.0 ports 10/100/1000Base-T Ethernet AirPort Extreme (built-in/nonremovable) Bluetooth 2.0	ExpressCard/34 slot 1 FireWire 400 2 USB 2.0 ports 10/100/1000Base-T Ethernet AirPort Extreme (built-in/nonremovable) Bluetooth 2.0
Video connectors	DVI (dual-link) VGA (with included DVI to VGA adapter)	DVI (dual-link) VGA (with included DVI to VGA adapter)
Video camera	Built-in iSight	Built-in iSight

MacBook Pro (17-inch)

MacBook Pro (17-inch 2.16 GHz)

Introduced	April 2006
Mac OS (minimum)	Mac OS X 10.4.6
Technical specifications	http://support.apple.com/specs/macbookpro/ MacBook_Pro_17-inch.html
Processor	2.16 GHz Intel Core Duo

MacBook Pro (17-inch 2.16 GHz)	
Cache	2 MB L2
Memory	1 GB PC2-5300 SO-DIMM two slots support up to 2 GB
Hard disk	120 GB Serial ATA
Optical drive	SuperDrive
Graphics	ATI Mobility Radeon X1600 graphics processor, 256 MB GDDR3 VRAM, dual-link DVI support
Expansion	ExpressCard/34 slot 3 USB 2.0 ports 1 FireWire 400 1 FireWire 800 10/100/1000Base-T Ethernet AirPort Extreme (built-in/nonremovable) Bluetooth 2.0
Video connectors	DVI (dual-link) VGA (with included DVI to VGA adapter)
Video camera	Built-in iSight

Lesson Review

1. Name as many of the MacBook Pro right side ports as you can. Use the Answer Key to fill in any you may have missed.

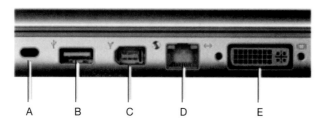

2. Name as many of the MacBook Pro left side ports as you can. Use the Answer Key to fill in any you may have missed.

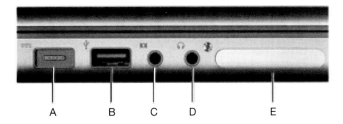

3. Match the installed memory to the MacBook Pro model.

    a. 512 MB

    b. 1 GB

    c. 2 GB

4. Which of the following is true?

    a. The MacBook Pro's Core Duo processors have one single processor chip containing two processor cores.

    b. The MacBook Pro's Core Duo processors have two processor chips containing two processor cores.

    c. The MacBook Pro's Core Duo processors have one single processor chip containing one double-speed processor core.

Answer Key

1. A. Security slot; B. USB 2.0 port; C. FireWire 400 port; D. Gigabit Ethernet (1000Base-T) port; E. DVI port; 2. A. MagSafe power adapter port; B. USB 2.0 port; C. Combined Optical Digital/Audio Line In port; D. Combined Optical Digital/Headphone Out port; E. ExpressCard/34 slot; 3. a. 1.83 GHz MacBook Pro (Jan 2006); b. 2 GHz MacBook Pro (Jan 2006); c. MacBook Pro 17-inch; 4. a

26

Reference Files	MacBook Pro service manual (macbook-pro.pdf)
Time	This lesson takes approximately 15 minutes to complete.
Goals	Install memory in a MacBook Pro

Upgrading a MacBook Pro

The MacBook Pro is the first Mac portable based on an Intel Core Duo processor. It sports a sleek, one-inch thick design that rivals dual-processor desktop performance. Despite having a similar exterior look as the aluminum PowerBook, in reality only the power cord "duckhead" and power adapter AC plug are the same.

This lesson explains how to install additional random-access memory (RAM) in the MacBook Pro to further enhance system performance. We will focus on the original MacBook Pro with a 15-inch liquid crystal display (LCD).

Servicing a MacBook Pro requires a precise and careful touch, as it is composed of many expensive components in a very compact form factor. Always exercise care and do not exert excessive pressure when working on its sensitive parts.

Given the experience gained in previous lessons in this book, you will be required to locate the online resources and sections in the service manual to accompany this text. The Apple Service Manual has been provided for you on this book's companion website, www.peachpit.com/ats.deskport3.

Because users of this computer are most probably professionals, ensuring a minimum of downtime for the customer is of utmost importance.

> **NOTE** ▶ Apple maintains an extensive online collection of instructions and videos for each Macintosh model's Do-It-Yourself (DIY) parts. End users can install these replacement parts and upgrades, as they require only a moderate amount of technical ability and common tools. For a complete list of DIY parts, visit www.apple.com/support and look for the Do-It-Yourself link.

Required Tools and Equipment

To complete this lesson, you need the following:

▶ Clean, non-marring work surface

▶ Soft cloth

▶ Phillips #0 screwdriver (magnetized)

▶ Electrostatic discharge (ESD) wrist strap and anti-static mat

▶ PC2-5300 small outline dual inline memory module (SO-DIMM) double data rate 2 (DDR2) memory modules

Before You Do Anything

Follow the normal antistatic procedures discussed in Lesson 4, "Safe Working Procedures and General Maintenance." It is vital that you follow these instructions and that you do so in the order presented. Take precautions, as ESD can do permanent harm to the computer.

Removing the Battery

Whenever you open any portable computer—whether to install memory or remove a faulty component—your first step is to shut down the computer and remove the battery.

1   Shut down the computer and wait 30 minutes before continuing to allow the computer to cool.

   WARNING ▶ Always shut down the computer before opening it to avoid damaging its internal components or causing injury. After you shut down the computer, the internal components can be very hot. Let the computer cool down before continuing.

2   Disconnect the power cord and any other cables connected to the computer.

3   Place the computer face down on a clean, flat surface.

4   Slide both battery latches away and lift the battery out of the battery bay. Removing the battery will prevent you from turning on the computer accidentally.

WARNING ► Removing the battery before shutting down your computer may result in data loss.

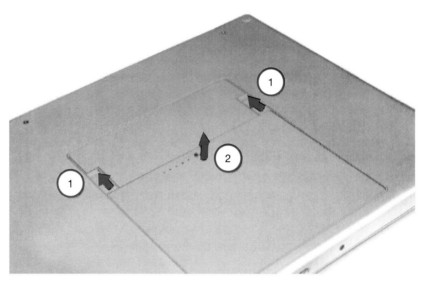

Slide the battery latches (1) and then lift the battery out of the way (2).

Installing RAM

The MacBook Pro comes with a minimum of 512 megabytes (MB) of 667 megahertz (MHz) DDR2 synchronous dynamic RAM (SDRAM) installed. Both memory slots can accept an SDRAM module that meets the following specifications:

► SO-DIMM format

► 1.25 inch or smaller

► 512 MB or 1 gigabyte (GB)

► 200-pin

► PC2-5300 DDR2 667 MHz

Depending on the configuration of the MacBook Pro, both memory slots may already be full. The maximum amount of memory that can be installed in the MacBook Pro is 2 GB, by using 1 GB modules in both memory slots. The MacBook Pro will run well with unmatched memory sizes, however by loading both slots with an equal amount of memory, you can take advantage of the system's dual-channel memory architecture, thus enabling the MacBook Pro to reach a memory throughput of up to 10.7 GB/s.

> **WARNING** ▶ Apple recommends that you have an Apple Authorized Service Provider (AASP) install memory. If a non-AASP attempts to install memory and damages the unit, such damage is not covered by the AppleCare limited warranty.

The following installation process is extremely simple. It assumes you have already removed the MacBook Pro battery following the steps in this lesson.

1   Using a Phillips #0 screwdriver, remove the three screws from the memory door and set the door aside.

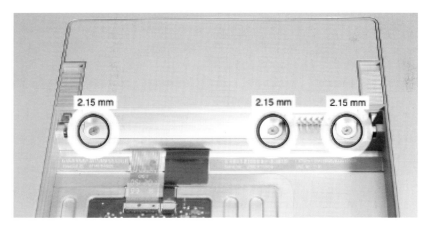

Three 2.15 mm screws (circled in blue)

NOTE ▶ If only one memory module is installed, the factory installs it in the bottom memory slot. Memory must be removed from the top slot before removing from the bottom slot. In the images that follow, both slots are filled with modules that must be replaced.

NOTE ▶ If performing a DIY, non-AASP installation (not using a grounding strap), touch a metal surface inside the computer to discharge any static electricity from your body, without touching any circuit boards or exposed components. An ESD wrist strap and mat are highly recommended.

2 To remove the memory modules, carefully spread the two locking tabs for the top slot away from the top module on both sides and allow the module to pop up slightly.

NOTE ▶ Handle the memory module only by its edges. Do not touch the gold connectors.

Spread locking tabs (1) away from top module; the module will pop up slightly.

3 Pull the module straight back and out of the memory slot at a 25-degree angle. Repeat steps 2 and 3 using the lower set of locking tabs to remove the module from the bottom slot.

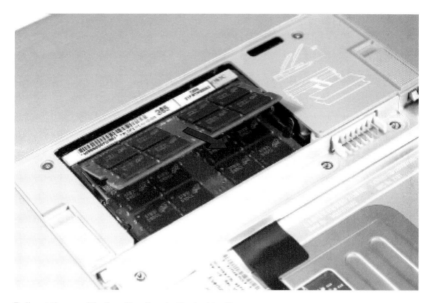

Pull out the card in the direction indicated by the arrow.

4 To install a memory card, align the notch in the memory module with the tooth in the slot, and then insert the module at a 25-degree angle. If installing the bottom module, insert it behind the locking tabs of the top slot.

> **NOTE** ▶ If installing two modules, be sure to install the bottom module first.

5   Firmly push the card straight into the slot until it is fully and securely
seated along its length.

> **NOTE ▶** If the back of the module drops down before it is fully seated,
> raise it up enough to push it fully into the slot.

Insert the memory module in the direction indicated by the arrow.

6   When the card is fully seated, push the card straight down until the tabs
click onto both sides of the card, locking it into place.

7   To ensure that the lower memory card is fully and securely seated, use a nylon probe tool (also called a black stick) or other non-conductive tool leveraged against the frame to evenly push along the back of the card.

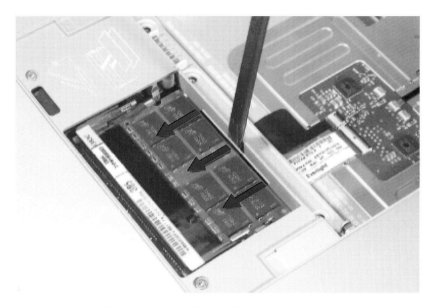

Gently push along the back of the card in the direction of the arrows.

8   To ensure that the upper memory card is seated properly, push with your thumbs to verify that the card is fully seated.

9   Check that the cards are secured by the brackets on both sides.

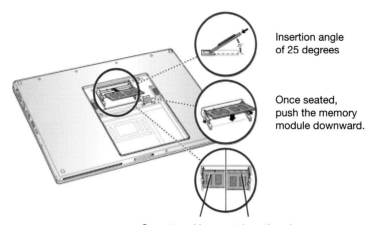

Insertion angle
of 25 degrees

Once seated,
push the memory
module downward.

Correct and incorrect insertion views

10   Install the memory door.

11   Replace the battery.

12   Position the computer in the upright position. Reconnect the power cord and remaining cables. Power on the computer.

13   After logging in, choose Apple menu > About This Mac. Click More Info, select the System Profile tab, and open the Memory overview to verify that the computer recognizes the newly installed memory.

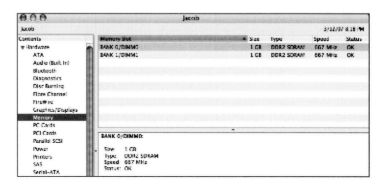

In this example, two 1 GB memory modules have been recognized properly.

Lesson Review

1. True or false: The MacBook Pro models use the same PC2-5300 DDR2 667 MHz type RAM as the MacBook (13-inch).

2. Which of the following tools is necessary when upgrading memory in a MacBook Pro?

    a. TORX T8 screwdriver

    b. Phillips #0 screwdriver

    c. Coin

3. How many SDRAM slots are available in the MacBook Pro?

    a. Zero

    b. One

    c. Two

4. True or false: Before installing memory in a MacBook Pro, you must remove the battery.

5. True or false: Before installing memory in a MacBook Pro, you should touch the gold connectors on the module to discharge any static electricity.

6. How many screws hold the memory door to the bottom of the MacBook Pro?

    a. Three

    b. Four

    c. Five

7. True or false: Top and bottom memory modules are inserted at a 35-degree angle in the MacBook Pro.

8. True or false: It is possible to remove the module from the bottom slot without first removing the module from the top slot in a MacBook Pro.

Answer Key

1. True; 2. b; 3. c; 4. True; 5. False; 6. a; 7. False, modules are inserted at a 25-degree angle; 8. False, removing the top module is necessary before accessing the bottom module.

27

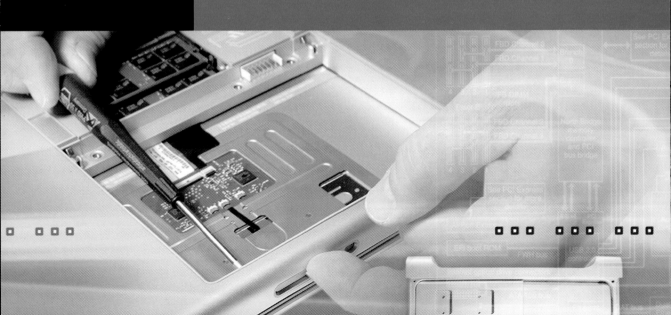

Taking Apart a MacBook Pro

In the previous lesson, you learned how to install memory in a MacBook Pro. Now you're going to become even more familiar with the MacBook Pro, taking apart all of the components necessary to remove a faulty logic board, one of several possible causes of a no video symptom that we will cover in Lesson 28, "Troubleshooting a MacBook Pro."

In the interest of conserving space, reassembly instructions are not reproduced on these pages but are included in the service manual on this book's companion website, www.peachpit.com/ats.deskport3.

Further, this lesson is meant to accompany the Apple Service Source manual, also provided on the website. If you are an Apple Authorized Service Provider (AASP), practice the Take Apart and reassembly at your own speed until you feel confident that you can replace any MacBook component to factory specifications. AASPs should download and refer to the latest service manual before servicing any Apple product. Non-AASPs should read the service manual and this text to become familiar with the procedures.

> **NOTE ▶** If anyone other than an AASP opens a MacBook for any reason, and any damage to the unit results, the repair of such damage will not be covered under the Apple warranty or the AppleCare Protection Plan.

Required Tools and Equipment

In addition to the standard electrostatic discharge (ESD) wrist strap and mat—which you should always use, following the guidelines discussed in Lesson 4, "Safe Working Procedures and General Maintenance"—you will need the following tools and equipment:

- ▶ Soft cloth and clean, non-marring work surface
- ▶ Multi-compartment screw tray (such as a plastic ice cube tray)
- ▶ Nylon probe tool (also called a Black Stick) or other non-conductive plastic flat-blade probe tool
- ▶ Phillips #0 screwdriver (magnetized)
- ▶ Torx T6 screwdriver (magnetized)
- ▶ Razor knife
- ▶ Needle-point metal probe
- ▶ Kapton tape (0.5-inch x 12-yard roll)
- ▶ Thermal grease
- ▶ Gasket kit
- ▶ Alcohol pads
- ▶ Apple Hardware Test (AHT) diagnostic disc for the MacBook Pro model

Taking Apart the MacBook Pro

At each stage of the Take Apart procedure, we'll let you know if there are special notes and information; otherwise, we proceed from component to component, from the outside in.

Proceed to page 99 of the service manual to review the preliminary steps for the logic board replacement. Use the service manual as your main guide and this text to accompany it.

Servicing a MacBook Pro requires a light touch, since it is comprised of many small, expensive components arranged in a compact form factor. Always exercise care, and do not exert too much pressure when disassembling a MacBook Pro.

Battery

Proceed to page 19 in the service manual to review the battery removal procedure. You should be familiar with this procedure from the preceding lesson. Whenever you open any portable computer—whether to install memory or remove a faulty component—your first step is to shut down the computer and remove the battery.

1   Perform step 1 on page 20 of the service manual to shut down the computer and wait 30 minutes to allow for cooling before continuing.

> **WARNING** ► Always shut down the computer before opening it to avoid damaging its internal components or causing injury. After you shut down the computer, the internal components can be very hot. Let the computer cool down before continuing.

2   Perform step 2 on page 20 to disconnect the power cord and any other cables connected to the computer.

3   Complete steps 3 and 4 on page 20 to place the computer face down and to perform the steps to lift the battery out of the battery bay, reading all notes that apply to these steps. Remember that removing the battery will prevent you from turning on the computer accidentally.

Memory

The memory door must be removed so that the top case can be removed. Proceed to page 21 of the service manual to review the memory module removal procedure.

1 Perform steps 1 through 3 on page 22 of the service manual to remove the three screws from the memory door, and set the door aside.

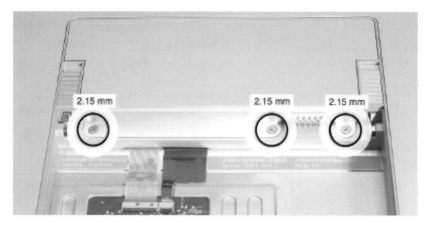

Three 2.15-mm screws

2 Perform steps 4 and 5 on page 23 to remove the installed memory modules.

Top Case

The metal top case and attached keyboard assembly must be removed to access various internal components, including the hard drive. For this procedure, we will be removing the top case only.

1 Perform steps 1 and 2 on page 28 of the service manual to place the computer upside down and remove the six screws, as shown on the following page.

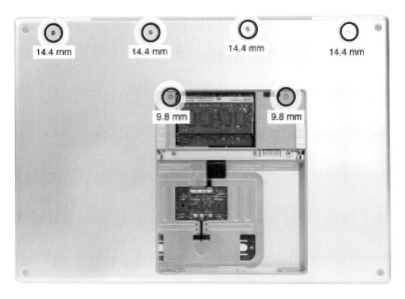

Four 14.4-mm screws are at top and two 9.8-mm screws are in center.

2   Perform step 3 on page 28 to rotate the computer and remove the two screws along the front of the battery bay.

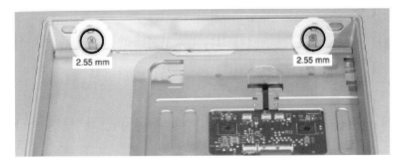

Two 2.55-mm screws are at top.

3 Perform step 4 on page 29 to remove the eight 3.4-mm screws from each side of the computer.

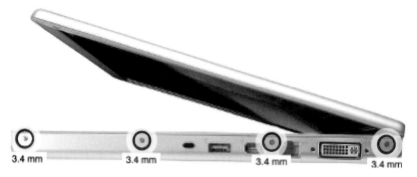

3.4 mm   3.4 mm   3.4 mm   3.4 mm

Four 3.4-mm screws must be removed from each side of the computer.

4 Complete step 5 on page 29 to remove two 3.2-mm screws from the back edge of the computer.

5 Complete steps 6 and 7 on page 30 to face the computer forward and loosen the top case along the rear of the left and right sides.

Gently loosen both rear sides of the top case.

6   Perform step 8 on page 31 to slowly encourage the snaps and screw tabs to release as you move right. Pay attention to the note for this step. A snapping noise as the snaps release is normal.

WARNING ▸ To preserve the delicate bead trim around the top case, try using your fingernails to gently loosen and pull up on the top case before using a nylon probe tool.

The tabs have released, but the top case is still connected to the bottom case.

7   Perform step 9 on page 32 to disconnect the keyboard flex cable from the logic board.

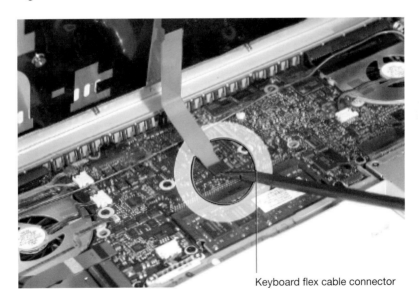

Keyboard flex cable connector

Right Ambient Sensor Lens

The right ambient sensor lens is actually part of the logic board. You will need to remove its dust cover. Proceed to page 83 in the service manual and perform steps 1 and 2 to carefully remove the right sensor's dust cover.

Right Speaker

Turn to page 94 in the service manual to review the right speaker removal procedure.

1   Perform step 1 on page 94 to remove the low voltage differential signaling (LVDS) grounding strap screw.

2   Once you have accessed the tape along the right side of the speaker, perform step 2 to pry up the tape with a nylon probe tool and allow the speaker to rotate.

Carefully use the tool to pry the tape.

3   Complete the speaker removal by performing steps 3 and 4 on page 95 to lift out the speaker and disconnect the thermal sensor, if required.

Fans

Turn to page 86 of the service manual to review the fan removal procedure.
Pay particular attention to any notes.

1   Perform steps 1 and 2 on page 87 to remove the right fan.

WARNING ▶ Be very careful in using a razor knife to cut the Kapton
tape. A small slip of your hand could seriously damage the logic board.

2   Perform step 1 on page 88 to disconnect the ambient light sensor flex
cable from the logic board.

The tight sensor flex cable connector is very fragile.

3   Perform steps 2 and 3 on page 89 to peel the flex cable from the fan cover, and then disconnect and move cables out of the way.

4   Perform steps 4 and 5 on page 90 to cut the Kapton tape from the fan and remove the three screws that hold the fan in place.

5   Complete step 6 on page 91 to remove the left fan from under the left speaker screw tab.

Remove the left fan in the direction indicated by the arrow.

Optical Drive

Turn to page 75 in the service manual and review the optical drive removal procedures.

1   Perform step 1 on page 76 of the service manual to disconnect the flex connector.

2   Complete the removal of the optical drive by performing step 2.

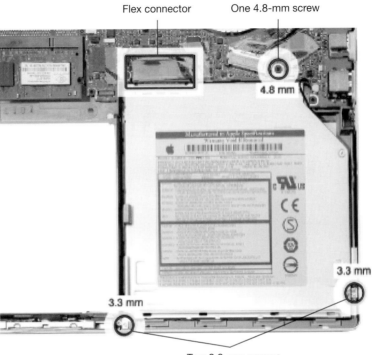

Flex connector   One 4.8-mm screw

4.8 mm

3.3 mm

3.3 mm

Two 3.3-mm screws

Logic Board

Review the logic board procedures in full starting on page 99 of the service manual. Pay attention to notes and warnings.

1   Perform 1 step in the procedure on page 100 to disconnect cables from the logic board.

2   Perform step 2 on page 101 to tape the sensor cable to the display assembly.

3   Complete step 3 on page 101 to remove 10 screws that hold the logic board in place as pictured below.

Note the location of the one screw that is shorter than the rest. Be sure to keep track of screw placement.

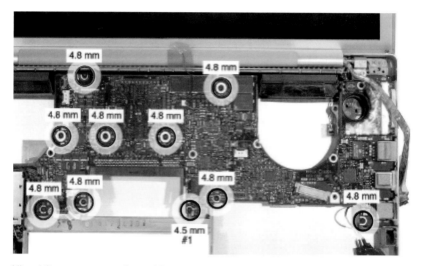

Nine 4.8-mm screws and one 4.5-mm screw on the logic board

4   Read step 4 on page 102 of the service manual. This step is extremely important.

5   Ensure that you have indeed removed all of the logic board screws, then perform step 5 to slowly begin to lift the logic board.

6   Without removing the logic board completely, perform step 6 on page 102 to remove the connector from under the board.

7   Perform steps 7 and 8 on page 102 to carefully lift the left side of the board to disconnect the thermal sensor cable.

Thermal sensor cable (circled in blue)

8   Review the warning note on page 103 and perform step 9 to remove the logic board. Set aside the logic board in an antistatic bag.

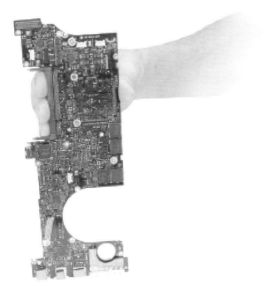

Logic board

The logic board replacement procedures are provided in the service manual beginning on page 104. Please review all steps in full before performing any procedures. Installation of EMI gaskets and new thermal grease is crucial to the proper operation of the unit.

When You Are Finished

1   Return the faulty logic board to Apple in the packaging provided.

2   Install the replacement logic board following the instructions in the service manual.

3   Verify that the system works correctly by starting up the system and running AHT, Apple System Profiler, and some common Apple applications that test the system's capabilities, including sound, display, and hard drive functions.

Lesson Summary

▶   Whenever you work on the internal components of any computer, it is imperative that you follow proper ESD procedures and follow steps in the service manual in the order provided.

▶   Each product has different Take Apart procedures that are explained in detail in its particular service manual. The information presented in this lesson applies to the MacBook Pro.

▶   Gaining access to a particular component often requires the removal of several other components first. Each component must be properly protected from damage as it is removed.

▶   You must unplug the power adapter and remove the battery to prevent the MacBook Pro from turning on during the Take Apart procedure.

▶   Some parts—such as thermal grease—must be replaced, not reused, when you reassemble the computer.

► Take precautions with fragile internal components to protect them from ESD and surface damage. Screws and other small objects can fall into the computer, shorting the components upon startup.

► Always exercise care and do not exert too much pressure when disassembling the MacBook Pro, as internal components are fragile.

► When taking apart components, pay particular attention to the routing of cables and connectors. Reassembly requires these to be in the correct place.

► Some connectors are very fragile and require special precautions.

28

Reference Files   MacBook Pro service manual (macbook-pro.pdf)

Time   This lesson takes approximately 1 hour to complete.

Goals   Given a MacBook Pro, locate service procedures, symptom charts, and service issues

Given a problem scenario or malfunctioning MacBook Pro and the Apple General Troubleshooting Flowchart, return the computer to normal operation

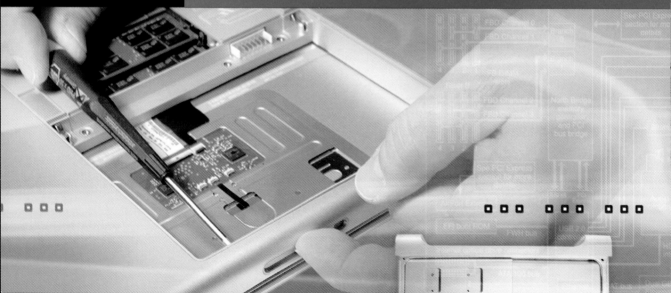

Troubleshooting a MacBook Pro

In this lesson, you'll find overview information about general trouble-shooting procedures and detailed symptom charts, both of which will help you troubleshoot and repair MacBook Pro computers. Being famil-iar with Apple technical resources and some of the underlying operations can help you troubleshoot and restore the computer to normal operation more quickly.

NOTE ▶ For more detailed information, refer to the Service Source manual for this unit, which can be found on this book's companion website, www.peachpit.com/ats.deskport3.

Servicing a MacBook Pro requires a light touch and precision. Be careful with sharp tools that can easily damage its components.

As you read this lesson, consider the symptoms (discussed in Lesson 27, "Taking Apart a MacBook Pro") that would lead you to conclude that a logic board replacement is necessary. Use best practices and Apple resources to set the example for others, because eventually, you will be the lead technician!

General Information

Wire and Flex Cables

Because of its extremely thin enclosure design and dispersed circuit board, the MacBook Pro utilizes a large number and variety of flex cables and wire cable harnesses. Many of these cables carry multiple types of signals.

The following is a list of the cables and the signals that run through them. If you notice a group of functions not working, it is likely that the cable is not properly inserted or the connector is damaged.

Cable or Flex Cable	Signal(s) Running Through It
SuperDrive flex	SuperDrive data, power, and control signals (cable select info)
Left I/O board flex	Audio in and out Left and right speakers Left USB (2 ports) ExpressCard data AirPort power and data
Power button cable	Power-on signal
Infrared cable	Infrared power and data
Hard drive flex	Hard drive power and data Sleep LED power Infrared power and data Bluetooth power and data
Sleep LED cable	Power to sleep LED
Ambient light sensor (left) flex	Left ALS power and data

Cable or Flex Cable	Signal(s) Running Through It
Main battery connector wire harness (to logic board and left I/O board)	Battery power to main logic board Power adapter power to battery and system
Speaker assembly cable	Left speaker audio Right speaker audio Internal microphone audio
Trackpad flex	Trackpad data and power Power-on button Keyboard backlight power Sleep sense signal Keyboard data
Bluetooth antenna cable assembly	Bluetooth radio signal
iSight video signal cable	Video power and signal from iSight camera
AirPort Extreme antenna cable	AirPort radio signal
Left fan cable	Power/control for left fan
Right fan cable	Power/control for right fan
Inverter cable (to logic board)	Display backlight control Inverter control signal (brightness)
LVDS cable	Video data
Thermal sensors (bottom case, heatsink)	Internal temperature data

Many of the MacBook Pro components are connected to each other by thin ribbon cables that can be easily creased, cracked, or torn, and they must be handled in a deliberate and cautious manner. Because ribbon cables are often wrapped around or threaded through parts in a specific path, carefully note the cable's path, so that you can reinstall it in exactly the same way.

In the MacBook and MacBook Pro systems, the case is very tightly packed with components, which means that cable routing can sometimes be complicated. Misrouting a cable during parts replacement can render the system defective.

Like the cables they connect, cable connectors are also fragile and can be broken easily. When a connector is inadvertently broken, the part containing the connector must be replaced. Some MacBook Pro connectors are not keyed, making it possible to install the connector backwards. Forcing an improperly connected cable can also short out other components. When repairing MacBook Pro computers, avoid costly errors by taking time to carefully and accurately attach each connector.

It is highly recommended that you trace cable routing inside the unit using a marker pen prior to removing a cable. This will enable you to put the cable back where it belongs with a minimum of guesswork.

Power Button Pads on Logic Board

With the top case removed, the power button is disconnected. Instead of having to reconnect the top case to turn on the system, there are two pads on the logic board that can be very carefully shorted across (with a metal tool like a flathead screwdriver) to act as the power button.

These pads are located near the edge of the logic board, just above the center of the hard drive. The pads are marked "PWR BTN" and are outlined and separated by a white line.

Power button pads

Resetting the Power Manager (SMC)

In Lesson 3, "General Troubleshooting Theory," resetting the power management unit, now called the System Management Controller (SMC), is a quick fix. The SMC reset sequence for the MacBook Pro is as follows:

1   If the computer is on, turn it off.

2   Disconnect the power adapter and remove the main battery.

3   Hold down the power button for five seconds, then release.

4   Install the main battery and connect the power adapter.

5   Press the power button to restart the computer.

Using Caps Lock LED to Check for Power

There are situations, after a system crash for instance, when the computer may seem to be shut down (no sleep light, no hard drive access, screen is dark, no fan, and so on), but the logic board is actually still running—drawing power and generating heat.

> **WARNING ▶** In this situation, if the computer is put in an enclosed environment like a carrying bag, the computer can overheat.

In this situation, press the Caps Lock key. If the LED glows, the power manager is running on the logic board. If pressing the Caps Lock key and other methods of waking it up fail (closing the lid to make it sleep and trying to wake it again, for example), hold down the power button for a full six seconds to force a shutdown of the computer. Restart the system to check if it boots up normally.

> **NOTE ▶** In previous PowerBook models, the keyboard was connected directly to the power manager, and this method worked under all conditions. However, the keyboard is now a USB device, and if the OS hangs, the keyboard may not be able to respond. So if the Caps Lock light does not come on, the computer still may be drawing power. If in doubt, hold down the power button for six seconds to force a shutdown of the computer.

Symptom Charts

The symptom charts included in this lesson will help you diagnose specific symptoms by following the guidelines set forth in the Apple General Trouble-shooting Flowchart. The steps listed to solve a particular problem are listed sequentially, in the order to be performed. Perform each step until the symptom is resolved. If a cure instructs you to replace a module, and the symptom continues to persist with the new module, reinstall the original module before you proceed to the next cure.

> NOTE ▶ These symptom charts are taken from the service manual that was current at the time of publication and which appears on this book's accompanying website. AASPs should always refer to the latest service manual before servicing any Apple product.

Startup

Startup sequence

The Intel-based MacBook Pro starts up very much like the previous professional Macintosh portable computers. If power is available to the system, pushing the power-on button will boot the system.

▶   As the system boots, it performs a power-on self test (POST).

> NOTE ▶ For a full description of POST error codes, kernel panic dialog, or flashing question mark, consult the startup symptom charts in the Service Source manual for this unit.

▶   Initially, the screen stays dark, and the sleep LED glows solid.

▶   Soon after, the boot chime sounds (if the sound is not muted), the backlight lights up a gray screen, and the sleep LED turns off.

▶   The Apple logo appears, and the turning gear animates below it.

▶   After that, the screen turns blue, and a system login dialog containing a progress bar appears.

▶   Finally, either a login dialog appears, or if auto-login is active, the user's desktop background appears, followed by Finder features such as the menu bar, the Dock, and desktop icons, some of which populate incrementally depending on how many startup items are loading.

The computer will not start up (no fan movement, no hard drive spin up, and display is not lit)

1   Remove any connected peripherals and eject any ExpressCard.

2   Press the button next to the LEDs on the battery to check whether the battery has enough charge to start the computer.

    At least one LED must light solid (not flashing).

3   Connect a known-good 85W power adapter and power cord or plug to a known-good power outlet; make sure the DC plug is properly inserted. The MagSafe connector LED should light up. If it does not light up, consult the Power Adapter troubleshooting section.

4   Try powering up without the battery installed. If it boots, replace the battery connector cable.

5   Reset the power manager (SMC). See new procedures in the "Resetting the Power Manager (SMC)" section earlier in this lesson.

    Boot up the system and watch the sleep indicator. If it turns on solid and turns off, the main logic board is getting power and completing the initial boot cycle. If the light does not turn off, the boot cycle is not being completed. This may be caused by the hard drive not being seen by the system, by corrupted system software, or by a hardware issue. Try booting off the Mac OS X Install Disc 1. If no video appears, there may be a hardware issue. See the following section.

6   Press the Caps Lock key to see if key light comes on. If it does, hold down the power button for six seconds to shut down the computer and restart.

7 If it still doesn't start, verify that the power button cable is connected properly to the top case flex cable assembly and that the flex cable is connected correctly to the logic board. If the power button is damaged or not functioning correctly, replace the top case.

8 Disconnect the keyboard completely. Inspect the connectors. Restart with the keyboard disconnected.

9 Remove any additional RAM.

10 Try removing the AirPort Extreme Card from its socket and start the computer. If it starts, shut it down and check the flex cable connector and the connector on the logic board and replace the damaged parts.

11 Reseat the following flex cables:

▶ Left I/O flex cable

▶ Hard drive flex cable (will boot to flashing folder if not connected or corrupt)

▶ Optical drive flex cable

▶ Trackpad flex cable

▶ Display LVDS cable

▶ Thermal sensor cables

12 If the computer starts up, inspect the flex cable connector and its terminal on the logic board for damage and replace the damaged parts.

13 Try a known-good left I/O board.

14 Replace the logic board.

Computer begins to power up, the fans and hard drive are spinning, pressing the Caps Lock key turns on the LED, but there is no startup chime or video

1 Reset the power manager (SMC). See new procedures in the "Resetting the Power Manager (SMC)" section earlier in this lesson.

2   Try connecting an external display to check for a video signal that is not being displayed on the LCD. If no external video appears, skip to step 4. Otherwise proceed to step 3.

3   Check all cable and flex connections to the logic board. Try restarting.

4   Replace the logic board.

System shuts down intermittently

1   Disconnect all external peripherals and eject any ExpressCard.

2   Make sure a known-good, fully charged battery is properly inserted. Check that the battery latch is fully engaged and is not broken or getting caught before fully catching. Check the battery connection to the logic board.

3   Inspect the battery connector in the battery bay. Make sure all blades are visible and not bent. If the battery connector is damaged, replace it.

4   Make sure the system is not overheating, the air vents are clear, and the unit was not used on a soft surface.

5   Make sure all feet are still on the bottom case. If not, order a foot replacement kit.

6   Check that the fan cables are connected and the fans are operational.

7   Remove the battery and connect a known-good 85W power adapter and power cord or plug to a known-good power outlet; make sure the DC plug is properly seated.

   The MagSafe connector LED should light up. If it does not light up, consult the Power Adapter troubleshooting section first to determine the issue.

8   Verify that both thermal sensors are well seated with no damage to the cables or connectors.

9   Verify that the left I/O board cable is securely connected and that the cable shows no signs of wear.

10   Try a known-good left I/O board.

11   Check that the thermal material between the heatsink and the logic board is making contact by unscrewing the logic board and gently pulling up on the left side to verify resistance caused by adhesion of the thermal material. If it's not making contact, replace the thermal material for the processor, control ASIC, and video chip (see the Logic Board take-apart chapter in the service manual).

12   Replace the logic board.

Computer shuts down almost immediately after startup

1   Disconnect all external peripherals and eject any ExpressCard.

2   Make sure a known-good battery is fully inserted. Check the battery charge and make sure that at least two LED charge indicators light; otherwise connect the adapter.

     The MagSafe connector LED should light up. If it does not light up, consult the Power Adapter troubleshooting section first to determine the issue.

3   After charging for a while, if the battery does not seem to charge, or if it is charged but quickly discharges, replace the battery.

4   Check the battery connection to the logic board, and check wire attachment to connectors.

5   If just before the system shuts down the sleep LED comes on briefly, check the thermal sensor connections to the main logic board. They should be fully seated with no damage to the wiring. If the thermal sensor cable or connector is damaged, replace the thermal sensor.

6   If a known-good battery does not charge, replace the left I/O board.

7   Replace the logic board.

Application quits, kernel panic, or other booting problems

1   If a specific application quits, reinstall or replace the application. Verify that the application is compatible with the current version of Mac OS X.

2   Clear parameter RAM (PRAM). Hold down Command-Option-P-R during startup until you hear a second startup chime. For more information, consult Knowledge Base document 2238, "Resetting Your Mac's PRAM and NVRAM."

3   Run Disk Utility from the Software Install and Restore DVD.

4   Perform a clean install of system software with the Software Install and Restore DVD that came with the computer.

5   Reboot the system. Run Apple Service Diagnostic in loop mode (Control-L) for an extended time to test the memory. If the test finds bad memory, replace the modules one at a time and test until all bad modules are replaced with known-good modules.

6   Replace the logic board.

AirPort Extreme

NOTE ▶ The AirPort Extreme Card is now separate from the Bluetooth module. In addition, the AirPort antenna is now in the clutch barrel behind the gray plastic window. The Bluetooth antenna is now separate from AirPort and mounted just in front of the hard drive.

AirPort Extreme Card is not recognized

1   In Mac OS X, use Software Update in System Preferences, or see the Apple Software Updates webpage, to make sure the latest version of AirPort Extreme software is installed.

2   Restart the computer.

3   Open Network preferences and make sure AirPort is on and a wireless network is selected.

4   Reseat the AirPort Extreme Card in its slot.

5   Remove and reinstall the AirPort Extreme software.

6   Replace with a known-good AirPort Extreme Card.

7   Replace the left I/O board.

8   Replace the main logic board.

AirPort connection is slow

1   Move the computer closer to the AirPort Base Station or other AirPort device.

2   Check the number of users trying to use AirPort in the area.

    Too many users accessing the network at the same time causes heavy network traffic and slowdowns. To improve network connection speed, consider adding AirPort Base Stations.

3   Check for other changes in the environment that may cause interference with the AirPort signal. For more information, consult Knowledge Base document 58543, "AirPort: Potential sources of interference."

4   Use Software Update in System Preferences, or see the Apple Software Updates webpage, to make sure the latest version of AirPort Extreme software is installed.

5 Restart the computer.

6 Check the AirPort Extreme antenna connection to the AirPort Extreme Card.

7 Reseat the AirPort Extreme Card in its slot.

8 Replace with a known-good AirPort Extreme Card.

9 Check the AirPort Extreme antenna wires coming from the clutch barrel for a nicked insulator or crimped wire. If the wires are bad, replace the AirPort Extreme antenna in the clutch barrel.

10 Replace the left I/O board.

11 Replace the main logic board.

Battery

Battery will not pop up

1 Flip over the unit and slide the battery latches.

2 If the battery does not pop up, use a small plastic flat-blade tool to pry up the battery around the battery latch.

3 Try a new battery.

4 Verify proper latch operation by exercising the latch. If it does not move smoothly or evenly, replace the bottom case.

5 If the latch does operate correctly, verify that the customer is not installing the battery with excessive force or the body of the battery has not been deformed around its perimeter. If there is no sign of abuse (dents or scratch marks), replace the battery under warranty.

WARNING ▶ If the battery plastic housing has been damaged, or the two halves of the housing have separated, the battery is unsafe for use.

Battery will not charge

1   Remove any externally connected peripherals or any ExpressCard.

2   Try a known-good power outlet.

3   Connect a known-good 85W power adapter and power cord or plug; make sure the DC plug is properly inserted. The MagSafe connector LED should light up. If it does not light up, consult the Power Adapter trouble-shooting section first to determine the issue. If the power adapter light is green, turn over the computer and press the battery button. The battery lights should glow green and stay on if the power adapter is operating correctly.

4   Try a known-good battery. If it charges, replace the battery. If doesn't charge, check the battery connector and its connection to the logic board.

5   Replace the battery connector assembly (requires removing the logic board).

6   Reset the power manager. See new procedures in the "Resetting the Power Manager (SMC)" section earlier in this lesson.

7   Make sure the left I/O cable is firmly connected. Look for damaged insulation or wires.

8   Replace the left I/O power cable.

9   Replace the left I/O board.

10 Replace the logic board.

Battery will not charge completely

If the battery appears to stop charging between 95 and 99 percent, this is normal operation. Refer to Knowledge Base document 88344, "Apple portable computer's battery does not show full charge in Mac OS X." The information in this article applies to the MacBook Pro as well.

Short battery life

Refer to Apple Knowledge Base document 86284, "Calibrating your computer's battery for best performance," for tips on extending battery life and explanations of some concepts of battery use.

There are three categories of scenarios to consider:

If there is a system issue (not the battery):

1   If you have the customer's power adapter, plug it into a known-good outlet and verify that it can charge the system. Make sure it is the correct 85W power adapter.

2   Plug a known-good 85W power adapter into a known-good outlet. Verify that the MagSafe connector is fully seated in the computer.

3   Check whether the customer's system is set up for heavy battery power use (AirPort on, Bluetooth on, optical media always in drive, Processor Performance set to Highest in Options pane of Energy Saver preferences, and so on).

4   Test the computer with all third-party devices removed.

5   Reset the power manager (SMC). See new procedures in the "Resetting the Power Manager (SMC)" section earlier in this lesson.

If the battery needs calibration or is nearing the end of its useful life:

▶ Calibration should be done when you first use the battery, and every few months after. It allows the battery to properly calculate how much power is left in the battery.

  NOTE ▶ Consult pages 194 and 195 of the service manual for additional information on how to perform the battery calibration procedure.

▶ The battery is a consumable part. You can charge and discharge it only so many cycles before it becomes depleted and can no longer hold a charge.

If the battery has a defect:

1 Symptoms include, but are not limited to, a relatively new battery that:

  ▶ Will not charge at all

  ▶ Displays an "X" in the Battery menu extra icon

  ▶ Has a status light on its case that will not go out

  In the first two cases, the battery may need calibration—try this first. In addition, after troubleshooting at the system level, if the battery causes abrupt shutdowns or goes to sleep without warning, the battery can be considered severely degraded; follow the procedure in the note below.

2 After recalibrating the battery, test it under the performance test specified in Knowledge Base document 86440, "PowerBook, iBook: Battery Life." If the battery lasts less than two hours, it is considered to have severely degraded performance.

  NOTE ▶ If the battery was purchased (either with the computer or as a standalone part) in the last 90 days and exhibits severely degraded performance (as defined above), provide an in-warranty replacement. If the battery was purchased between the last 90 to 365 days, have the customer calibrate the battery. If, after calibration, the battery still exhibits severely degraded performance, then provide an in-warranty replacement. If the battery was purchased more than 365 days ago, the customer must purchase a new battery.

Bluetooth

NOTE ▶ Unlike the previous PowerBook G4 (15-inch Double-Layer SD), the AirPort Extreme and Bluetooth 2.0 functions are on separate cards.

Bluetooth preferences does not appear in system preferences

1 Check for software/firmware updates using Software Update.

2 Check the Bluetooth card flex cable. Make sure the cable is not damaged and is fully seated.

3 Check the hard drive flex cable to the main logic board.

4 Replace the Bluetooth card.

5 Replace the hard drive flex cable.

6 Replace the logic board.

Other devices do not recognize Bluetooth card

1 Open Bluetooth preferences and make sure that under the Settings tab, Discoverable is selected.

2 Make sure the Bluetooth antenna is properly installed and connected to the Bluetooth card.

3 Replace with a known-good Bluetooth card.

4 Replace the logic board.

Display

Display latch not working

When the display is being closed, two latch hooks in the top of the display housing should be magnetically pulled down through the slots in the top case and secured by the latch mechanism. When the latch button is pushed, the hooks should release and retract into the display housing. If the latch hooks are broken, replace the display latch hook assembly.

When displaying a single color over the screen area, the LCD panel shows one or more pixels that are not properly lit

To determine whether or not the display has an acceptable number of pixel anomalies, consult the service manual on pages 196 and 197.

ExpressCard/34

ExpressCard will not insert into the ExpressCard slot

1   Make sure the ExpressCard is 34mm in width. 54mm ExpressCards will not fit in this slot.

2   Make sure the ExpressCard is right side up (cards are keyed and cannot be inserted upside down).

3   Verify the ExpressCard is not warped or damaged in any way. If so, replace the card.

4   Try a different ExpressCard.

5   Carefully raise the ExpressCard slot cover and check for a foreign object inside the slot.

6   If the slot cover is preventing the card from being inserted, reseat the ExpressCard on the left I/O board by making sure the cage is closer to the main logic board. The door may catch on the top of the ExpressCard mechanism.

7   Replace the ExpressCard cage.

8   Replace the left I/O board.

ExpressCard does not mount to the desktop

1   Make sure the ExpressCard has its drivers installed.

2   Check if a known-good ExpressCard works in this slot. The ExpressCard may be bad.

3   Check the left I/O board flex cable connection to the logic board.

4   Try inserting the card without the ExpressCard cage installed on the left I/O board. If the card is recognized, reinstall the ExpressCard cage with the card in place.

5   Replace the ExpressCard cage.

6   Replace the left I/O flex cable.

7   Replace the logic board.

Hard Drive

Internal hard drive will not initialize

1   Make sure the hard drive is a cable select drive set as a master (0).

2   Start up from the MacBook Pro Mac OS X Install Disk 1 disc that came with the computer (hold down the C key during restart).

3   When the Installer opens, select Open Disk Utility from the Installer menu.

If the hard drive is recognized, format it under the Erase tab.

If the hard drive is not recognized, reseat the hard drive flex cable, or replace if needed.

4   If still not recognized, replace the hard drive.

5   Reinstall system software using the MacBook Pro Mac OS X Install Disc 1, which came with the system.

> **TIP**   If you have crucial data and require disk recovery services, an option would be to visit www.drivesavers.com. For additional information, refer to Knowledge Base document 31077, "DriveSavers: Hard Drive Data Recovery & Warranty Implications." Mention of third-party products or services is for informational purposes only and constitutes neither an endorsement nor a recommendation on the part of any party associated with this book.

Apple Remote

Remote won't communicate with system applications such as iTunes or iPhoto, or with the optical drive

1   Make sure of the following when using the Apple Remote:

▶   You are within 30 feet of the front of the computer.

▶   You have an unobstructed line-of-sight to the front of the computer.

▶   You are pointing the lens end of the Apple Remote directly at the front of the computer.

▶   The computer is powered on and awake.

▶   The "Disable remote control infrared receiver" checkbox in Security preferences is *not* selected.

▶   Make sure the active application works with Apple Remote. Apple Remote uses Front Row, and from Front Row it can access DVD Player, iPhoto, iTunes, and QuickTime Player.

▶   Make sure the remote is paired with the computer. Open Security preferences and select Unpair if available. Close Security preferences and re-pair the Apple Remote with the computer. Consult Knowledge Base document 302545, "Pairing your Apple Remote with your computer."

2   Use a digital camera to test your Apple Remote. If you have a digital camera or DV camera with an LCD display, you can use it to see if your Apple Remote is emitting a signal. Infrared beams are invisible to the human eye, but most digital cameras and video cameras use Charged-Coupled Device (CCD) chips or image sensors that are sensitive to infrared light.

To use a camera to test your Apple Remote, follow these steps:

a   Turn on your digital camera or DV camera and remove any lens cover.

b   Point your Apple Remote toward the display latch button.

c   Press and hold the Menu button on the remote while looking at your camera's LCD display.

d   If you see a faint blinking light coming from the Apple Remote in the camera's LCD, the remote is working properly.

e   If you don't see any blinking light in the camera's LCD, replace the battery in your Apple Remote and then test it again with your computer.

3   Replace the Apple Remote battery.

NOTE ▶   To replace the Apple Remote battery, consult Knowledge Base document 302543, "How to replace the Apple Remote battery."

4   Replace the Apple Remote.

Infrared Board

Supported applications do not respond to input from the remote control.

1   Make sure the "Disable remote control infrared receiver" checkbox is not selected in Security preferences.

2   If Unpair is available in Security preferences, another Apple Remote may be paired to the computer. (Pairing allows only one Apple Remote to control the computer.) To delete a pairing between the remote and the MacBook Pro, click Unpair. (You may have to enter your Administrator password to make changes in in Security preferences.)

3   Perform the checks in the preceding section to verify that the Apple Remote is functioning correctly, and retest.

4   Check that the infrared board cable is connected to the hard drive flex cable and infrared board.

5   Verify that the infrared sensor can be seen in System Profiler. Open System Profiler and click the USB section. If you don't see the infrared sensor, replace the infrared board and retest.

6   Replace the hard drive flex cable and retest.

7   Replace the logic board.

Built-in iSight Camera

The built-in camera is not recognized

1   Boot the MacBook Pro to the desktop and launch iChat AV.

> **NOTE** ▶ You do not need to be connected to a network to use iChat AV to troubleshoot. Verify that the correct versions of Mac OS X and iChat AV are installed. Reinstall or update software as needed.

2 Open the iChat AV preferences and click the Video icon. Verify that the camera is recognized by the iChat AV software.

3 Check the camera connection to main logic board.

4 Check the camera connection to the camera board (in the display assembly).

5 Replace the camera (part of display bezel).

Camera image quality poor

1 Verify that the lens assembly for the iSight camera is clean. Fingerprints and other contaminants can affect image quality. Clean the lens using a lint-free lens cleaning cloth, being careful not to scratch the lens.

2 Verify that there is sufficient lighting to produce a good-quality image. Lighting comparable to that found in a well-lit office will produce a good-quality image. If possible, avoid having a brightly lit background. Diffused lighting is preferred over direct lighting.

3 Launch iChat AV and open the iChat AV preferences. Click the Video tab. Is the video quality acceptable?

Yes: The camera is functioning normally. The image quality problems may be caused by bandwidth limitations when using iChat over the Internet. Instruct the customer to use the iChat AV connection doctor feature to verify that there is sufficient bandwidth to have a video iChat session without a significant degradation of image quality.

No: The camera may not be functioning normally. Replace display assembly and retest.

Camera is recognized but no audio

1 Open Sound preferences. Verify that the built-in internal microphone has been selected as the device for sound input. Verify that the volume settings (on the slider bar) are appropriate.

2   Launch iChat AV and open the iChat AV preferences. Click the Video icon. Speak into the microphone while monitoring the microphone level indicator. If the line meter responds, it was a settings problem.

3   Check that the speaker assembly (includes the microphone) is plugged in.

4   Replace the speaker assembly.

Audio quality is poor

The camera is recognized but the built-in microphone's audio quality is poor.

1   Open Sound preferences. Verify that the internal microphone has been selected as the sound input port and that the input volume settings are appropriate. Use the volume level meter to verify settings.

2   Open iMovie and create a new project. Click the Audio button and record a sound sample. If audio quality is fine, it was a settings problem.

3   Check that the speaker assembly (includes the microphone) is plugged in.

4   Replace the speaker assembly.

Keyboard

No response from any key on keyboard

1   Remove any connected peripherals and eject any ExpressCard.

2   If only numbers appear, check if Num Lock (F6) is engaged.

3   Open System Profiler.

4   Attach an external USB keyboard. If it doesn't work, go to step 6.

5   Turn off the computer. Check the keyboard flex cable connections to trackpad and main logic board for proper seating and/or damage.

6   Start up from the MacBook Pro Mac OS X Install Disc 1 that came with the computer (hold down the C key during restart, if possible) to verify that it is not a software problem.

7   Replace the internal keyboard.

8   Replace the top case.

9   Replace the logic board.

No keyboard illumination

1   Open Keyboard & Mouse preferences and make sure the "Illuminate keyboard in low light conditions" checkbox is selected. Try using system in a dimly lit environment.

> **NOTE ▶** The keyboard illumination is not bright enough to be seen in most well lit spaces. In order to view the key being illuminated, the ambient light needs to be dim.

2   Check the keyboard backlight cable connection to the top case flex cable.

3   Replace the keyboard.

4   Replace the top case.

5   Replace the left ambient light sensor.

6   Replace the logic board.

Keyboard is partially illuminated

1   Check the keyboard backlight cable connection to the top case flex cable.

2   Replace the keyboard.

3   Replace the top case.

Microphone

The microphone is not working

1 Open Sound preferences and verify that the selection under the Input tab is for the built-in microphone.

2 Check the signal level and level meter and adjust the gain.

3 Reset the PRAM. (Shut down the computer, press the power button, then hold down the Command-Option-P-R keys until you hear the startup chime at least one additional time after the initial startup chime.)

4 If there is no sound output from the internal speaker, and the microphone is not working, verify cable connections.

5 Replace the speaker assembly (which contains the microphone).

6 Replace the left I/O flex cable.

7 Replace the left I/O board.

8 Replace the logic board.

Modem (External)
MacBook Pro does not have a built-in modem. Apple offers an optional external USB modem. Consult page 202 of the service manual for additional information.

Optical Drive

Optical drive not recognized

1 Make sure the optical drive is a cable select drive set as a slave (1). ATA ID 1 is slave mode and the hard drive is usually set to ATA ID 0, which is master mode.

2 Make sure the optical drive flex cable is undamaged and properly installed. If it's damaged, replace the flex cable.

3 Replace optical drive.

The optical drive does not accept CD or DVD disc (mechanical failure)

1 Verify disc is not warped and is a 12-cm circular disc.

2 Check that a small disc or other foreign object is not stuck inside. Remove drive from system to extract disc.

3 Verify that the disc is pushed almost all the way into the slot.

4 Make sure the optical drive flex cable is undamaged and properly installed. If damaged, replace the flex cable.

5 Replace the optical drive.

The optical drive does not eject CD or DVD disc

1 Verify the disc is not in use by quitting any applications that may be using the disc.

2 Press and hold the Media Eject key at the upper-right corner of keyboard. If that does not work, hold down the Function (fn) key and Media Eject key.

3 Drag the disc icon to the Trash, or select it and press Command-E.

4 Choose Restart from the Apple menu, holding down the trackpad button during boot.

5 Reseat the optical drive mechanism. Make sure the drive is oriented toward the back of the computer and that all four corners are seated so that the drive sits flat in its bay.

6   Replace the optical drive. (See "How to remove a stuck disc from the optical drive" in the Optical Drive chapter in the Take Apart section of the service manual.)

The disc icon does not show up on desktop, or a dialog appears to initialize disc, when inserting a read-only disc

1   Verify that the correct type of disc is being used.

2   Use Software Update to check for updated firmware.

3   Try cleaning the disc. If it is dirty or scratched, it may not mount.

4   Try a different disc.

5   Replace the optical drive cable.

6   Replace the optical drive.

Difficulty writing to optical media

1   Verify the correct type of disc is being used.

2   Try a different brand or speed of CD-R disc.

Some brands of 24x or 32x CD-R media may not work with the SuperDrive.

There are two factors in the ability of the optical drive to write to media:

▶   First, there are varying qualities of blank optical media. Some media are made to such low specifications that the ability of the drive to write to it is marginal. There are variations in optical media even under the same brand. Some brands source their optical media from a variety of manufacturers, so there may be variations in the quality.

▶ Second, an optical drive that supports writing to a CD-R/RW or DVD-R/RW disc requires a special writing algorithm for discs from each disc manufacturer. There are hundreds of disc manufacturers; it is impossible to implement writing algorithms for each disc manufacturer. Usually drive manufacturers implement special writing algorithms for discs from major disc manufacturers. For discs that are not supported by the drive with special writing algorithms, the drive will use a generic writing algorithm to write the disc. In this case, the writeability and readability may not be optimal.

3 Replace the optical drive flex cable.

4 Replace the optical drive.

Ports

A USB port is not recognizing devices

1 Shut down the computer; then press the power button to start the computer.

2 Use Software Update to check for the latest software.

3 Test USB ports with an Apple keyboard or mouse.

4 If the left USB port is not recognized (and the right USB ports are), check the left I/O flex cable's condition and connection. If the cable is damaged, replace it.

5 If the left I/O flex cable is fine, replace the left I/O board.

6 If the right ports are not recognized, check the backup battery flex cable and connections. If damaged, replace the backup battery.

7 If all USB ports are unrecognized, and System Profiler does not recognize the bus, replace the logic board.

A USB device is not recognized by the computer

> **NOTE** ▶ If you are trying to use a serial device with a USB/serial adapter, check with the manufacturer of the adapter for compatibility.

1   Shut down the computer; then press the power button to start the computer.

2   Verify that the current driver for the device is installed.

3   If the device is a camera, turn on the camera after initiating the download with the camera application.

4   Try other USB ports.

5   Try a different USB device on same port.

6   Eliminate any USB chains by plugging in only one peripheral.

7   Try a known-good Apple USB keyboard or mouse to verify that each port is working properly. If a port isn't working correctly, see the preceding section.

A FireWire port is not recognizing devices

> **NOTE** ▶ In FireWire target disk mode, a MacBook Pro cannot be mounted on systems with Mac OS X 10.3.9 or earlier. Refer to Knowledge Base document 303118, "Intel-based Macs: About using target disk mode with Mac OS X 10.3.9 or earlier."

1   Test the FireWire port by connecting to another computer using FireWire Target Disk Mode. Refer to Knowledge Base document 58583, "How to Use FireWire Target Disk Mode."

2   Verify that drivers are installed properly for third-party devices, if needed.

3   Make sure the cable is firmly attached.

4   Try a different cable.

5   If the device is self powered, make sure that the power supply is connected and the device's LED indicates it is getting power.

6   Replace the logic board.

Power Adapter

The power adapter LED does not turn on

1   Confirm that the power adapter is connected to a known-good 85W outlet.

2   Try replacing the AC plug or the AC power cord. If the adapter works, replace the appropriate plug or cord.

3   Check the pins in the power adapter DC plug for pins that are stuck down.

If a pin or pins are stuck down, try cleaning the contacts or working the pin to release it. Remove debris with a soft, non-electrostatic generating (nonplastic bristle) brush. A tool such as a cotton swab may introduce foreign material that will cause the pins to seize up.

4   If pins are missing or bent, replace the power adapter.

5   If the LED on the MagSafe connector does not turn on, there may be con-tamination in the computer port, and/or the contact pins are dirty. It can be cleaned with a soft brush. Do not use liquid. In addition, foreign mate-rial may be covering the contacts or preventing the connector from seating far enough for the sense pin to connect to the system. The center pin is the sense pin.

6   Remove the battery and connect the power adapter. If the adapter turns on and boots the system, replace the left I/O board.

Sound

No sound heard and the Output tab in Sound preferences incorrectly indicates that an external device is plugged in (to the headphone jack or USB ports)

1   If nothing is plugged into the headphone jack or USB ports, the Output tab of Sound preferences should be set to the internal speakers.

2   If nothing is plugged in, and Sound preferences is set to provide audio to the external speakers, try plugging in an external device such as headphones or external speakers, restart the computer, then remove the device you had plugged in.

3   Reset the PRAM. (After restart, hold down the Command-Option-P-R keys until you hear the startup chime at least one additional time after the initial startup chime.)

4   If the system continues to indicate a phantom device plugged into the system, replace the left I/O board.

5   Replace the logic board.

No sound from internal speaker(s)

1   Use Software Update to verify that the latest audio update has been installed.

2   Press the F3 key (with the fn key pressed and not pressed) to verify that mute mode is not enabled.

3   Press the F4 or F5 key (with the fn key pressed and not pressed) to check the volume setting.

4   Verify that no external speakers or headphones are plugged in.

5   Check the Output tab in Sound preferences to confirm that the software is correctly sensing that there are no external speakers or headphones connected.

6   Shut down the computer and restart.

7   Reset the PRAM. (After restart, hold down the Command-Option-P-R keys until you hear the startup chime at least one additional time after the initial startup chime.)

8   Verify that the speaker cable is connected properly to the left I/O board.

9   Check the speaker cable itself. Verify left and right cable connections.

10 Check sound with headphones or external speaker. If audio is heard, replace speaker assembly.

11 Replace the left I/O flex cable.

12 Replace the left I/O board.

13 Replace the logic board.

Distorted sound from internal speakers

1   Verify sound is correct with external speakers/headphones. If sound is correct, check speaker wire and connections.

2   In the Output tab of Sound preferences, check the Balance setting.

3   Compare the same audio with two different units to make sure that the sound is distorted on both.

4   Check speaker wire. If damaged, replace speaker assembly.

5   If the distortion is coming from the right speaker with sound balance shifted toward the left, remove the right speaker. Check the gasket in the speaker housing. If the gasket is deformed, move the gasket back into a circular shape. If gasket cannot be fixed, replace the housing. You need to order the speaker assembly.

6   Replace the left I/O flex cable.

7   Replace the left I/O board.

8   Replace the logic board.

Trackpad

The pointer does not move when you are using trackpad

1   Verify that no USB device is connected.

2   Boot from the Software Install and Restore DVD to verify that it is not a software problem. If the trackpad works, restore the system software.

3   Reset the power manager (SMC). See new procedures in the "Resetting the Power Manager (SMC)" section earlier in this lesson.

4   Check the trackpad flex cable connection to the logic board.

5   Replace the top case.

6   Replace the logic board.

The pointer intermittently does not move or moves erratically

> **NOTE ▶** User must touch the surface with only one finger at a time and point directly down. When running Apple Hardware Test or Apple Service Diagnostic, the trackpad will respond to very small movements of the pointer. This behavior is normal.

1   Clean the trackpad surface (with the computer off, using a non-static-inducing material).

2   Shut down the computer; then press the power button to start the computer.

3   Reset the power manager (SMC). See new procedures in the "Resetting the Power Manager (SMC)" section in earlier in this lesson.

4   Make sure the power adapter is using the AC power cord, not the AC plug (also known as the "duckhead"). If the intermittent behavior goes away, recommend using the AC cord, because it provides a ground path for static.

5   Disconnect the power adapter and run on battery power only. If the problem goes away, replace the power adapter.

6   Place the MacBook Pro Mac OS X Install Disc 1 in the optical disc drive, restart, and hold down the C key. Check the pointer movement to see if the problem is software.

7   Check the trackpad flex cable connection to the logic board.

8   Replace the top case.

9   Replace the logic board.

Video

No display, or dim display, but computer appears to operate correctly

1   Remove any connected peripherals.

2   Make sure the F1 key is not stuck down.

3   Press the F2 key (with the fn key pressed and not pressed) to increase screen brightness.

4   Reboot the computer holding down the Control and Command keys and pressing the power button. Or if necessary, press and hold the power button for 5 to 10 seconds to shut down the computer, and then press the power button to restart. Let the system run for an hour so the panel can warm up.

5 Verify that the inverter cable and LVDS cable connections are seated properly and are not damaged.

6 Replace the inverter board.

7 Replace the display assembly.

8 Replace the logic board.

Computer appears to work, but no video on external device connected to the S-video/composite port of the optional DVI-to-video adapter

1 The device must be connected to the S-video/composite port while the MacBook Pro is sleeping or off for the device to be recognized.

2 Verify that the test monitor is a known-good device and supported by this computer.

3 Try a different DVI-to-video adapter.

4 Replace the logic board.

No video on an external VGA device connected to the external monitor (DVI) port

1 Verify that the test monitor is a known-good device and supported by this computer.

2 Try another DVI-to-VGA adapter cable.

3 Restart the computer and test again.

4 Replace the logic board.

No display, or dim display, but the computer can display external video

1   Remove any connected peripherals.

2   Try adjusting the brightness using the F2 function key.

3   Open Keyboard & Mouse preferences and adjust the brightness. If it works, replace the keyboard.

4   Check the inverter cable connection to the main logic board.

5   Check the cable connections to the inverter board and from the inverter board to the LCD.

6   Replace the inverter board.

7   Replace the display assembly.

8   Replace the logic board.

Display has repetitive patterns or shifted color pattern

1   Check for the latest system software update.

2   Check that the LVDS connection is fully seated on the logic board.

3   Replace the logic board.

Display has permanent vertical or horizontal lines

1   Check for the latest system software update

2   Replace the display assembly.

3   Replace the logic board.

Miscellaneous symptoms
Consult pages 212 through 213 of the service manual for information.

Lesson Review

1. True or false: It is impossible to turn on a MacBook Pro when the top case is removed.

2. True or false: resetting the power manager (SMC) also resets Date & Time preferences.

3. True or false: The MacBook Pro may give indications that it is shut down when the logic board may actually be running.

4. What type of power adapter is recommended for a MacBook Pro?

   a. 45W

   b. 65W

   c. 85W

5. True or false: If a MacBook Pro will not start up, the ExpressCard might be responsible.

6. True or false: When the AirPort Extreme Card is removed, the Bluetooth module will not function.

7. What key, when stuck down, might make a MacBook Pro appear to have a dim or broken display?

   a. F1

   b. F2

   c. F12

8. You are troubleshooting a MacBook Pro that fails to respond to any key on the keyboard. What does Apple suggest as the first procedure?

   a. Attach an external USB keyboard.

   b. Remove any connected peripherals and eject any ExpressCard.

   c. Restart the computer.

9. True or false: You can control the keyboard illumination feature of the MacBook Pro in Keyboard & Mouse preferences.

10. True or false: The optical drive in the MacBook Pro can accept mini-CDs less than 12 cm in diameter.

Answer Key

1. False, the power button pads on the logic board can be carefully shorted to act as a power button; 2. True; 3. True; 4. c; 5. True; 6. False, the AirPort Extreme Card and Bluetooth module are separate parts; 7. a; 8. b; 9. True; 10. False, CDs and DVDs must be 12 cm in diameter.

Index

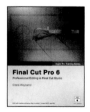